AFTER THE NATION-STATE

AFTER THE NATION-STATE

Citizens, Tribalism and the New World Disorder

MATHEW HORSMAN
AND ANDREW MARSHALL

HarperCollins*Publishers*

THIS BOOK IS DEDICATED TO
NANCY, JOE, EILEEN AND THE MEMORY OF RONALD

HarperCollins*Publishers*
77–85 Fulham Palace Road,
Hammersmith, London w6 8jb

Published by HarperCollins*Publishers* 1994
1 3 5 7 9 8 6 4 2

Copyright © Mathew Horsman and Andrew Marshall 1994

Mathew Horsman and Andrew Marshall assert their moral right to
be identified as the authors of this work

A catalogue record for this book is available
from the British Library

ISBN 0 00 255145 4

Set in Linotron Janson by
Rowland Phototypesetting Ltd
Bury St Edmunds, Suffolk

Printed in Great Britain by
HarperCollinsManufacturing Glasgow

CONTENTS

ACKNOWLEDGEMENTS

This book began life on the back of an envelope in London in the spring of 1990 and was finally completed in Montreal and Brussels in early 1994. We are first and foremost grateful to our employers during that period for their patience and tolerance. The support of our colleagues on the *Financial Times*, the *Financial Post*, *The Independent* and *The Independent on Sunday* and at the Institute for Research on Public Policy was vital to completing the book. Working for these organizations also gave us the opportunity to witness some of the events we have mentioned, and supplied the many benefits that working journalists take for granted. Particular thanks are due to David Walker and David Lennon of the FT, Neville Nankivell of the FP, Godfrey Hodgson and Harvey Morris, successive foreign editors of *The Independent*, and Monique Jérôme-Forget of the IRPP.

The book was written in London, in Vauthion and the Mas du Viala in France, and in Brussels and Montreal. We are particularly grateful to Jean Denieuil and Christian Gros, whose warm hospitality we enjoyed in France. Thanks also to Colette Camil, Pierre Denieuil, the Denieuil and Berger families, Harriet and Deborah Logan, John Dunton-Downer, David Sturgess, Georgia Glynn-Smith, Francis Hamel, Mark Devine, and Katelijne De Backer who were all unceasingly kind and tolerant. Marye Bos proof read significant portions of the manuscript. Equally, the project would never have materialized without the practical assistance of JDF Jones, the technical wizards of the FT, Pat Salter, and Clive Frampton. Felicity Bryan, our agent, and Philip Gwyn Jones and Stuart Proffitt at HarperCollins took us in hand and have done a fine job.

Guidance, ideas and criticism that helped shape the book came from Aron Rodrigue, Anna Cancogni, André Raynauld, Dalton Robertson,

Beatrice Riddell, Stephen Scott, Jerri-Lin Scofield, David Owen, Edi Smockum, Miguel Casas, Paul Fox, Mark Nicholson, Neil Ascherson, Annika Savill, Dominic Simpson, Brian Cathcart, Sarah Lambert, Peter Torday, Steve Crawshaw, Richard Davy, Michael Dynes, Hugh Stokes, Paul Murphy, John Ridding, John Crabtree, Peter Stevens, Duncan James, and many other colleagues and former colleagues at the *Financial Times*, *Financial Post*, *The Independent* and *The Independent on Sunday*, The Institute for Research on Public Policy, Oxford Analytica and Hudson Research International. A week spent at Klingenthal with the 21st Century Trust was a particularly useful opportunity to discuss some of what follows with William Wallace, Hagen Schulze, Sir Michael Weir and participants from all over Europe and the US.

A book of this kind owes a great deal to the work of many other writers and thinkers. More than usual, readers are directed to the notes where we list the main sources. Friends and contacts in officialdom and the private sector have provided many insights over the past four years. These people are responsible for the good things about the book; for the bad things, the fault is ours.

Montreal and Brussels, February 1994

INTRODUCTION

'The nation-state offers most of its members a
stronger sense of security, belonging, or affiliation,
and even personal identity, than does any alternative
large group.'   KARL DEUTSCH[1]

The traditional nation-state, the fruit of centuries of political, social
and economic evolution, is under threat. Changes in the structure of
the international economy, technological advance, and the end of
the Cold War together will force – indeed are already forcing – a
realignment of the relations among states, citizens and the international economy. The origins and character of that realignment are
the subject of this book.

Historians speak of long and short centuries, playing with beginnings and endings of quite arbitrary hundred-year periods in an effort
to imbue them with significance. We all understand the centenarian
impulse. We like the shorthand of referring to a 'nineteenth-century'
phenomenon, or of saying, 'welcome to the twenty-first century.' Historians do not always agree on the dividing dates, of course. But most
say the nineteenth century ended with the outbreak of the Great War
in 1914, even though the significance of the juncture was lost on many
at the time. In our day, the end of the twentieth century seems rather
easier to pinpoint. The year 1989 was a watershed year – the end of
a bipolar global political accommodation based on the strength of the
superpowers. A new world order – not the one former US President
George Bush hopefully hailed – was ushered in with the end of the
Cold War. Unlike those who contemplated the aftermath of global

ix

battle in 1918 we have the luxury of knowing, if not *how* things are changing, then at least that they *are* changing in radical ways. The elites of Europe believed, after the First World War, that they could re-establish the stability and structure of late nineteenth-century society. On the threshold of our new century, we now know for sure we cannot remake the world in the image of some less chaotic past.

Consider the apparent contradiction between two trends readily observable in the world around us. First, states seem to be giving up sovereignty in their rush to sign regional trading and political agreements. Second, groups are agitating for greater sovereignty within existing states, intent on some measure of independence. Is the world becoming more integrated or is it becoming more fragmented? Are we becoming more international or more tribal? The answer, in both cases, is manifestly yes. The North American Free Trade Agreement, the single European market and the new General Agreement on Tariffs and Trade are all steps toward greater integration. The international economy's move toward globalism is inexorable. Consumerist capitalism needs ever-expanding markets and ever more efficient ways of producing and distributing goods and services. Transnational companies are becoming increasingly adept at finding ways of circumventing national borders in their search for cheap labour, and efficient sourcing of raw and processed materials. Equally, Georgians, Tartars, Ukrainians, Serbs, Slovenes, Croats, Slovaks, Chechen and scores of others have won or are battling for greater independence within existing states, even at the price of transitory economic privation. Examples of tribalism can also be found in Britain, France, Canada, Spain, even in the US.

(By tribalism, we mean the retreat by individuals into communities defined not by political association or by the state borders that enclose a political nation, but by similarities of religion, culture, ethnicity, or some other shared experience. The retreat is driven by fear and confusion, and fed by the reassuring 'sameness' of others in the group.)

What do these two trends have in common that might allow us to understand them not as contradictory processes but as complementary ones? We argue here that tribalism and globalism, fragmentation and integration, are responses to various, sometimes contradictory, impulses: changes in the nature and reach of capitalism; technological advance and market deregulation; the altered relations of citizens to their governmental structures; and the lack of one or more hegemonic powers that might sponsor a global system. Such changes represent a direct threat to the identity of the classically constituted nation-state. We suggest that while the most durable form of political, social and economic organization is being weakened by both centrifugal and centripetal forces, no effective candidate to replace it is emerging. The result is likely to be a period of prolonged instability and un-certainty. There is an urgent need to find new means of collective representation, intervention and assistance.

The fundamental political structure that underpinned capitalism's earlier phases, and which has channelled nationalism for two centuries is under immense pressure. When the global economic system required a measure of personal freedom, a general lack of constraint on the individual's pursuit of profit, and social stability in the absence of old hierarchies, the nation-state was an elegant answer to that need. It replaced communitarian, feudal affiliations with national ones, co-opting populations by providing a sense of membership that often transcended local concerns. But national politics – inflamed by mass democracy and newly freed from the clutches of the Cold Warriors – now often gets in the way of the global economy. The effects of this shift have been made manifest by the altered roles of the US and the states of the former Soviet Union as guarantors of global stability. A world dominated by two superpowers could go on pretending that the classic nation-state – charged with protecting national citizens within secure borders and with the conduct of national economic policies – was the rational, inevitable political structure. Blinded by security needs, and sponsored by the US, the western world could act as if nation-states, and the balance of power among them, counted for something, no matter what the underlying realities might have otherwise imposed. In the decades immediately following the Second World War, the US was the globe's most important power by far – awkward, naive, blundering at times, but no less powerful for that. However, the US economy alone is no longer equal to the challenge of sponsorship, at least not on the old terms of a liberal international order. Pax Americana, the forty-year period of western stability after the war, was also an era of mass consumption born in America, and Americans did best out of it. No longer able, on its own, to finance its role as superpower, and steadily losing ground as an industrial behemoth, the US is in relative decline. At the same time, communism in its Soviet form has lost its battle with the West. With the end of the Soviet Union's control of its East European satellites and with the unwinding of the Union itself, the one remaining nineteenth-century empire has crumbled. These events had obvious implications for the international security order. What was less obvious in 1989 was that they also marked a watershed in the international economic order, a point of transition from a system that still had its roots in fundamentally dated ideas of production and consumption.

The faces of integration and globalization are most evident in the spheres of production, finance and commerce. Despite the lip-service paid in the 1980s to the classical liberal economic tradition of the nineteenth century, no economy can any longer rely primarily on the entrepreneur and his skilful manipulation of the factors of production. The great age of bourgeois stability, so convincingly sketched by Eric Hobsbawm in *The Age of Empire*, is not returning.[2] Arguably, the world economy has not been so constituted since the First World War. Reaganite and Thatcherite nostalgia in the 1980s could not hide the characteristics of the emerging world economic order. The top five hundred international companies are responsible for a huge and increasing share of global production. Entrepreneurs do not run these giants; bureaucratic management does.

The nature of economic production is changing. Although claims that we have entered the reign of 'post-industrial' capitalism are difficult to sustain in the light of the industrial profiles of many developing countries, the share of world Gross National Product represented by traditional manufacturing is nonetheless declining in relative terms. Less labour-intensive transformative processes take up an increasing share of overall industrial output, while the service sector represents a large and growing share of GNP, particularly in the developed economies. Industrial goods are giving way to new products in the international marketplace. Knowledge-based industries trade in words, ideas and images, not in physical goods. It is only in the last ten years that the political implications of these changes have become clear, though their hazy outlines were discerned by some writers and politicians in the preceding decades.[3]

Technological change, in the communications industry particularly, and extensive financial deregulation over the course of the 1980s in the leading economies have begun to render the very concept of 'borders' obsolete. Technological advance has given us effortless data transmission across boundaries; television signals do not respect frontiers; telephone conversations are not necessarily carried over physical lines but via border-crashing satellites. Financial institutions transmit funds electronically; investors trade simultaneously on markets thousands of miles apart.

This 'techno-economic' revolution is beginning to alter the very concept of 'work' in a modern economy, and that fact has huge and troubling implications for social organization. The Fordist paradigm,[4] in which workers were paid enough to be able to buy the sorts of products they had a hand in making, and could give up a share of their income to finance an extensive welfare system for the unemployed, the retired, and the ill, is no longer tenable. Globalization has meant that factory workers in the US cannot compete with their counterparts in Korea and still maintain a high and growing standard of living. It has meant that governments cannot afford to administer huge social programmes on the proceeds of a declining manufacturing sector. Finally, it has meant new kinds of jobs in the West – in finance, real estate, computer software – for which an industrial workforce is untrained.

The global economy relentlessly passes judgement on governments and societies. It is no longer possible to sustain a monetary policy at odds with trends in the leading economies; financial markets extract a heavy penalty from those who stray. Consider the lessons learned by a representative middle-ranking nation such as France. Following attempts to reflate in the early 1980s, despite the worldwide recession, the Socialist government in France accepted it could no longer go it alone. It subsequently embraced a form of economic liberalism as assiduously as did the rightist opposition. This policy, based on a strong currency tied to the European monetary system, was then badly damaged in a few days of concerted action by the foreign exchange markets in August 1993.

The emerging consensus on capitalism has left little room for radical alternatives, certainly at the domestic level; capitalism has become a game that is virtually impossible not to play. Countries such as Mexico, which a decade ago relied on state control and ownership, are privatizing heavily; Thailand is balancing its budget; Peru is lowering tariffs. Liberalism – not the nineteenth-century individualist credo, but rather a modern variant much influenced by the hallmarks of the twentieth century – has apparently won the day, and on economic terms anyway the world is finding common ground. That variant, in the ascendancy virtually everywhere, is committed not to pure, unsullied capitalism but nonetheless sponsors a great measure of economic freedom. Twentieth-century economic liberalism champions private ownership, a reduced role for the state in business, fewer trade barriers, lower taxes, and a general reliance on the market as the most efficient distributor of resources in a given economy.

But the political corollary of this apparent shift toward economic liberalism is proving far more complicated. If the hallmark of the late 1980s was the turn to the market, in politics it was the revival of nationalist tensions on a grand scale and the weakness of the institutions charged with handling the world economy. Some efforts have been made to create new political structures that transcend national borders. The European Union* instituted a Single Market within its twelve member countries at the end of 1992. In addition, it is struggling to create a political and monetary union with the underpinning of economic co-operation. Far Eastern governments are discussing plans that would increase political co-operation within the region, in line with growing economic ties. The US, its Free Trade Agreement with Canada and Mexico already in place, is now ready to extend the FTA concept to South America as well. Such trading links will be followed by attempts to fashion a political element. Efforts to introduce such liberal tenets throughout much of the developed and developing world (notable exceptions such as Iran, sub-Saharan Africa, and embattled outposts of eastern Europe aside) have made it easier for regional economic bodies to emerge elsewhere. These regional bodies can be seen as the embryo of a multinational political correlative to the increasingly global economy.

But the erosion of nation-state sovereignty has created a democratic deficit. Citizens continue to hold their national governments accountable on issues over which states have no autonomous control. The strong sense of allegiance to the nation-state borne by its citizens, and developed over the past two hundred years, has not yet weakened in line with the diminution of the autonomy of national governments. Despite the advent of the 'global village', individuals so far feel little more than token allegiance to emerging supranational bodies such as the European Union. There is as yet no sense of 'belonging' to an efficient superstate. Where is the reflection of self, of the group, of the nation?

International and regional organizations also face more fundamental problems in seeking to manage the global economy. The crisis in

---

* The European Community is now known as the European Union (or EU), following passage of the Maastricht Treaty.

the European Monetary System from 1992–3 underlined the difficulties of accommodating an internal shock as great as German unification. The General Agreement on Tariffs and Trade spent seven years negotiating an accord that was supposed to be finished in five, and one that falls far short of the original goals. The US-Canada Free Trade Agreement and the subsequent North American Free Trade Agreement aroused strong opposition and its much-vaunted disputes mechanism did not pre-empt tit-for-tat trade measures. A global economy with ineffectual political oversight risks leaving citizens of all social classes disenfranchised. Individuals will retain some limited power as consumers, but will have less obvious influence on the political structure that underpins the international economy. As the diminution of single-state power becomes evident, and as the embryonic supranational political arrangements come only slowly into being, citizens will tend to think more closely – again – about their own communities (variously defined, as we shall see), seeking local political reflections of their concerns, even as the economies in which they are consumers move ever closer toward global integration. They will seek political solutions, and democratic accountability, at ever more local levels as the world economy moves towards an even greater level of integration. That this is already true to some degree can be seen in the proliferation of ethnic and other inter-group tensions, not just in the developing world and in the states of the former Soviet bloc, but in the West as well. It is seen, for example, in the degree to which individuals in many western countries already seek local solutions in a growing number of areas such as community-based health care and social services, training and education. It is our contention that these localist tendencies, many of them obvious for years, have become far more important, and will attract increasing interest as the individual loses hold of the political anchor that helped him make sense of his world.

There are many dangers in this. The very changes this book addresses are an invitation to a return to ethnocentric, xenophobic political formulations, as individuals, disenfranchised by the emergence of a truly global, borderless economy, seek familiar forms of protection from the effects of such a world-shaking transformation. Individuals in the West will be worried by the presence in their midst of people from other cultures, who are there in part because of the fall-out of imperialism but just as much because of the trend towards globalism, intensified by rapid population growth and polluted environments. The danger to minority populations is obvious. Most western nation-states have evolved to embrace the theory that citizenship can be, perhaps should be, more important than, say, race or religion. This theory has been severely tested throughout the world, as people migrated from East to West, from Europe to North America, believing they would be accepted as citizens in the new nation of their choice. Tribalism flies in the face of tolerance.

The rise of virulent strains of nationalism was assisted by the sudden decompression in the states of the former Soviet bloc, in Europe, Africa and Asia. The end of the Cold War loosened the ties that had bound together multi-ethnic states, or that had at least kept them from flying apart. In the former Yugoslavia this finally led to bloody civil war. In the Baltic states it exposed the Russian minority, and in the Central Asian republics of the former USSR it produced cross-border conflicts. The transformation of 1989, while opening up the world to economic liberalism, thus also laid the foundations for a contradictory and illiberal political reaction.

There is no denying the power of nationalism. But it is important to understand the basis of its political empowerment in the modern age, and to reflect on its relatively brief history. The nation-state as it developed in the course of the nineteenth century is a pact between citizens and governments within geographically distinct borders.[5] To warrant the hyphen, the nation-state requires a self-conscious belief on the part of its citizens that the collective has a power greater than the mere agglomeration of a given country's population. The nation-state represents the citizen, gives him a sense of belonging to a coherent whole. It requires the marriage of civil administration and self-conscious patriotism. The nation-state embodies the hopes and aspirations of its citizens, who owe it allegiance. It is a pure form of co-option. At its simplest level, a nation-state is an abstract construct for which citizens are nonetheless willing to die.

Fundamentalist Islam offers similar assurances as a model of social organization. So has communism, at least at certain times in history. And many nations without states have managed to imbue members with a similar willingness to commit themselves to an abstract ideal. A sense of community, rooted in the land, has long been a hallmark of human interaction. 'Our' hills, 'our' fields, 'our' streams and rivers – man has long been laying claim to his natural environment. But until such belief-systems are married to a formal state, with legal jurisdiction and common laws of citizenship, they cannot be considered in the same category. Hence the efforts of stateless 'nations' to lay claim to specific territories, and to people them with the ghosts of their own past histories.

The idea of the state is centuries old, if by that word we mean the basic structures of civil administration. But the idea of the nation-state, to which all citizens feel committed, much as they once did to their family or local community or church, was more recent in coming to prominence. In fact, it was really only with the introduction of mass education in the nineteenth century – and with it the imposition of a standard language and a credo of civic responsibility – that a sense of citizenship could be extended to every individual within the borders of a given state. The nineteenth century also confirmed the role of the state in representing a national economy, despite the likelihood that capitalism could be more efficient on a global basis, even then. The development of national economies from 1800 on led to a world of great complexity, wherein nationalism, national economic rivalry, and ultimately imperialism intermixed to help create the recognizably modern characteristics of the nation-state.

In the early years of the twentieth century, the principle of nationality was enshrined as the obvious and most stable basis for the organization of states worldwide. It became the framework of diplomacy, the irreducible building block of the international economy. After the First World War, itself ignited by nationalist tensions, US President Woodrow Wilson could argue for national self-determination as the basis for the organization of nations, underlining the view that common culture, history, and ethnicity were the natural constituents of human association. In the Third World, the states were often completely imagined by colonial masters. But this has not precluded a desire in Africa, for example, to transform colonial states into nation-states, despite persistent tribal conflicts. Most African nations that won independence in the mid-twentieth century retained the borders drawn by colonial masters. Any change might have set off uncontrollable tribal divisions: indeed, lingering cultural and geographical anomalies have dogged virtually all the African countries.

These reflections serve as a reminder that the nation-state as it developed in Europe and subsequently around the world did not *a priori* require a people with a self-perceived common ethnicity and culture. This is not to suggest that ethnicity did not play a role in the determination of allegiances: there are clearly differences among people that underline a shared sense of community. Yet the mixture of cultures and indeed ethnicity in Europe is such that no nation-state could ever claim to be peopled with those of 'pure' stock. The nation-state was nonetheless required to create a myth of 'nation' to attract each succeeding generation to its bosom. In this way, a shared history, a mythified past, a series of rituals, common attitudes and invented traditions[6] are created and disseminated in relentless fashion.

Peter Alter has offered some useful definitions of the various forms of nationalism. His schema identifies two broad forms into which nationalist agitations fall. The first, Risorgimento nationalism, posits that not only does every nation have a right to independence via a state but every member of that nation-state equally has the right to self-expression, freedom and the possibility of development. This form of nationalism was dominant within the transnational empires of east and central Europe at the end of the nineteenth century.[7] Alter's examples include the efforts of Prince Alexander Ypsilanti, who urged Greeks to declare self-consciously independent status from the Turks in the early nineteenth century.

Alter's second category, integral nationalism, posits the one nation as absolute and superior. It entails expansionism and validates colonialism. Its earliest variant is probably *Italia irredenta* (Italy unredeemed) whereby it was believed that parts of the 'real' Italy were under control of the Hapsburg monarchy and had to be recovered. This movement reached its height under the Italian dictator Benito Mussolini, when *mare nostro* was extended to include the entire Mediterranean and not just the Adriatic, and in Adolf Hitler's quest for *Lebensraum* (living space) during the Third Reich.

In most cases in Europe, and subsequently in its colonies, the structure of the state has come first, and a sense of nation and therefore nationalism second. 'It is the state that makes the nation and not the nation the state,' said Polish liberator Józef Pilsudski.[8] Modern nationalists, encouraged by the early twentieth-century acceptance of national self-determination, routinely mine history and folklore to demonstrate the inevitability of claims for a nation-state. They point to common culture, language and traditions, a specific territory, and a 'golden age' deep in the past, and imply that these elements of nationality have existed always. But the nation-state is, as we shall see, a relatively modern phenomenon. The modern states of Iraq and Syria have only been independent countries since the inter-war years, and were hardly nations-in-waiting before that. Yugoslavia was once divided between the Ottoman and Hapsburg empires, within which nationalism was encouraged to develop as a sign of dissatisfaction with the ruling state. One can trace the creation of the nation through the efforts of administrative states and through the work of the intelligentsia, to some degree the repository of collective memory – real or imagined. It was through the efforts of academics, linguists, and philologists, for example, that modern Czech, Flemish, and Romanian were elevated from the status of peasant dialect to national language. With the growth of mass print media, and the extension of literacy through state education, a national language became the vehicle for the conception and dissemination of shared values. Common expression could help underpin claims for a nation-state.[9]

The nation-state was primarily a way of ordering relationships: of locating authority and channelling power. Authority is central to economic organization, to political management, to security and to international order. We imagined the nation-state, and its constituent communities, in response to economic, technological, social and political change. Now we must imagine once again: this book sets out the basis of that reimagining – anchored inevitably in the past – and the forms it is likely to take. In the first of three parts, we explain the genesis of the nation-state, its rise as a form of organization, and its expansion from Europe to the new nations of America, Asia, and Africa. This process was by no means inevitable; nor did the nation-state take the same form everywhere. The bases of the nation-state are explained: the ideological and cultural ties that legitimized nationalism; the economic expansion that underpinned unity; and the political structures that emerged, whether democratic, authoritarian or admixtures of the two. We next sketch the emergence of an international order from the chaos of the inter-war years which sought to tame the explosive forces of nationalism and social unrest, while opening up the world economy to trade and investment. Finally, we explore the declining salience of borders and territoriality in the post-Cold War age.

In Part Two, the fissures and fault lines of the post-war era are spelt out. These culminate in the political developments of the 1980s, which made change inevitable. Events in the Soviet Union characterized a period of spectacular upheaval which led to the joint cry from Moscow and Washington for a New World Order, one that would transcend the logic of superpower confrontation. Yet the political structures that were supposed to accommodate that change – the international organizations spawned by the post-war order – have clearly been inadequate to the challenge. The sudden unravelling of established but unstable states in Europe and the Third World has presented the West with a series of dilemmas which it has yet to confront in a systematic way, and the expansion of a global economy has outpaced efforts to create institutions.

At the same time, economic and social changes make a return to exclusive reliance on the nation-state impossible. The expansion of the international marketplace has made the pursuit of national economic goals impractical. The ideological revolution of the 1980s has undermined attempts to put the interests of the state ahead of those of the market. And the growth of new communications technologies has increased the possibility for cultural and intellectual heterogeneity within nations. The formation of economic blocs and regional alliances has been an attempt to deal with these processes in a rational way, yet these have so far only experimented with political forms that ultimately transcend the nation-state.

In Part Three, we look at the clash between late twentieth-century capitalism, which searches for a borderless world, and the impulses of nationalism and tribalism, which often seek to repudiate the imperatives of the marketplace. We argue that the new world order will be a shifting and complicated one, at once tribal and international in character. Such shifts will ultimately affect the relationship of citizens to states, and hence the character of community. Finally, we argue that these shifts are likely to generate opposition. There may still be room for a sustained critique of liberal capitalism that is avowedly anti-market. New communities may reflect a growing dissatisfaction with the global system and with efforts to provide political management. These 'rival' communities are only now coming into view but may form a potent force against those who, too early, triumph in the end of history and the global victory of liberal capitalism.

PART ONE

The Nation-State from Westphalia to the Wall

1

When and Why Was the Nation-State?

> 'Nationalism sketched out a new order for state and
> society which enveloped individuals who had been left
> to fend for themselves.'   PETER ALTER[1]

The formation of the nation-state, the single most important institution of the modern era, can only be explained by reference to its
historical origins.[2] Through long periods of steady evolution, punctu-
ated by revolutions and wars, Europeans fashioned for themselves a
political system that could be relied upon to order domestic, political
and economic life, and it provided all members of society with a sense
of their place in the larger community. The birth of the nation-state
is closely related both to an emerging pattern of relations between
states, an international system, and to the growth of commercial
relations across the world – a global system.

Something like the modern political system only emerged in the
West at the end of a relatively static period wherein economic life was
structured around land and agriculture, and around direct agricultural
consumption. Trade took place on the Mediterranean, in Asia and
across Africa between kingdoms, city-states and fragments of the
empires, largely in foodstuffs and a small range of luxury items. The
early western European system revolved around what Immanuel
Wallerstein has described as 'a series of tiny economic nodules whose
population and productivity were slowly increasing, and in which the
legal mechanisms ensured that the bulk of the surplus went to land-
lords who had noble status and control of the juridical machinery'.[3]

The feudal 'crisis' of the fourteenth and fifteenth centuries brought

3

together two separate developments: ever more-expensive wars between princes, and a point of saturation in agricultural production.[4] The results were stagnation, peasant revolts, and increasing demands by courts on nobles to pay for waging wars. Order only returned in the early fifteenth century, when the courts of western Europe finally imposed something like central control on their noble countrymen. Of course, the trappings of state control had been built up in previous years: particularly the capacity to raise arms to fight a series of territorial battles. Paul Kennedy suggests that it was in times of war that the early European state took on its obviously modern features. While agreeing that it was the gradual breakdown of feudalism ('and the concomitant shift toward a more secular, vernacular basis of social organization') that helped engender the nation-state, Kennedy argues that it was the pressing need to finance wars that tipped the balance toward an administrative model based less on seigneurial right than on the legitimacy of the nation. 'It was war,' Kennedy writes, 'and the consequences of war, that provided a much more urgent and continuous pressure toward "nation-building" than . . . philosophical considerations and slowly evolving social tendencies.'[5] Charles Tilly puts it even more succinctly: 'War made the state and the state made war.'[6]

The Renaissance saw the birth of statecraft in its recognizably modern form. In Italian city-states such as Venice and Florence, independent political power was carved out, linked to specific territory and legitimized by the threat and use of force. The spread of Renaissance ideas, aided by the revolution in printing ushered in by Gutenberg's invention of movable type, helped plant this system in the soil of western Europe.

The growth of trading routes in sixteenth-century Europe, first along the Mediterranean but extending, ultimately, across the Atlantic, helped finance not only the royal courts of Europe but its elites as well. This emerging system has been dubbed a 'capitalist world economy, vast but weak' by Fernand Braudel.[7] But the state that developed with early capitalism was no nation-state: it ordered internal and external relations on behalf of a monarch; the vast majority of the inhabitants of Europe had no relationship to that state, except one of explicit subordination. Their relationship to each other and to the social hierarchy was defined by a mix of feudal law and religious stricture.

With the widening of economic relations, and the prospect of competition from neighbouring powers, the state became the focal point of international treaties, alliances, and other political arrangements, and fulfilled the bureaucratic function of a war cabinet in the series of battles fought between rival monarchs. The early state system reached a point of maturity with the signing of the Treaty of Westphalia in 1648, an agreement that signalled the end of the Thirty Years War. The Treaty confirmed that sovereignty should be ascribed not just to the sovereign but to the particularity of his territorial holdings; that the nation – still not its nationals – was sovereign and irreducible. Key elements of the agreements ratified in Westphalia survived hundreds of years of turbulent history, and codified some of the basic elements of the modern system: non-interference in the domestic affairs of other states, the concept of diplomatic immunity, and the recognition that only states (i.e. not the Church) were able to exercise political control.[8] The hundred years following the signature of the Treaty saw the development of an international system recognized as legitimate by monarchs, and able to withstand frictions and the odd, limited war. This system – and the bureaucracy it nurtured – gave monarchs a relatively secure basis on which to develop power domestically.

Nowhere was the evolution of a royal bureaucracy more complete than in France. King Louis XIV systematically stripped local aristocrats of power and made Versailles the unchallenged centre of the emerging French nation. Through the *intendant* system, every region of France was linked to the monarchy. There were intermediaries between the people and the representatives of the state – in the form of the 'notables', the Church, and the local aristocracy, not to mention the *fermiers*, who bought from the state (at a discount) the right to collect taxes throughout the countryside. But a structure was emerging that would accrue to it a series of monopolies – to tax, to adjudicate, to use violence legitimately – and through which every individual could eventually find a sense of communal belonging, once he was convinced he wanted to.

It took a popular revolution to create the conditions for the emergence of a distinctly modern nation-state in France. The French Revolution of 1789 marked a watershed: in its aftermath, the nation was not just the king, his territory, and his subjects. In France, the cradle of the modern nation-state and of the principles of nationalism, the *patrie*, in the view of the revolutionaries, was not strictly the country but its people – all its people. The nation was a pact between the

sovereign people and the state, and defence of the *patrie* was defence
of the right of the people to impose their will. In his seminal tract,
'What is the Third Estate', Sieyès wrote, 'The Nation exists before
all things and is the origin of all. Its will is always legal, it is the law
unto itself.'[9]

Nationalism was not tied up with ideas of ethnic purity and common
language and culture. How could it be, given the number of culturally
and linguistically distinct tribes that made up France – Bretons,
Normans, and the like? Nationalism was, instead, a belief in the
political nation. The state itself became the repository of nationalist
sentiment, and was, in turn, transformed by the very allegiances it
won from its citizens. Common ethnicity was not a requirement for
the nation-state: as Anthony Smith has written, the claim of the
nation-state to legitimacy 'is based on the aspiration of a heterogeneous population to unify in terms of public culture and political
community'.[10]

In the years directly following 1789 the state was already able to
call on the mass of French people to rise up in defence of the Revolution. This call was not everywhere heard; the counter-revolution was
fought just as hard within France – by the peasants of the Vendée,
for example, who resisted the dictates of the Paris government – as
at her borders. But the '*levée en masse*' worked well enough to send
French troops deep into Europe, thereby inciting anti-French feeling
and stirring nationalist sentiment elsewhere, particularly in the states
that would later become Germany.

The French Republic helped nurture a nationalist spirit and allowed
it to spread throughout the country, co-opting the farmer, the artisan,
even the beggar, regardless of their economic interests. The nation-
state, over time, turned peasant and lawyer, Breton and Norman, king
and serf into citizens. It would take another hundred years, and massive and unprecedented urbanization, before most western European
states consciously and consistently viewed themselves as the sponsors
not just of the administrative, juridical elements that make up national
government, but of nationhood itself. It would take that long too for
citizens of every social class to look predominantly to the state for
confirmation of their place in the nation. But, already, amidst the
fervour abroad in revolutionary France, early attempts to marry the state
and an emerging nation were evident, and at least some of the population were prepared to replace traditional affiliations – to the Church,
to the sovereign, to a master – with a generalized commitment to *la*

patrie. And, aided by the explosion in printing, the proliferation of newspapers, gazettes and treatises, that message spread quickly, first to neighbouring countries soon to be targets of French expansionist design; later to generations of Europeans, Asians, and Africans attracted by its egalitarian tone and messianic power.

The revolution in France marked the first self-consciously modern agitation for a new political system. 'If the economy of the nineteenth century was formed mainly under the influence of the British industrial revolution, its politics and ideology was formed mainly by the French . . . France provided the first great example, the concept, and the vocabulary of nationalism.'[11] As such it became a model for other countries, or at the very least a concrete example of how power and authority could be wielded in the absence of feudalism and an absolute monarchy. But it is, as Hobsbawm tells us, the English industrial revolution that shows how important a role economic transition plays in the development of political systems, and how quickly social and political structures are shaped by economic change. England's Civil War in the 1640s settled a host of questions about the relationship of the monarchy to its subjects, and gave the English elite a taste for a greater measure of power. By executing King Charles I in 1649, Parliament had claimed a moral right on behalf of the ruled to punish wayward rulers. But more importantly, the period from 1640, the year of the first sitting of the Long Parliament, until 1660, when the monarchy was restored, provided incontrovertible proof that royal powers could be circumscribed. The Glorious Revolution of 1688, in turn, marked a further evolutionary stage – in England's creation of a constitutional monarchy, under which the king owed a large measure of his legitimacy to Parliament. In the century that followed, Parliament confirmed its right to create legislation, impose taxes, and sponsor and make subsequent changes to a legal system that applied to all citizens equally. By the eve of the industrial revolution, England and its dependencies, Scotland and Wales, had achieved many of the hallmarks of a modern state.

England's was not the first 'capitalist' economy, but England's was the first economy to develop into industrial capitalism. This was the result of a particular conjunction of structural conditions, of which the transformation of agriculture was perhaps the most important. By removing land from the community through widespread enclosure of fields and commons formerly held collectively, England created a rural population indentured to the landowning class. That led to the production of food for the market, not just for the subsistence of agricultural labourers, as surpluses were channelled toward the non-rural population, with the profits accruing to the landowner. Coupled with efficient farming techniques, the new agriculture produced a large number of displaced labourers, many of whom drifted towards cities and towns in search of work.[12]

The English nation-state proved far more supple than its continental counterparts in subsuming the entrepreneurial classes into the political order. Its earlier history, particularly the accommodations of the seventeenth century, helped pave the way for a relatively smooth incorporation of the middle class into the political elite. The process would be far more difficult and violent on the continent. At the same time, the system itself managed to create a wholly different form of allegiance within the state. The individual was pre-eminent, the collective less important. The middle classes were allowed political representation without having to ask for it too loudly, and without having to enter into a strategic alliance with the working class. In sum, England's success as a capitalist power owed much to the evolving nation-state that supported and channelled the interests of a rising middle class and that co-opted the political agenda – partly through institutional violence against the agitations of the small but growing working class. A strong political class was created that helped make it possible to extend the democratic franchise only fitfully through the nineteenth century. There was a built-in paternalism, fuelled and financed by economic success, that helped wed citizens to the state, underpinning political stability.

With the exception of the Low Countries, mainland Europe was slow to follow the English example. One reason was the relatively slow rate of urbanization, owing to the persistence of the old-style mode of agricultural production. Equally, few countries had created a class of entrepreneurs willing to risk capital to develop new manufacturing processes. The countries of continental Europe had also yet to create truly national markets – with the exception, partially, of France. Toll roads and customs barriers littered the landscape in the German states and in the Italian duchies and kingdoms. At the same time, wealth was even less evenly distributed on the continent than in England, and those mainland European landowners with a claim to the lion's share of national wealth were slow to invest outside land-based industries – for example, agriculture, mining, and metallurgy. Finally, the extent to which the continental economy was still dominated by agricultural production meant that the landowning classes were unwilling to contemplate a world in which rural labourers were swallowed up by the city.

All the same, the English industrial example was followed, slowly at first, fitfully certainly; but other nations had no choice. So successful was the English capitalist system that no country in Europe could compete unless it was prepared to emulate it.[13]

Britain itself was antagonistic toward continental economic designs, and passed laws, as did other countries, limiting the export of industrial techniques and emigration by skilled entrepreneurs. It fought hard against the French Revolution, partly because England and France had traditionally competed, but also to limit any economic advantage an enthusiastic French state might derive from expansionism. The British opposition to the French Revolution had a more obvious political element as well. Although there were several supporters of the French experiment in republicanism – not least an enthusiastic William Wordsworth, at least until the Terror – the British establishment found the anti-revolutionary critique of Edmund Burke to be more persuasive. His view sat more satisfactorily with the received wisdom that there must be a political class to represent the interests of the nation, and that experiments in popular democracy risked upsetting the social order.

Most continental European nations were still hidebound by functional divisions among aristocrats, journeymen, rural labourers and the like. In most cases, absolutist states dominated, and the societies they governed were deeply conservative. The French Revolution was certainly not popular in the capitals of absolutist Europe; but nor, everywhere, was England's emerging political liberalism. The state was to go through a major transition, and not just in England, over the course of the nineteenth century. It would develop firmer forms of political co-option, and tap richer veins of nationalist spirit. It would create citizens of every class, teach them allegiance to the nation and to its political expression, the state.

As the nineteenth century dawned, the hallmark of the modern world, nationalism, was not yet firmly in view. What we understand today by the term had not yet fully emerged as a basic consideration of statecraft: at the Congress of Vienna in 1815, the Great Powers set out to re-carve up Europe on the basis of diplomatic accommodations not national self-determination. This marks the start of the Concert of Europe, under which the five Great Powers (England,

Russia, post-Revolutionary France, Austro-Hungary, and Prussia) dictated terms within the continent – and later abroad – on the basis of the interests, strengths and weaknesses of the dominant military and economic players. The philosophy behind these changes had little to do with modern concepts such as national self-determination or the principle of nationality. It had everything to do with the balance of power among great states. The redrawn map was dedicated to the principles of order and stability: it was meant to last.

The nineteenth century was the great epoch of nation-building; the era saw the emergence of the nation-state system we today view as natural and eternal. The 1800s saw the beginnings of mass education, and the rise in influence of the masses through democratization.[14] It was a time when capitalism changed character, becoming increasingly dominated by combines and joint-stock companies, vying with the self-made entrepreneurs and family firms. Economic advance was inexorable: industrialization continued apace; railways spread throughout Europe and parts of the developing world as well; communications improved, and great inventions appeared with regularity, particularly toward the end of the century. There may not have been a mass market in modern terms, but in the leading countries of Europe the capitalist marketplace had become a commonplace. There were pockets of 'backwardness', notably in Russia, the Balkans, parts of Italy, the Iberian peninsula. But by the 1880s, in the core states at least, the industrial-capitalist model had triumphed.

In western Europe, the 1800s marked the deepening of national awareness, conditioned by the trappings of the modern nation-state and infused, ultimately, by growing nationalism. Elsewhere, particularly in eastern and central Europe, nationalism would take on a far less liberal, more exclusionary character. But even in the states of western Europe, nationalism had a particularizing effect on the political structure. For everywhere, fuelled by the mythifying of historians, politicians, poets and folklorists, national self-consciousness became inextricably linked with a perceived need for the state to sponsor an awareness of common history, and ethnic and linguistic ties. Informed by the experience of France particularly, national movements sprang up throughout the Ottoman and Hapsburg empires, encouraged by the work of scholars who attempted to find the origins of the claim to nationhood in the deep past. This was the century of 'national history'; most of these efforts revolved around ethnicity as the determining feature of nationalism. Common ethnic roots – represented by language, popular culture, maybe even food and drink – were meant to prove that nationalism was the natural ideology of humankind. The unification of both Italy and Germany was the product of the tireless efforts not just of statesmen and private capital – although both played a role in forging on the one hand a single political entity and on the other a single national market – but of myth-making members of the intelligentsia.[15] Peter Alter[16] calls these writers the 'awakeners': men such as Johann Gottfried von Herder in Germany, the linguist Adamantios Koraïs in Greece, and the poet Adam Mickiewicz in Poland. Their messages spread more quickly as literacy levels climbed throughout most of Europe and printing technology was further refined.

Key to the success in changing attitudes as surely as economic structures was the introduction of mass education in most European countries in the nineteenth century, and with it the imposition of a standard language and a credo of civic responsibility; a sense of citizenship could be extended to every individual within the borders of a given state, while a labour force could be better prepared for the kinds of jobs the economy supplied. Coupled with censuses, military conscription and the growth in the state's role as documentor of its citizens' movements, mass education, and the mass literature it spawned, helped spread the cult of the nation.

Religion and ethnicity are key determinants of a sense of community, and are regularly used even today to justify a politics of exclusion and narrow nationalism. In Belgium, Ireland, and Quebec, for example, the Church played an important role in helping develop nationalist allegiances. But one of the strongest glues of the nation-state, as found in the European model of the eighteenth and nineteenth centuries, was undoubtedly the emergence of a common, national language. Language reflects the public sphere of government above all. The tentacles of the state – tax collection, postal service, a host of regulations and permits – required a common administrative medium, regardless of what people spoke at home. But economic growth, and the concomitant expansion of the activities of the modern state, particularly by the nineteenth century, meant that more and more people were required to operate fluently in their public language. At the time of Italian unification, it is estimated that between two and three per cent of the population spoke Italian. Despite the persistence of regional tongues and argot, the national language has triumphed; the Italian language, in sum, is the *sine qua non* of modern Italy.

Remember Italian statesman Massimo d'Azeglio's famous phrase, uttered on the eve of unification: 'We have made Italy; all that remains is to make Italians.'[17]

The cult of the nation was easier to spread as a result of the migration from country to city which all Europe witnessed during the nineteenth century. In England and Wales, the urban share of total population rose to forty-one per cent by 1850, up from twenty per cent in 1800. In France, similarly, almost fifteen per cent lived in cities of ten thousand or more by 1850, up from eight per cent at the turn of the century. What was, in 1871, to become Germany lagged somewhat further behind: the urban population was five per cent of the total in 1800, and only eleven per cent fifty years later. Overall, Europe saw the rate of urbanization increase inexorably throughout the nineteenth century: from ten per cent in 1800, the urban share of total population in north, west, and central Europe rose to thirty per cent by 1890 (although admittedly the periphery of the continent was far more resistant than the centre to the trend). Stripped of the support structure of the countryside, with its communitarian, familial comforts, these city-bound men and women were forced to seek other forms of social reassurance. As citizens – answerable to the law but protected from arbitrary actions – Europeans had taken the first steps towards replacing the old ways. Therein lay one solution to the anomie felt by former peasants in the large towns and cities. By becoming Germans or Frenchmen, they could begin to accommodate themselves to the social structures of a new way of life.[18] The process took time: it was certainly far from complete even in the final quarter of the nineteenth century, when mass education preached citizenship to all, and when anti-clericalism in those countries still in the grip of the Church dealt the first of several blows to the vestiges of rural commitment to religion as a political agent.

The nineteenth century also confirmed the state in its role as representative of the national economy; this key alteration ushered in a world of great complexity, wherein nationalism, national economic rivalry and, ultimately, imperialism intermixed to help create the recognizably modern characteristics of the nation-state system. *Laisser-faire* capitalism found a political correlative in the British political system. The 1800s spawned a huge literature on the benefits of liberalism and on the precise nature of the relationship between individuals, the state, and the economy. Much of this was intricate and elegant in nature, stressing the balance between the rights and the responsibilities of the citizen in a modern nation-state. John Stuart Mill's *Principles of Political Economy* is perhaps the best example. His singular contribution to the study of economics was to claim – *pace* Ricardo – that only production followed established rules of economics. Distribution – what we did with goods once we made them – was a political rather than an economic question. This had the effect of reinjecting a sense of morality into what had been a rather soulless and nasty conception of economic competition, wherein man exploited man and there was little society could or should do about it.[19]

But other works were far more unthinkingly triumphalist, heralding the start of a golden age when man would go from strength to strength, building a perfect society of acquirers and consumers in a fully competitive world. The state was to do as little as possible so as to leave the nation's merchants, industrialists and financiers a free hand.

However, it was not everywhere the case that the nation-state championed political and economic liberalism; in continental Europe, the free-trade ideology had far weaker roots than in Britain. It was opposed by those thinkers, notably German, who believed that the route to nationhood lay in protection and the creation of a strong, dominant set of state institutions, and that the steady advance of the British industrial giant had by all means to be thwarted – by tariffs and by state-sponsored industrial development for example. Nor were continental nationalisms so deeply rooted in liberal sentiments. Their aims were often couched in terms of expansion, aggrandizement and violent confrontation between nations. But all countries to a degree accepted the industrial-capital model: private property, legal even-handedness and reference to the market were the minimum prerequisites for success. In this sense, and because the world's richest country was imbued with the politics of classic liberalism, the liberal ideal derived great strength from the ever-firmer hold of industrial capitalism in Europe and beyond.

The nineteenth century saw the emergence of a continental economy in the US, in an environment particularly conducive to successful capitalism. The American nation-state had taken its first bold steps while in the throes of the revolutionary war with Britain in the 1770s, and from the start placed the sovereign people at the very centre of a new politics.

The evolution of the state was a qualitatively different process in the US from that undertaken in Europe and the result was to create a radically different idea of the nation. The US was the product not just of a revolution but of a war against colonial control (and subsequently of a bloody civil war). It was also a nation-state carved out of near-virgin territory and an unprecedented mix of ethnicities and religions, and so sought to establish a common perception of 'being American' that all immigrants, many escaping despair in their home countries of Europe, could embrace. It did not inherit all the vestiges of previous social communities – religious, hierarchical, and static – but instead welcomed individuals who chose to come, who felt they had some sense of what they would find. The population of North America in 1800 totalled about seven million; by 1900, it had risen to eighty million. Throughout the century, despite another war with Britain in 1812 and a series of war scares as European events threatened to interfere, the American economy expanded massively. The US was to come into its own in the nineteenth century, when an expanding population and the rush to secure territories to the west and south combined to set its economy booming. But the political structures and ideals that developed out of the revolutionary war, refined through the struggles between federalists and republicans in the early 1800s, were to provide an excellent medium for frontier capitalism: jealously guarded state independence balanced, eventually, by effective central government policy and the phasing out of interstate barriers to commerce; wide suffrage; a consensus on the advantages of economic continentalism; a very real, if not always consistent, commitment to political liberalism. Rugged individualism also engendered a readiness, in the period of rapid industrialization in the nineteenth century, to promote mercilessly a national culture to all who arrived on American shores.

The first half of the nineteenth century also saw the creation of independent states in Latin America; but the British colonies of Australia and Canada were not yet independent, China and Japan had not yet opened up to western influence, and Africa was not yet divided up by European imperialists. In Europe itself, Greece, Serbia and Belgium had won independence, but, on the whole, the continent was as it had been in 1815: nearly everywhere, monarchies held power; with the exception of the British case, the middle class had little direct political power. Throughout the 1840s, pressures were building for political reform, particularly on the continent. The moves coincided with increasing social tensions between poor and rich, as the industrial revolution extended its influence in Europe and in the US. In the

1850s and 1860s, virtually every west European country introduced liberal reforms, ranging from the creation of central banks and a professional civil service to the lowering of tariffs and the creation of parliamentary governments elected on limited suffrage. Each of these reforms strengthened the state and the climate for industrial capitalism. Meanwhile educational and military reforms, in particular, helped co-opt ever greater numbers of 'citizens' into the superstructure of the developing nation-states.

The age of liberal stability was not to last and the 1870s were a turning point. The commitment to narrow suffrage, and a parliament of the wise, was increasingly untenable. With the first signs of economic downturn in the by now well-established capitalist system of Europe, emerging working-class movements encountered the conditions that would radicalize them. The Great Depression of 1873 had the effect of encouraging the erection of tariffs, although free-trading Britain was resistant. The national-economy system, meanwhile, meant that capitalism sought a range of self-consciously national solutions to the problem of declining profits, particularly in the form of mergers and consolidation. The latter part of the nineteenth century was the start of the Trust period in the US, when huge conglomerates were built by strong-willed capitalists. Europe was not immune. To a large degree, world capitalism was a victim of its own roaring success. Technological development made production ever more efficient. Yet a true mass market had yet to emerge, and there were too many goods chasing too few consumers. Until a mass market could be created, capitalism sought efficiency through oligopoly, and new markets through imperialism.

At the same time, nationalism began to evolve a darker, less liberal identity in the late nineteenth century. In earlier centuries, patriotism – love of country – was not based primarily on ethnicity or language. By the 1880s in Europe, conservatives saw in theories of ethnic purity and in the concept of race a barrier against the onslaught of an increasingly complicated and fragmenting world and as a weapon for the assertion of identity on a wider stage. Nineteenth-century nationalism became, particularly for the right wing, the natural extension of man's communitarian nature rather than an extension of his individual right of self-determination.[20] The manipulation of the popular sentiment, most obviously in the fanning of nationalist fervour, may at first have ensured the success of the nation-state against vestiges of the old order, and so protected and enhanced the national economy it represented and helped nourish. But mass democracy also led to demands on the elites of European countries to soften some of the more troublesome edges of capitalism, and made it increasingly difficult to impose anything like the pure-market system.

The previous hundred years had seen Britain win and embellish the mantle of world's leading economic power. But now it was no longer alone: indeed, it was losing ground against its competitors. British industrial production grew by between three and four per cent annually between 1820 and 1870 but only by 1.5 per cent a year through to the 1890s.[21] By the turn of the century, Germany produced more steel than Britain; while the US was ahead of both in the production of coal and pig iron.[22] Japan embarked on a programme of rapid industrialization, although it impinged little on European consciousness until the early years of the twentieth century.

Industrialists themselves were clamouring for protection from competitive foreign firms. The classical liberals began to lose the debates about the role of national governments in the economy. Demands on states to protect national industries and agricultural producers led to a blossoming of tariff wars; even in federal Germany, where the member states still retained large powers and made common cause difficult to achieve, Bismarck managed to push through protectionist legislation. Governments, their costs rising, sought sources of financing that increasingly flew in the face of doctrinaire liberalism. Imaginative taxes were coupled with nationalization of railways in the major European countries.

All the same, the 1890s marked the start of a boom that lasted, despite fits and starts, through to the outbreak of the First World War. There were slowdowns and some spectacular financial failures, particularly in the US, but industrial capitalism made steady, in places heady, progress.[23] By the turn of the century, nation-states explicitly competed economically, and when they could not compete, they erected barriers and imposed tariffs, particularly on commodities. Britain resisted this impulse, as the pre-eminent trader of goods and services. Economic concentration increased virtually everywhere in the developed capitalist world: the new norm became oligopolist or 'organized' capitalism – in steel, in oil, in coal. The management of these large companies was professionalized relentlessly, as members of founding families were replaced by salaried presidents and expert financiers. In the US, the trend toward concentration encouraged legislators to act in the early years of the twentieth century, introducing anti-trust laws. In Europe the response varied, with the German government actively sponsoring the growth of a private monopoly in coal. Even firms that operated internationally, particularly the large banking groups, were careful to maintain ties to a single country, under the sponsorship of a single nation-state that would protect them.

Finally, and most damaging to the liberal ethos, increasingly powerful states continued to jockey for position in diplomatic as well as economic terms. The second half of the nineteenth century saw what Adam Watson terms a 'loosening'[24] of the Concert of Europe: the emergence of new nation-states, particularly Germany, undermined acceptance of the *diktat* of the traditional Great Powers. Liberals had welcomed the national liberation movements, arguing that democratic nation-states would not go to war against each other. As Watson writes, liberals believed that 'what had once been a sovereigns' club would become a family of independent nations'.

Despite the rise of the US as an economic power, the European state system continued to dominate. What had been a formal, quasi-hegemonic concert of great powers had been transformed utterly by the rise of the nation-state and the growing economic interdependence of nations in the world economy; all the same, the assumptions that underlined nineteenth-century international politics remained largely intact, even if the 'great powers' themselves could not dictate terms as they had a hundred years previously. The European system had become a world system by 1900, and if Europe did not explicitly rule it, European values infused it.

The early years of the twentieth century and the last decades of the nineteenth were marked by often vicious arguments, war scares, a massive build-up in armaments, and the conduct of secret diplomacy. Germany was the source of particular worry in Europe: it had grown impressively, particularly after 1880, and was soon to rival Britain, whose long, steady, relative decline dates from the end of the nineteenth century. Competition extended overseas, in the rush to claim colonies in Africa, the Middle East, and Asia. This was the great age of imperialism, although the tidal wave had begun to gather momentum earlier in the century. By the eve of the First World War, virtually every inch of the world had been carved up by the European nations, the US, and Japan. The jockeying for power, coupled with secret alliances aimed at containing distrusted neighbours, would ultimately lead to the hostilities of 1914–18, the first war on such a scale among nation-states, rather than among competing sovereigns and narrow elites. Imperial conquest played an important role in determining the features of the modern state: external representations of a nation's power were testimony to the state's robustness, and helped convince citizens they were members of a club worth belonging to.

Imperialism, and the mythification of the nation and its overseas dependencies was also to have an important if far from lingering effect on the growth of internationalist working-class movements in Europe. These were arguably the biggest threat to the political elites, if only because the ideology of a global working class was at root antithetical to the functioning of the liberal nation-state. The trade union movement that developed in the latter part of the nineteenth century maintained at least a surface commitment to internationalism, and at any rate the level of militancy if anything increased. The turn of the century saw a high incidence of trade-union activity, including crippling strikes and violent clashes between workers and strike-breakers (aided on numerous occasions by the police or the army). Trade-union activity became even more radical as industrial processes became standardized: the assembly-line pioneered by US car maker Henry Ford in 1905 found its way into even underdeveloped regions of Europe soon after the First World War, introducing far greater opportunity for the use of semi-skilled labour in manufacturing and a consequent downward pressure on industrial wage bills.[25] Class war seemed just as possible as war among states.

Socialism and communism proved a potent rival to economic liberalism in many European countries, and found supporters not only among workers but among teachers, clerks, and other members of the middle classes. Left-wing organizers were effective and persuasive: they posited not just reform but a revolution in the way the economy was managed. Antithetical to political liberalism, antithetical indeed to the prevailing economic system itself, left-wing ideology, strengthened by the 'scientific' theories of, particularly, Karl Marx, derived much of its power from the sheer extent and all-embracing nature of its vision. It was not about tinkering; it was not about minor reform. Socialism and communism both proffered a world view, and as such were a major threat to liberal capitalism. Socialists rejected the essential contention of liberalism – that enlightened self-interest and individual freedom would together lead to the greater good. It was conflict between classes, rather than the individual's pursuit of profit, that was the primary engine of economic, and hence social, change.

Governments were beginning to realize that the solutions to their domestic problems could not be found overseas, although they were loath to abandon their imperialist programmes. The costs of empire, particularly of wars (such as that between the English and the Boers of South Africa) were much higher than the return in purely economic terms. The very conservatives that had trumpeted empire as a way of advancing the cause of the nation-state found that they had created insoluble budget crises and precipitated a loss of confidence among voters. Some traditional liberals, who had already worried about the incompatibility of empire and classic liberalism, were prepared to abandon the mainstream political parties. In 1905, left-leaning governments made inroads throughout Europe.[26]

Through the 1890s and up until the eve of the war, the state's role grew apace. Germany had, in the 1880s, offered some measure of state protection against sickness and old age, ushering in limited welfare programmes paid for by the state. In France, the programme of the Solidarists was accepted in large measure by the Republican government in the 1890s, and slow progress was made in introducing health services for the poor and encouraging the development of pension schemes. In the US, informal welfare was dispensed by the party machines, particularly in the big cities. It was paid for in part through the extraction of bribes from corporations looking to buy land or to establish new companies; the funds thus raised helped local politicians develop infrastructure – lights, schools, hospitals – and to find jobs for friends and supporters. Serious calls for national government intervention in the economy only emerged in the very last years of the century, during the Progressive era, and even then the most important legislation enacted by Theodore Roosevelt's administration was aimed at extending the federal government's regulatory power and improving the lot of consumers (but not, specifically, of the industrial working class). Only with the advent of the activist presidency of Woodrow Wilson were the first important curbs on the capitalist system introduced, and federal-government policy tools such as the Federal Reserve created.[27]

Most European governments were now prepared to legislate for a range of social protection. They accepted the need to extend the power of the state to intervene in the economy, to provide limited welfare to those without jobs, to improve living and working conditions in the cities, to extend the concept of compulsory education. The state, then, was to help mediate between the classes. But to do so, it would need some way of financing itself. The Right was willing to support the introduction of an income tax; and the citizenry appeared willing to pay it – provided much of the money went to armaments. The traditionally pacifist Left accepted the price that came with the power to tax and spend, and even the liberal political elite in Britain, uncomfortable with both imperialism and militarism, acquiesced.

Even without the powers it would win later in the century, the state by 1910 was already huge and omnipresent. It operated on behalf of citizens and the nation-state, and in the 'national interest', sponsoring a limited number of social programmes and protecting national industry. It re-armed in part to further the power and independence of its territory, and so supported a large, private-sector national defence industry; it was ready, ultimately, to go to war. That decision would be broadly supported by conservatives in most European countries whose nationalism was strong and growing. It would be fed by a sense that the world had become too chaotic – social categories were too fluid, trade unions too boisterous, foreign competition too challenging. The cult of nationalism so carefully nurtured in the nineteenth century, and invoked with increasing hysteria when the 'socialist threat' looked serious, made war seem natural: made it seem, indeed, something of a relief.

The proximate causes of the war are well known, if still much debated even today: the great-power alliances, the arms race, perceptions of German belligerence in the east, the slackening hold of the Hapsburg and Ottoman empires on their multinational constituent parts, the nearly universal commitment to the balance-of-power system. The flexible concert of the nineteenth century had become hardened into the rigid alliances of the early 1900s: diplomacy could not cope. The war enhanced the power and role of the state – the war economies of Europe required strong central administrative control and a measure of tax reform – and presaged a social revolution in attitudes towards women and indeed towards class. It gave birth to the first communist state, in Russia. But it did little for the stability of the international system. The inter-war period would be one of crisis, of rampant nationalism, of fascism, of a collapse of international order.

The war, and the period immediately following it, settled one issue. Bourgeois liberalism, the quintessentially nineteenth-century view of progress, of peace, of reward for hard work, represented by good, non-interventionist government in the service of elites yet with due regard for the rest of the population, was dead. It had already shown signs of weakness in the critical thirty-five-year period from 1880, when the middle classes in many European countries could be seen to be suffering from a form of political and moral uncertainty. Modern life in the Belle Epoque looked and felt, to many, ordered, stable, and above all increasingly comfortable for the bourgeoisie. Belief in progress, particularly scientific progress, was still strong, and the arts flourished. But far too visible were the poor and huddled workers in city ghettos and far too audible were the rabble-rousing trade unionists and socialists.

The assertion of a new, modern age had enormous consequences for intellectual life. The fear of being swamped by 'mass' culture, which by now included among its clients the petty-bourgeoisie and the educated working class, helped push 'high' culture towards the self-consciously avant-garde and selective. But these forms were increasingly alien to the cultured classes. The birth of the 'modern' – sometime in the first decade of the twentieth century – established a gap between bourgeois taste and the avant-garde that was never really to be bridged again. The issue became moot with the introduction of truly mass culture, in the form of recorded music and films. The dance hall and the 'musical entertainment' of the nineteenth century had already shown the way; technological innovation and capitalism's power to harness cultural expression would do the rest. The 'modern' brought with it new philosophies – of time, of the physical world, of the psychological workings of the mind.[28] Far from fomenting cohesiveness, communal experience and comprehensibility, the modern world henceforth would be fractured, and humankind relentlessly individuated. Such philosophies were in keeping with the end of the age of the bourgeois and the rise of a society of consumers. In 1918, the automobile was still a plaything for the rich; within a decade, it would be symbol of consumerism *par excellence* – distance would be redefined, isolation difficult to maintain. Soon, radio would reach millions and its message, too, would be pulsatingly modern. The world as it was becoming would have its elites, its social distinctions, its owners and employees, its advantaged and disadvantaged. But the certainties of a bourgeois world order – and its precise hierarchy and political outlook – were gone.

The conflict marked another caesura, the passing of the European Age. The war not only confirmed the US as an important military power and an unequalled economic competitor but also ushered in the first American-assisted attempts to forge a new international system, a new world order. It was to founder, in part because the US itself refused to sponsor the system so carefully outlined by President Woodrow Wilson, but the 1919 restructuring of the western world was to have a profound effect on the inter-war years, and on the final form of the American hegemony that followed the Second World War in 1945. Wilson came to Paris in 1919 with his famous fourteen points, enshrining, notably, the principle of national self-determination. Intending his new world order to be broadly democratic, Wilson evidently believed his goal was achievable through the recognition of the right of peoples to govern themselves.

The years after 1919 proved, however, that the dream of creating viable, ethnically determined nation-states throughout Europe remained elusive. In the twentieth century, new orthodoxies would be needed to head off the challenge of socialist radicalism and to sponsor capitalism. Ironically, one of liberal capitalism's natural enemies – the nation-state – would give it a new lease, by finding a new balance between liberalism, capitalism and democracy, under the direct and careful watch of a sponsoring hegemon.

2

A World of Nations, a Society of States

'Harrow the house of the dead; look shining at
New styles of architecture, a change of heart.'

W.H. AUDEN[1]

The form of the nation-state created in Europe over the course of
the seventeenth, eighteenth, and nineteenth centuries remains the
model for the institution of today. But similarities in basic architecture
should not obscure the massive changes that took place in the decades
following the Great War. It is as if we were to look at a cluster of
houses that once formed a village and are now part of a great city,
and say: nothing has changed. It is not just the scale of development,
but the qualitative changes that are important.

Three momentous changes took place as a result of the inter-war
crisis, the Second World War, and the long 'peace' that followed.
Firstly, the nation-state system that had its origins in Europe was
generalized to the whole world, but under the disciplines enforced,
ultimately, by the two superpowers. Secondly, a global economy
emerged which enforced significant limitations on the ability of even
the most powerful states to dictate their own policies. Thirdly, the
expansion of both the global economy and the international political
system knitted states together in a tighter embrace, creating new forms
of international co-operation.[2]

The European crisis which took up the first half of the twentieth
century led to a dramatic reshaping of the environment within which
states operated. Europe was removed from the centre of the world
stage, the European empires collapsed, and control passed to the two

23

superpowers. As a result, a global political system was created for the first time.

The balance among the European Great Powers had proved ineffective in preventing the outbreak of the First World War, but nothing else had been conceived to fill the gap in the inter-war years.[3] The destruction of the Great War created a climate of public opinion in many countries against armed conflict, and hence the post-war period began with high expectations that the slaughter could be redeemed through a more just liberal world order. The League of Nations was the principal standard-bearer of this optimism. Woodrow Wilson 'came to Europe to replace traditional great power diplomacy, not to make it work more effectively'.[4] But Wilson's assertion of the principle of national self-determination legitimized bitter struggles without putting forward any rational or effective process for resolving them, while the First World War itself engendered fierce rivalries and hatreds. These could only be exacerbated by the political nonsenses that the territorial settlement created. The framework of small, isolated states which the Peace of Paris had set up was designed to reflect national self-determination; but it left unredeemed minorities everywhere, and a patchwork of grievance.[5]

The inter-war period was in many respects the apogee of the instability and bloodshed we associate with nationalism. The struggle between liberalism and nationalism that had intensified in the second half of the nineteenth century reached its violent and bloody climax. Fascism found its motive power in the rejection of both liberalism and socialism; but also in a critique of the liberal internationalism of Wilson, expressed in the peace settlements, and in the inadequacies of the fragile democracies of the post-war era. Mussolini was the first leader to take advantage of the chaos of the period; but it was Hitler's regime that typified fascism's power. Its nationalism was racist, violent, and ultimately genocidal. Loyalty was owed to the state, to the nation, to the leader, to a new world order. Totalitarianism was combined with a view of the individual and his relation to society that was utterly unfamiliar to liberalism and that was unyielding to the structures so painfully created at the end of the First World War. In the face of the driving harshness of the regimes that sprang up between the wars, the old diplomacy was powerless.

The League of Nations was poorly designed to remedy the lack of overall structure in the international system – structure that was crucial if stability were to be maintained. The United States and the

Soviet Union were not engaged in the League; it lacked any powers of enforcement; and with each of the key European states distracted by its own domestic crises, as well as by a plethora of international challenges, the prospects for its successful operation were small. The League failed, comprehensively, and its failure had resounding and enduring consequences. After the Second World War, the new United Nations paralleled the League in organization; but it also sought to avert the problems that had beset its predecessor by, for example, making the decisions reached by the Security Council binding on all members. More importantly, however, the UN put most of its influence into the Security Council, which was, of course, dominated by the Permanent Five members (the US, the USSR, Britain, France and China), rather than the General Assembly. While the UN was to serve as a meeting place for all states, a universal institution, it was thus clear from the beginning that great power sensibilities and security demands were to be pre-eminent.

The details of the dispositions of the peace in 1945 rapidly came to matter less than the overriding feature of the post-war settlement: the establishment of two poles of massive power, the Soviet Union and the US. Very quickly, the promise of world institutions that could bring all nations together dissolved under the pressure of superpower conflict. 'The globalization of politics . . . destroyed one of the essential premises of the system: that the new central political institution could act as an impartial judge of the misdemeanors of one or two squabbling, misbehaved delinquents. The central institution was not above the conflict, able to maintain order by injunctions from afar. It was the central arena within which the conflict took place.'[6] No fewer than 279 vetoes of Security Council resolutions were cast during the Cold War.[7] Despite earlier plans, the UN had no forces of its own and was largely powerless to arbitrate between its two most important members.

Instead, conventional forces and nuclear weapons provided the glue that kept the blocs together, and also the divide that kept them apart. The emerging antagonism between the West and the East, and the desire of both sides to make a stable settlement, had led to the formation of spheres of influence as early as the Yalta conference. In the immediate post-war years, these were formalized and deepened: the US thus became the central power within a bloc of like-minded states, as did the Soviet Union. 'The two superpowers were not "bookends" holding together a single closely involved society of states; they were centres round which largely separate societies developed, locked against each other strategically but insulated by geography and ideology.'[8]

The role which America took on in 1945 drew lessons from its failure to assume responsibilities during the inter-war years, but also from what American policy makers saw as the greatest weakness of the inter-war period, the lack of any systematic leadership. In the West, the states that emerged from the war under its hegemony were to be democratic, capitalist and relatively open to the world. The US achieved this principally through the support of local politicians committed to democratization and liberalism. Where there was doubt or opposition, as in Italy in 1948, the US used covert action and support of political and extra-political forces to ensure the outcome. Security within these states, as well as between them, was necessary in order to maintain the greater struggle with the East. Allies were brought together in collective security organizations, such as Nato; provided with military aid and *matériel*; and assisted in rearming – even, after a decent interval, in West Germany. As well, the US assisted and encouraged the continent's experiments with political and economic unity.

The political stability of the states in the US sphere of influence was underpinned by a new approach to economic management, gleaned from the lessons of the inter-war failures. In the West, the paradigm was set by Keynes and the new economics. The techniques of demand management were intended to prevent the dramatic and unsettling fluctuations that had upset national economies in the previous decades, in turn the cause of so much social unrest. Stability would provide an even pitch for democracy, which depended on a reasonable expectation of economic success. Equity was sought through ambitious welfare programmes, and through redistributive taxation. Industrialization and modernization proceeded rapidly.

Keynes had recognized what was implicit in his theories. 'The central controls necessary to ensure full employment will, of course, involve a large extension of the traditional functions of government', he wrote in the General Theory. With that modest phrase, Keynes launched a revolution in thinking about the state just as he had launched a revolution in economic thought. 'The most significant and revolutionary feature of Keynesian macro-economic analysis lay in the beneficent role it indicated for direct government intervention in the modern market economy.'[9] Government spending, including deficits, and government intervention in private industry were legitimized as the way to reconstruct and develop economies. The state provided a stable macroeconomic basis; it evened out the business cycle; it provided trained labour, kept fit and healthy by new provision of state services; and it ensured that sufficient capital was provided to lubricate the wheels of industry.

The social changes that accompanied this shift were as profound as the economic changes. Consumption spending was a key part of the formula for post-war growth, and the encouragement and facilitation of consumer spending were achieved hand in hand with the private sector. The US led the way in putting the consumer at the forefront of society. 'When, during the so-called Eisenhower recession of 1957–8, the President took it upon himself to advise the public to buy, and was asked what, he answered, "Anything!" In the same way, Harold Macmillan is said to have sent a memo asking: 'Who are the middle classes and what do they want? We shall try to give it to them.'¹⁰ The shift in economics thus fed a political change: towards democracies that had a broad, stable base in middle-class acceptability, delivering to voters and co-operating with the various interest groups that made consumerism work. Pluralism was the counterpart to the mixed economy, filling in the gaps left by traditional allegiances. In the pursuit of social peace a more solid, consensual relationship was established among the state, the private sector and the unions.

Consumer society did the work that capitalism had previously been unable to accomplish. It went even further in breaking down the traditional societies that remained in Europe; it put the home and car at the centre of existence, shifting the communal ethic towards civic privatism – the idea that personal acquisitions were the goal of existence and that life was to be lived at home. Economic growth, combined with the growth of the institutions of civil society, provided a legitimizing basis for the extension of the state, and for a new, more stable form of democracy.

In the East, the Soviet Union carved out its own sphere, maintained, in the extreme, by force not pluralism. For the Soviet Union, the motive was to create a bulwark against any revival of German power, and to establish a place at the centre of any post-war order. Excluded from the management structures of the inter-war era, Moscow had little reason to trust the western states, or to put its faith in multilateral diplomacy. Instead, it established a zone of security and dominance. The Soviet Union carried out a much bloodier job of harnessing territory to its own ends, starting with its occupation of the defeated territories and continuing with the establishment of party rule at the expense of democracy. This was maintained by military and police force, including interventions in Hungary in 1956 and Czechoslovakia in 1968 and the threat in Poland in 1980. The pre-war institutions of society were bulldozed: the party took over, monopolizing political power and the right of social organization.[11]

The economic ties the Soviet Union created with eastern Europe were on an entirely different model, that derived from Stalin's surge for growth. The private sector was gradually abolished and state ownership extended; a premium was put on heavy industry and intensive growth; consumer industries took second place in the command economy. The aim, again, was growth, and, as in the West, the aims were primarily political. But the methods were entirely different, and the goal was to produce a homogenized society, not the bourgeois individualism of the West. The Soviet Union, when it occupied Czechoslovakia, Poland and Hungary, was taking control of states that had been nearly as wealthy as their western counterparts; but their pre-war industrial and commercial strength was stripped away, and industry was pointed in new directions. That direction was, overwhelmingly, east: just as the states reliant on the US turned to Washington for finance, trade and aid, so the states of the East were forced to look to Moscow.

The creation of the two blocs effectively sealed the end of Europe's existence as a single entity. By effacing the power of the traditional European states, the superpowers also laid down the basis for a far-reaching change in the rest of the world. The Second World War resulted in the dismantling of the European overseas empires and the creation of dozens of new nation-states. This had its beginnings in the move towards decolonization begun by the League, and in the trusteeships it established. After the Second World War, European colonialism unravelled rapidly, and out of the control (in many cases) of any external force, hostile or allied. The European states were increasingly unable to keep hold of their far-flung territories; the growth of nationalist movements throughout (in particular) Asia during the War made life increasingly difficult; and the US, through the new United Nations system, was keen to establish the principle that these territories be given their right of self-determination.

The nationalist movements in the Third World had their roots in opposition to the cruelty, exploitation and increasing weakness of the colonial regimes. The movements which had sprung up since the nineteenth century made their appeals, as the European states had before them, through a wide range of imagery – historical, political and cultural – to a lost past, an ethnic unity, and the illegitimacy of foreign domination. The 'nations' for which sovereignty was claimed frequently had little meaning; different ethnic, religious and social groups were lumped together into areas with little historical experience of unity or independence. The borders that had been artificially created by the European powers, however, became the limits of striving for the new nationalist movements. And the techniques which the colonial powers had used to weld unity out of disparate provinces were now turned against them, often by the local elites that they had sought to co-opt.[12] 'Seek ye first the political kingdom, and all else will be added unto it,' said Kwame Nkrumah.

The new nationalism of the Third World appeared to present a threat, not just to the traditional dominance of the European powers, but also to the international system of states created in their wake. The new nations fiercely resisted outside intervention and activity, repelling efforts at domination by other states, throwing out western-owned companies and seeking to nationalize their economies. Equally, they frequently flirted, more or less seriously, with associations that went beyond sovereignty, with the aim of forming more lasting federations – through, for instance, Pan-Africanism, expressed in the Organization for African Unity, or Pan-Arabism. But the threat was more apparent than real; the new states in fact replicated the important aspects of the European states system, clinging to an idea of sovereignty that had changed little. As Peter Calvocoressi points out, 'the OAU was an association of sovereign states in a continent which, in the wake of decolonization, was becoming more fragmented than it had been under foreign rule. The OAU established particularism in Africa in the same way as the UN accepted it in the world at large.' Pan-Arabism had a similarly chequered career as a concept. Overall, the authoritative judgement on the result is that 'It is the traditional society of states which has had the greater impact on anti-colonial nationalism, rather than the other way round.'[13]

Nor did the new states remain outside the orbit of the superpowers. Instead they became part of a peripheral zone, where the conflicts were fought out, the resources mined, and the surplus stock sold off. The formation of blocs and groupings among the Third World states, an ambitious project to combat both their own disunity and the economic and political dominance of the North, never realized its potential. The non-aligned movement made little progress in breaking the deadlock of the superpowers. 'Non-alignment was originally as much

a geopolitical and strategic concept as a political one, but it recommended itself to many anti-colonial governments because they
interpreted the western alliance as the military infrastructure of the
world capitalist system.'[14] The non-aligned movement reached its
height in the 1970s, with the demands for a New International Economic Order, but crumbled under the disunity of the states involved,
and their uncertain interpretations of 'non-alignment'.

Economic policy in these states was guided by the necessity for
development and modernization, not just to reverse the patterns of
dependency that had been established by the colonial powers, but to
stabilize the often fragile relationship between the ethnic groups which
were brought together in individual states. The new decolonized states
built on the colonial structures that had forged primary-product
economies for a century or more, economies centred on the large-scale
production for export markets of primary goods. Onto this foundation
were grafted systems of welfare and subsidy on the one hand, and
state-owned industrial corporations on the other. In the Third World,
the imperative of national integration was if anything more pressing
than in the First World or the Soviet Union. In Africa, Asia and the
Middle East, newly independent countries, often with borders that
enclosed widely varying populations and vast social inequalities,
needed to weld national unity out of diverse elements. But this was
done – in most decolonized states – with a greater attention to the
role of the state than to the international economy and with less room
for the private sector than in the West.

The world that emerged out of the ruins of the Second World
War was thus recognizably shaped by what had gone before, by the
European system of inter-state relations, by the traditions and forms
of the European nation-states, and by the idea of sovereignty that had
been developed since the Peace of Westphalia. But 'while the rules
and institutions of the worldwide society emphasized continuity, the
pressures of the system were now too altered for a restoration to be
possible. The reality was not a diffused hegemony over the system;
nor was it a tightly knit international society based on voluntary commitment according to the theoretical design of the League and the
United Nations; nor an anarchy of multiple independencies. Its
characteristic was the dominance of the two superpowers, and the
separation of the two systems which they proceeded to construct.'[15]

The point is, for our concerns, that the growth of this international
system put some stiff limits on the autonomy of nation-states. Bipolar

domination imposed strict disciplines on what could be countenanced in the way of pretensions to sovereignty, nationalism or national self-determination. These impulses were always subordinated by the super-powers to the greater needs of international stability and order. The antipathetical relationship between the US and the Soviet Union was characterized by regular interaction, rules of engagement and a diplo-matic closeness that ensured conflict could be regulated.[16] The separ-ation of the two systems, though informal, was in general respected by both sides. Though both were prepared to contribute to tensions in the other's sphere of influence by stoking nationalist fires, neither would go all the way, a modern form of the principle that had been established at Westphalia. Within these spheres of influence, both exercised a hege-monic influence, with differing degrees of intensity, and the legitimacy of this was broadly recognized by both sides. There was little western attempt to support the uprisings in Hungary, Czechoslovakia or Poland. In the same way, Soviet attempts to undermine US hegemony in the heart of its sphere of influence, western Europe, were rare; sup-port for foreign communist parties continued throughout the post-war period, but Stalin was loath to destabilize to the point where it would attract US intervention. Equally, there was little pretence in the first years following the war of respecting the principles of national self-determination. In the same way as the UN sought to minimize the fissiparous tendencies of the League by putting more weight on the Security Council than the General Assembly, the post-war border settlement was dominated by the considerations of the two major powers. Hence Germany was left divided, with zones of control for Britain, France, the US and the Soviet Union, the first three eventually pooling their holdings into the Federal Republic; Korea was split in two. The Soviet Union's wartime acquisitions – the Baltic states, the eastern half of Poland, Bessarabia and northern Bukovina, and Karelia – were annexed and little complaint was heard from the West.

This lack of respect for national self-determination was equally common within the broader spheres of influence established by the superpowers. The US rapidly shifted away from its emphasis on break-ing the back of European colonialism, pushed by the need to secure bases for its forces, and resources and markets for its companies. 'To nationalists in Asia and Africa, the change of mood amounted to some-thing between evasiveness and betrayal. It placed the United States alongside, if not actually in, the ranks of the imperialists, and it was the beginning of the decline in the high standing of the United States in the minds of what was coming to be called the Third World.'[17] Soviet support for nationalist revolutions was limited to those that could be useful. Its attitude was tempered by its own nationalities problem.

Decolonization in many respects assisted in the freezing of the map that was consequent on the new balance of power.[18] Each new state resisted breaking up the borders set by colonial powers, and denied claims by neighbouring states on its territories. Many of these borders had been drawn up under colonial rule, or between colonial states at the times of much earlier imperial break-up, such as the Sykes-Picot agreement between Britain and France which set out the boundaries of modern Iraq. Only in rare cases – the partition of India and the creation of Pakistan for example – did post-colonial states permit further fragmentation. Secessionist movements had a low rate of success. Groups such as the Kurds were exploited by regional and global powers for their use in local wars, but there was never any real attempt to secure a homeland for them.

The counterpart of the new international political system was a reshaping of the international economic system. In much the same way that the old European political order had failed, while the League of Nations had proved too weak to sustain peace, the nineteenth century economic system had died in the First World War, but nothing had been found to take its place. The international political liberalism of Wilson had been accompanied by an attempt to revive the old economic liberalism of the pre-war period. There was a prevalent belief that 'Once the peace treaties had been signed and Europe had been sorted out, the vanquished had been penalized, the war-time economic restrictions abandoned and the great god of gold had been restored, life could carry on as before.'[19] The result, in the absence of any leadership by either the United States or Britain, had been the rapid collapse of the system after the Crash, the nationalization of economic policies and erection of tariff barriers.

The new orthodoxy after 1945 in the managing of national economies was far more interventionist. 'We curbed monopolies, we encouraged labour unions, we regulated competition, we intervened in the business cycle, we did a thousand and one things to make the economic game yield the results we wanted of it – not the result it would have brought had we done nothing.'[20] At the same time, greater attention was paid to the subject of international economic institutions and mechanisms. The system that emerged was a hybrid; it took some years for the framework established at Bretton Woods to have any meaning at all in the confused conditions of post-war Europe, and by the time an international system was up and running it was barely related to the schemes dreamt up by the likes of Keynes and White. But its general principles were an open international economy, with the newly founded General Agreement on Tariffs and Trade to promote successive lowering of trade barriers and a system of fixed exchange rates based on the dollar's link to gold. There had been a plan for a broader system, but the supranational elements required to run it were never effective. 'The arrangements . . . so patiently negotiated remained mostly imaginary.'[20] The IMF and World Bank had been meant to be supranational experiments; they ended up as American institutions. The GATT had been intended as the first step towards an International Trade Organization; this did not materialize. Instead, it relied for its effectiveness on management by the US.

This system, which survived numerous upsets for twenty years, gradually showed the strains of national management, however. The point at which it became manifestly dysfunctional was 1971, when the US pulled the plug on the Bretton Woods agreement. Once fixed exchange rates were gone it was hard to maintain other financial fictions. The collapse of the managed exchange-rate system was accompanied and partly caused by the rapid growth of global financial markets, which yielded little to international regulation. This began in the 1960s in London, and was concentrated on the trading in dollar balances in London, built up as a result of switching of accounts out of New York by some European governments, US military spending abroad, and the investments of US corporations and banks. As the 1960s turned into the 1970s, other centres of trading emerged, other currencies were traded, and the phenomenon exploded. 'The development of a free Eurodollar and Eurocurrency market during the 1960s undeniably gave international capital flows a big boost. The *dirigisme* which had hitherto characterized the world economy now made way for a system of free international capital transactions.'[21] The Eurocurrency market grew from $3bn in 1960 to $75bn in 1970 and over $1 trillion in 1984, fed by the recycling of oil money after the great oil price increases.

The dismantling of the US-managed international financial system was closely related to a change in the relationship among nation, state and economy which had been so painstakingly assembled in the post-war period in both the command economies of the East and the market economies of the West. The proximate cause of the breakdown was inflation, as states sought to finance growing deficits, and workers sought higher remuneration. The state suffered because of the mounting levels of national debt, which became increasingly unmanageable. State-owned enterprises that had been created lost money hand over fist, whether they were competing with private-sector business abroad or locked into national protectorates. The welfare systems sucked in cash and rising expectations kept the bill high. Corporations responded by raising prices.

The decision to shift away from state control was partly an economic argument. 'The events that brought inflation to the top of the agenda of governments in capitalist economies in the course of the 1970s destroyed their residual confidence in the efficacy of demand management for reducing unemployment and stimulating productivity growth and persuaded them that attempts to control the foreign exchange values of their currencies were not only ineffectual but potentially harmful in their side effects.'[22] On the one hand, growth had been allowed to subordinate the traditional aims of price stability and balance-of-payments equilibrium. On the other hand, it became increasingly obvious that the diverse aims of national economic management could not all be achieved at the same time. Indeed, each required different, often competing, sets of tools. Keeping the national model on the road in the face of diverse priorities was a problem not just for econometric calculation but for political management and one that states found all but impossible to solve.

There was thus an explicit political argument about the state itself, and its role in both the economy and the lives of citizens in the shift away from the post-war orthodoxy. The principal problem was the political 'asymmetry' of the Keynesian formula, as J.K. Galbraith, one of the foremost Keynesians puts it. 'Deflation and unemployment called for higher expenditure and lower taxes, which were politically very agreeable actions. Price inflation, on the other hand, called for lower government expenditure and higher taxes, which were far from politically agreeable.'[23] Managing national economies relied on the creation of a national political consensus which was increasingly difficult to support. The structures of macro-economic management that had been built up in the 1950s and 1960s also proved inadequate. In co-operation with the private sector, the state was a weak actor; in competition, it was likely to lose. The damaging battles that resulted sparked a new, sceptical approach to the benevolent and paternalist claims of the state. Its crusaders – Margaret Thatcher in Britain and Ronald Reagan in the US – went from being fringe figures to leaders of their countries, overturning many of the shibboleths of thirty years. The result was not just electoral change but also a change in the ideology of government. The catastrophic inflation of the 1970s, which brought social revolt in its wake, returned to power conservative, market-oriented governments throughout the West and forced liberal or socialist governments to change their policies.

The gradual abandonment of attempts at national economic management became recognized as one of the sea-changes of late twentieth-century politics. Privatization, a market-driven approach to currency management, and the dismantling of the welfare systems which had been erected in the previous decades became the new orthodoxy. The return of straightforward *laisser faire* was most marked in the United Kingdom, the country which had led the world into the age of national economic management. The British push towards privatization, allowing market forces into the state sector, was accompanied by a more pro-business attitude towards the economy and a confrontational approach to labour relations. In the US, there was little to privatize, but the market was given a freer hand in running the currency and in social affairs. In France, after the crisis of 1981–3, orthodox financial attitudes prevailed in the management of the economy. In Europe as a whole, the shift toward an emphasis on freer markets, trade and liberalism found its expression in the project to tear down internal barriers, creating a single market. The energies and the abilities of the continent's largest companies were to be stimulated by increasing competition, not by state intervention.

Privatization, the liberalization of capital markets and the increasingly open stance towards the world economy helped to feed another powerful dynamic of the new global changes: the growing importance of foreign investment as well as trade. Transnational corporations (TNCs), spreading networks of corporate ownership, competition and co-operation that confounded national attempts at management, had flourished in the post-war boom, and now they took off. The first wave of transnational investment was in the 1950s and 1960s, as US companies entered the buoyant European economy and the new states of the Third World. In 1980, America still dominated foreign direct investment (FDI) flows, generating half of all outgoing FDI. Foreign investment soared in the 1980s, as billions of dollars went into new investment, mergers, takeovers and joint ventures. In the five years to 1989, FDI grew by twenty-nine per cent a year to $1.5 trillion (three times the rate of trade growth). FDI grew at twice the pace of GNP growth in the 1960s; in the 1980s, the increase was fourfold. By 1989, the EU's FDI flows were on a par with America and Japan is set to catch up within five years with the EU and the US. Having tripled between 1984 and 1987, worldwide outflows of foreign direct investment increased by another twenty per cent in 1988 and 1989 to reach an absolute level of $196bn; by 1989, the worldwide stock of FDI stood at $1.5 trillion.[24]

Since 1983, FDI outflows have increased four times faster than the growth of world output. One expert suggests that 'as a means of international economic integration, foreign direct investment is in its take-off phase; perhaps in a position comparable to world trade at the end of the 1940s.'[25] Indeed FDI expanded three times faster than trade in the period 1983–91.[26] Peter Drucker dates the creation of the global economy to the early or mid-1970s,[27] around the time that the fixed exchange-rate regime collapsed, and the oil shock sent national economic demand management into a flat spin. He is of the opinion that the beginning of financial deregulation in the US combined with the new *laisser faire* ideologies of the West to create a strong dynamic for the globalization of economic activity. In the process, 'business has shifted from being multinational to being transnational,' inducing change not just in the large companies whose expansion characterized the 1960s, but also in what had been smaller, local concerns.

The impact of these changes in the world economy was limited, initially at least, to the developed countries and particularly the cluster of Europe, the US and Japan. The market turn in the developed world was only slowly diffused through the rest of the economic system. For both political and economic reasons, developing countries persisted for much longer with state-oriented, managed systems that conceded less to the marketplace and more to the imperatives of national political development. There was a backlash against western involvement; and TNCs in the developing world were nationalized wholesale during the 1970s. The Third World was also able to continue with its policies partly because financing from abroad continued to be available, especially to those with valuable natural resources to trade against debt. The Third World experiment with national economic management had been so dependent on incoming capital flows that it should have come as little surprise to anybody when the international debt crisis exploded in 1982. The result of the lack of economic co-ordination and weak management of national policy in the West was a sudden jump in interest rates in the early 1980s, as both Britain and the US put the brakes on inflation. This triggered a recession in both economies; it also led to a calamitous fall in commodity prices. The financial response of the banking system was to draw in its horns abroad and capital flows all but dried up.

The shock in the Third World, when it came, was more abrupt and more catastrophic than it had been in the developed countries.[28] It necessitated more far-reaching changes in economic policy over the following decade, as countries pursued capital to make the books add up once more. It led to radical economic policy shifts in Latin America, in particular, as right-wing or economically liberal governments moved into power, abandoning state ownership and taking up market-driven policies. The shift of policy in the Third World all but reversed the hostility to western involvement and in particular to foreign investment which had been voiced in the preceding decades.[29]

The spread of market principles, integration in the world economy and private investment came last and most dramatically to the Soviet Union and its satellites. 'The Stalinist development model . . . was in essence based on an autarkic industrializing process . . . foreign trade was given little attention, being regarded purely as a means of obtaining vital imports.' Trade within the Soviet bloc was achieved through Comecon, a highly inefficient and ineffective system based on yearly agreements and fixed prices, run in transferable roubles that were in practice all but useless. The result was to lock the bloc out of world trade. In 1977, when the Comecon area accounted for thirty per cent of world industrial production, it accounted for less than five per cent of total world trade.[30] This share actually declined throughout most of the post-war period. Though bilateral agreements emerged as a means of buying materials and technology, these were always very limited in scope. Political restrictions in the West limited commercial ties even further.

The Soviet bloc, less linked to the world economy, had been relatively insulated from change. But it too had seen declining growth rates. From the 1960s its exports no longer covered its imports and it was forced to borrow. Food imports, and later technology and investment accords and trade agreements, broadened the interaction. This allowed the wall that separated it from the capitalist system to be breached. The explicit recognition that the Soviet bloc had lost its economic independence was delayed by the ossification of the political process.[31] But the debt crisis of the 1980s forced some eastern bloc countries, in particular Poland, to cut wages, consumption, imports and investment. Other states adopted less draconian, but more effective, economic measures to cut down trade with the West. In April 1985, the Soviet leader Mikhail Gorbachev launched the economic reform programme which became known as 'perestroika',[32] and in subsequent years he moved to reform the foreign trade and investment rules and abandon the autarky which had characterized the Soviet system.

The advance of market capitalism helped to create, by the end of the 1980s, the foundations of a truly global economy: one from which no state could opt out, one that to varying degrees touched all decision makers, all consumers and all producers. But in the same way as the creation of a global political system created apparent 'gaps' between the assertion of state sovereignty and the reality, the growth of a global economy also created looming contradictions. On the one hand, the state was more powerful than it had been at any time. But its autonomy, its ability to de-link from other states and determine its own future, was repeatedly undermined and the new ideology stressed the limits, not the aims, of state intervention. Instead, 'the transnational economy has become dominant, controlling in large measure the domestic economies of the national states.'[33]

Together, the evolution of an international political system under the superpower hegemony and the rapid expansion of the international economy had helped to create a new type of international system, one that was truly global. The world was in a sense 'full'. There were no more playgrounds for great powers that had not been filled already by nation-states, and expansion had become a zero-sum game. The presence of two large players with nuclear weapons in global rivalry had filled the world in a second way: it had reduced the possibility of opting out of the great power game, and had generalized the risks of a breakdown in state-to-state relations. The other face of this global system was the growth of interlinkages, social and political but above all economic, among all the states. These enforced a severe price on any state which sought to 'opt out' of the global system; but also offered benefits to those that could skilfully manipulate their place in the world.

The global nature of the system contributed to a type of stability. The element in superpower competition that did most to affect the pattern of international relations was the weaponry with which the two blocs threatened each other. The nuclear bomb revolutionized the nature of warfare: it afforded both the Soviet Union and the United States the ability to unleash massive destruction almost instantly. This opened up the whole world as a battlefield; but it also reduced the benefits of aggression between the two major powers. It thus contributed to the sudden decline of warfare in what had hitherto been the main battlefield of the Great Powers – Europe. The costs were simply too great. War seemed to be on the way out as a way of attaining state goals. 'The key reasons,' wrote one analyst, 'are the destructiveness of nuclear weapons and to a lesser extent other factors such as the fragility of modern technological civilization, the higher priority assigned to economic welfare, the high costs of military occupation in the age of the nation-state, and liberal democratic inhibitions.'[34]

The use of force, whether nuclear or conventional, became far less likely partly as a result of the process of modernization itself, and the intricate networks of communication, trade and interaction that came with it. 'Employing force on one issue against an independent state with which one has a variety of relationships is likely to rupture mutually profitable relations on other issues. In other words, the use of force often has costly effects on non-security goals.'[35] Thus the effect of nuclear weapons could be just as profound for those states which did not possess them. Perhaps as important as the nuclear revolution was a revolution in surveillance through the development of satellites, which permitted not just a more realistic approach to gauging others' readiness for war, but also provided the means for the policing of arms control agreements.[36]

Equally, the threat of nuclear war, and the military and political difficulties which sprang from it, was an important spur to cooperation. Defence and mutual security pacts, however, accounted for only a small minority of the international organizations which sprang up after the war. The increase in the number of intergovernmental organizations has been phenomenal. In 1909, there were 37; by 1951, after the post-war reconstruction, there were 123; by 1984, the number had reached 365.[37] The constituency of these organizations varied widely: the UN, with universal scope encompassing many agencies of its own; regional bodies, such as the European Community or the Organization of African States; and a host of sectoral bodies and others with limited agendas and mandates. These organizations came, over the 1980s, to encompass not just the states of the West but, increasingly, the South and the eastern bloc as well.

With these organizations came another slow change, but one which its advocates thought could have a more profound effect: an attempt to introduce rules into international relations, in the form of a profusion of treaties and agreements between states. One study indicates that around six thousand bilateral treaties came into force in the period 1946–55; ten thousand between 1955 and 1965; and fourteen thousand in the decade that followed. In the first decade international organizations were party to some six hundred treaties; in the second, over a thousand; and in the third, over two thousand. Most of these concerned economic subjects – co-operation, trade, aid and communications. Some, such as the United Nations Declaration on Human Rights, and the agreements of the Council of Europe, were devoted to incorporating an element of morality in international relations. The result was a gradual enmeshing of states in treaties, organizations and regular meetings.

It was evident, of course, that though the post-war period had created a strong dynamic for international co-operation it had not eradicated the more fissiparous tendencies of a world built on nation-states. There was no emergence of 'world government' in any form. The ethnic and religious splits that had characterized the inter-war period were ever-present, if less obvious. The creation of dozens of new independent states in the Third World had done little to dissolve sovereignty. New nations were jealously protective of their sovereignty; more so than many of the states that had previously been imperial masters. The interference of the two superpowers fed and fed on the tensions that the imperial nations had left behind. But the post-war period was one of the longest without major war in the history of the world. The pacts that it spawned – notably Nato and the Warsaw Pact – were similarly of historic duration. Particularly among liberal advocates of change in international relations, politics, economics and society, this fed a degree of optimism about the prospects for a safer, more stable world. That was only underlined by the great shifts of the late 1980s, a time of great hopes and grand rhetoric.

Given that the primary threat to peace, the principal international division, the remaining obstacle to the spread of capitalism, appeared to be the division of the world into two superpower blocs, it was not surprising that the events of 1989 should have engendered such optimism. But of course, it wasn't as simple as that. The years since have proved difficult: triumphalism has shrunk in the light of economic dislocations, tribal conflict and political upheaval. The 'new world order' looks increasingly disordered and dangerous – not only for liberal capitalism (the putative 'winner' of the Cold War) but for democracy too.

3

Breaking Down the Borders

'It was an ancient tradition, that when the Capital was founded by one of the Roman kings, the god Terminus (who presided over boundaries, and was represented according of that age by a large stone) alone, among all the inferior deities, refused to yield his place to Jupiter himself.' EDWARD GIBBON[1]

Berlin still held power as a symbol of the Cold War at Checkpoint Charlie on a cold night in January 1990. But the ease with which the border crossing was accomplished – a simple wave of the guard's hand once he had given passports the merest of glances – proved that if the Wall was not yet removed, then the bricks, mortar, and barbed wire had at least been stripped of much of their ominous meaning. Only three months earlier, the crowds had swarmed across, and the guards had stood by, watching. It was now only a matter of time before the thing itself was removed.

Next morning, on the eastern side of the crumbling divide, Berlin looked a tired, soulless city. Wide avenues, bordered by sombre post-Second World War architecture and the remains of Berlin's nineteenth-century grandeur, cut a swathe through an even less pleasant urban landscape. The shops were dingy and bare; few pedestrians walked the cold, inhospitable streets. In government offices, wary bureaucrats, only a few of them ready to accept the inevitability of the changes sweeping through Germany and eastern Europe, said that their country's economy *would* be transformed, but it would be done slowly, and with respect for the egalitarian nature of the state-planning system. East German politicians said the changes would be accomplished without the heavy hand of West Germany.

Erhard Schmeling, director-general of the East German Foreign Trade Ministry, insisted that state ownership in some form would continue to exist. 'But we must considerably reduce the role of central planning.'[2] He believed in that 'we'. He refused to think that forty years could be brushed aside with a flick of a West German finger.

In the western sector, along the Kurfurstendamm, the cold weather did little to ward off shoppers and strollers. West Berliners wore smiles of quiet satisfaction, their poise punctured now and then – usually late at night – by the rowdiness of the swaggering, alarming young, singing and swigging beer in early celebration of the end of an era. West Berliners weren't yet talking about the 'lazy' East Germans who were arriving in their thousands now that the Wall was punched with so many holes it ceased to count as a barrier. Nor yet of the Poles, Czechs and Hungarians who would come by the busload to buy western goods with hoarded convertible currency.

That day in East Berlin it was clear that the world was on the verge of a radical revolution. Not one that would see barricades, deaths and sudden reversals of policy – although all that seemed somehow likely too – but one that would change forever the way Europeans (and indeed everyone else) viewed the world and their place in it. The two Germanys were on their way towards being reunited, the Soviet Union had let its satellites go, the US was fast becoming a junior partner in Europe and appeared less and less able to finance its self-appointed role as global policeman. These were incredible developments. Nowhere were the changes unveiled with such rapidity, with such euphoria, as in Berlin, the Cold War's headquarters, the delicate point of balance between East and West, between the US and the Soviet Union, between capitalism and socialism. A divided Berlin was the price paid for forty years of peace in Europe, or so Allied and Soviet officials alike believed. But now the Wall was coming down.

The remains of the border between the two Germanys are still there, though one must look quite closely to see them. There are concrete blockhouses, standing strangely isolated in the middle of fields; watch-towers that now observe only the toing and froing of rural life; and large empty complexes that stand forlorn alongside the motorways, awaiting transformation into service stations or out-of-town supermarkets.

Once, the wire fences, border posts, machine-gun nests and minefields marked the limit of one world and the beginning of the next. Depending on your standpoint – though not necessarily upon which side of the Wall you stood – the border between East and West Germany was either a symbol of the need for vigilant defence against rapacious western capitalism and its political agents, or of the need for struggling socialism to keep its sons and daughters under lock and key.

Now there is little to mark its passing. Traffic on the motorways from west to east passes unrestricted, with no intrusive searches, no passport controls, and no dramas, except private ones. The border still exists in the minds of those who live to its east and west: those marked by its creation or destruction, who lived in its shadow or who worked to perpetuate it or to bring it down. One sign of this: four years after the Wall came down, East and West Berliners were still reading different daily newspapers, sticking to the ones they knew in the divided era.

But even these mental divisions will be slowly erased. Many of those who lived in the former East Germany moved west in the chaotic days before the collapse of the East German regime, and many more have subsequently followed them. Capital has been transferred east to improve the infrastructure and raise the living standards of the new German states, and eventually, whether it takes twenty or thirty years, the differences between Wessis and Ossis, so salient in the early 1990s, will fade. That does not mean that new borders, new boundaries and new differences will not be created.

Already, the German administrative state has created a new set of boundaries, setting up *Länder* – states in the federal system – where before there were but weakly defined political units. Though they are called 'the new states', these correspond in some cases to the oldest geographical units in German history: Thuringia, Saxony, Mecklenburg-Vorpommern. Some villages in the former West Germany have undone decades of administrative convenience by choosing to return to the regions in which they were once situated, deciding that they belong in Mecklenburg-Vorpommern, a state in former East Germany, rather than Schleswig-Holstein, a state of the old West Germany.

The gigantic geographical game played out in Germany is more than anything else a testament to the forces that have been at work reshaping political geography in the past decade. So far, it has been most obvious in Europe, where the Cold War carved stark divisions into the map, which the European Union is now trying to elide, to change or in some cases to remove. The arbitrary lines drawn up by the post-war settlement have been undone by the force of humanity on the move, asserting both an older reality and a new truth: that the borders imagined by man can be reimagined by man.

The line drawn across Germany was once earmarked for the single greatest defining event of the twentieth century, the one that did not take place: a war between Nato and the Warsaw Pact. The area is still thick with troops, although the Russians are slowly returning home and the West is now ready to drop its guard. The presence of troops is evidence of past history, not a pointer to the future. The significance of national borders for western Europe, as for other developed regions of the world, has been vastly reduced by the three forces of military change, economic development and modern communications technology.

Frontiers define nation-states. They mark the edges of national authority, the point at which the traveller and the businessman pass from one jurisdiction to another. They are the object of national defence, they mark the boundaries of national resources, and they have excluded and included those individuals who form the '*patrie*'. The modern nation-state is a territorial entity, which guards its sovereignty jealously at these points of intersection. Hence the assumption that removing borders, by allowing a freer flow of goods, ideas, people and cultures, would help to reduce clashes between states and erode the differences between nations.

The territoriality of the state was the first condition of its existence. If the definition of the state was to be found in its right to a monopoly on the use of force in a given area, then the delineation of that area was of crucial importance. These boundaries in many cases predated the rise of nationalism. The wars of early modern Europe, tracing the lines of a new kind of spatial authority, were repeated wherever nationalism spread. Often superimposed on older divisions, these claims were given added weight by the new linkage which nationalism formed between a people and its homeland. This was no longer contingent, as it had been under the old empires of pre-modern Europe, or administrative, as it was in the new empires in Latin America, Africa and Asia. It was necessary: for every people, there had to be a homeland.

By the time the process had finished, virtually every square centimetre of the world had been carved up among nation-states, each claiming a unique tie to its resources, its landscape, its adjoining seas and its rivers. The government of men, associated with the pre-modern state, had become the government of things, which requires clear cut divisions and distinctions as to ownership and control.

Territoriality is also closely tied to the political drive for nationhood through relentless reference to common 'culture'. The physical aspects of nationalism pervade its mythology. This is not just the remembering of great historical events which took place at specific locations, but the reverence for landscape, for the environment in its broadest sense.

The existence of borders is first and foremost a function of the need for the state to defend itself. The frontier is the point beyond which foreigners may not go without permission; they may be resisted militarily should they attempt to do so. Thus the concept of the 'natural' frontier – whether a river, mountain range, ocean or other geographical obstacle – has been crucial to most states. Given the tendency of the peoples of Europe to live in inconveniently scattered communities with little regard for these niceties, it is not surprising that the history of the continent is littered with border conflicts and wars devoted to establishing firmer frontiers.

But national borders also mark the points of absurdity, contradiction and danger in the national idea. They divide communities; they are the flashpoints of expansive nationalism; and they are fault lines. This is primarily because the lines drawn by men on maps have not corre-sponded to the realities of human development, particularly in the pre-modern era. The patterns of settlement in Europe have never been geometrically convenient: ethnic minorities are not just scat-tered, but often scattered village by village, street by street, farmhouse by farmhouse, as in the confused battleground of Bosnia. If the draw-ing and redrawing of borders under the inspiration of nationalism has meant anything, it has meant the continual movement of large numbers of human beings to fit in with new states or the dismem-bering of old ones. Where individuals conflict with the principle of nationhood, it is individuals who must load up the handcart and move.

There has always been a tension between the fixed, durable and inflexible requirements of national boundaries and the unstable, transi-ent and flexible requirements of people. If the principal fiction of the nation-state is ethnic, racial, linguistic and cultural homogeneity, then borders always give the lie to this construct. The construction of a frontier always divides some fraction of an ethnic group, as Europe discovered after the First World War. It hampers trade. And it imposes barriers between people with much in common. Border regions, where they exist between countries that are in opposition or in dispute on key issues, are unstable, transient, and lacking in prosperity. In the conventional territorial state, the metropolis – the capital and its hinterland – is the source of prosperity. In these senses, nationalism helped to create a new geography: first in western Europe, as borders were drawn, redrawn, fought over and resurrected, then in Latin America, then in Africa, where vast tracts of land were carved up between colonial empires. Borders beget a hierarchy of core and periphery.

This tendency has been frequently repeated wherever Europeans have spread their colonies. Latin America is a particular example. Administrative boundaries set up by Spanish and other European colonists served as the basis for the wholesale creation of new states which took place in the early nineteenth century, regardless of the illogic of considering that Ecuadoreans were any different from Colombians or Venezuelans. The attempts of Simón Bolívar to persuade the continent that it was one united federation were in vain. Neither was the existence of numerous tribes, extending over vast areas of several of the new countries, considered any impediment. The result has been one and a half centuries of international conflict over strategic resources, access to the sea, slights that extend back centuries, poorly delineated frontiers and half-marked boundaries.

The concept of the territorial state has thus become tightly interwoven with expansionism and self-aggrandisement. Sometimes, this is spurred by the presence of national minorities elsewhere who must be joined to the homeland. Sometimes, it is connected to the desire to gain physical security for the existing state, by annexing strategic heights, coastlines, or mountain passes, as in the continual conflicts over the Rhineland or Israel's annexation of the Golan heights.

As well as its pre-eminent security function, the border has also always played an economic role. It is the point of control for movements of goods and capital in and out of countries, the point at which taxes can be levied. It also marks the limits of national control over natural resources. A boundary in an oilfield or a gold reserve is a valuable thing, to be contested with neighbouring countries, as the conflict between Yemen and Saudi Arabia over desert oilfields demonstrated. Economic nationalism has always been associated with the fortress state, with autarky and the avoidance of external contact.

Territoriality, then, has been a crucial feature of the modern nation-state. Its pre-eminence helps to explain many of the key features of the international system as modified by nationalism, and many of the main principles of national government. It shapes our perception of what a nation-state is: a determinate physical structure which can be seen on an atlas, a patch of the earth's surface dominated by one people, one government, one army, one economy and one foreign policy. When we now speak of a nation – of the US, of France, of Sudan or Chad – we mean precisely this coloured splodge on the map. That is what politicians seek to influence with policy, that is what economists measure, and that is what people believe they belong to.

It is, like most of the epiphenomena of nationalism, a very convenient illusion, and one which is increasingly difficult to maintain. The assumptions upon which the territorial state is based are increasingly irrelevant.

Most national governments in the nineteenth and twentieth centuries regarded the frontier as an economic bastion against imports. But as the main plank of external economic policy became trade liberalization, this was unsustainable. Tariffs, the main policy tool for defence against imports, were progressively reduced. Non-tariff barriers related less to border controls in any case; and these were also reduced, culminating, in Europe, in the creation of a customs union, a barrier-free market. Where there are no trade barriers, the justification for physical obstructions disappears.

Equally, the rise in global security threats – in the Gulf, in Africa, in eastern Europe – and the growing awareness of environmental risk have helped undermine the physical separation of states: both fail to recognize these neat lines on maps.

But the primary weakening of the bordered state has been technological: the shrinking of the globe under the influence of, initially, air transport, and, later, satellite and missile technology. In the first place, this made transportation of physical goods and people across borders a much more complex task. The monitoring of frontiers became less meaningful when the border extended across the whole country. But this could be checked by the use of radar to detect incoming aircraft, by the creation of large national airports to funnel incoming and outgoing traffic, and by control of national airspace.

However, air transport also brought with it the first weapon of global warfare: the bomber aircraft. Bombers, used first in the Second

World War, brought with them the possibility of delivering explosives across huge distances, taking war away from the trenches of frontiers. Bombers were swiftly overshadowed by the development of intercontinental ballistic missiles carrying nuclear warheads. These could not be shot down; could rarely be prevented from reaching their target; and could wield sufficient force to win wars single-handedly.

The nuclear age in this sense removed one of the key aspects of the territorial state: its ability, under any circumstances, to defend itself alone. Distance was not just shrunk but eroded forever as an overriding factor in strategic defence. There was no such thing as a natural frontier against nuclear attack: there was no longer any high ground.

Nuclear warfare thus, firstly, put the premium upon the political means of preventing war, taking the emphasis away from territorial defence. Secondly, it emphasized the logic of communication between enemies in the interests of deterring and preventing conflict. And it weakened the arguments for strong fences making good neighbours. The fence was useless, and the neighbour might be on the other side of the globe.

To this strategic argument was added a second as the countries of the developed world gradually settled down to more or less peaceful coexistence. The need for Maginot Lines and similar constructions of border security decreased, in western Europe in particular, as it became accepted that there was no need to defend against fellow European countries, but rather to share defences against a common threat – the Soviet Union. In this case, the defensive line was to be drawn not on national frontiers, but wherever the Soviet threat might be halted. George Kennan, the architect of America's containment policy – a policy born of the 1940s – required that such assessments be made on a case-by-case basis, to reflect perceptions of important interests and significant threats. That was too complex for some of his colleagues: instead, a perimeter was drawn, a new border: around the 'free world'. In the 1970s and 1980s, even that definition became less salient.

Linked to the expansion in the availability of border-busting military hardware in the post-war age is the revolution in civilian communications. It has affected the daily lives of citizens more than any other single technological change this century. It is at the cutting edge of the global market economy. Radio, television, and telecommunications cross borders effortlessly, beaming information and images into homes on either side of a concrete divide. Businesses keep in constant touch with subsidiaries on the other side of the world, while stock traders operate twenty-four hours a day through sophisticated electronic links. In addition, the real costs of these communication links have decreased over time, allowing broader use and constant refinement.[3]

The communications revolution has been particularly important to the growth of the transnational corporation (*we shall often abbreviate this to TNC hereafter*). The TNC relies explicitly on the basis of such communication links, and on its ability to tap and exchange information. Its access to knowledge is central to its success: to its production techniques, to its distribution and marketing, to its financial operations. In the service industries, communication links are of signal importance. In sectors ranging from financial services to management consultancy to commodity trading, there is no longer 'production' as it is traditionally understood. There is only 'information', communicated efficiently within, between and among companies.

The emergence of a world economy dominated by TNCs has further reduced the salience of borders. The touchstone for the TNC is the open economy. There are three golden rules. First, an open market for goods and services must obtain: market access is the key which unlocks the world. In the first wave of TNC investment, some companies sought access by investment where they could not export. Thus General Motors and Ford both invested in Mexico. Once the market was opened, they campaigned actively for easy trade access to the US. It is no surprise to find TNCs lobbying actively for trade liberalization, and arrayed in support of any new round of international trade talks.

The second golden rule: TNCs require open regulation – the so-called 'level playing field' where 'foreign' companies are to be treated as equals with local competitors. If a local bank can run a securities operation, then why can't a foreign bank? But they also want equal regulation across borders. If the standard for hooking up a computer to a telephone line is different in every country, computer manufacturers lose out, since they must produce a different model for every market. That gives an advantage to the small local competitor. In this particular case, as communications is the key to transborder operations, every other transnational also loses out: they must buy different equipment for every market, and consequently their costs rise.

The final rule: any TNC economy is typified by a need for wide, open capital markets. TNCs spend vast amounts on running their international empires, and this requires the ability to raise money swiftly and transfer it easily. TNCs also feed off an active market for corporate buying and selling. Large corporations seek to expand not just by green-field investment, but also by takeover. They are buying not just a place in the market, but a slice of that market, and the skills and technology that go with it.

The expansion of the Eurocurrency markets in the 1960s thus helped corporations, especially but not exclusively those based in the US, finance their expansion abroad. The currency instability generated by, first, the break-up of the dollar standard and, second, the end of managed floating may have played a role by making investment preferable to trade, since foreign direct investment removes some of the uncertainties surrounding devaluation. If it hampered investment, as others have suggested, the creativity of the banks soon ironed out any problems by creating new techniques for handling risk.

These changes have contributed to a steady shift in the composition of FDI. As the world economy has expanded, the transnational corporation has become more sophisticated; and its focus has changed. Declining investment in raw materials has meant that those TNCs trading in such commodities comprise a smaller and ever-declining proportion of the total. 'During the 1950s, foreign direct investment was concentrated in raw materials, other primary products and resource-based manufacturing; today it is mainly in services and in technology-intensive manufacturing.'[4] Partly this is the result of the nationalization of some foreign-owned Third World plants, mines and production facilities. But it also reflects the long-term collapse in world commodity prices, occasioned by their decreasing desirability, and the falling percentage of costs represented by commodity inputs. Resource companies have diversified from primary production into higher value-added, but related, businesses; for example, oil companies have bought chains of petrol stations, while pulp & paper companies have diversified into packaging.

But the structure of manufacturing investment has also changed. The salience of cheap labour has declined as improvements in productivity decrease the value of the labour component in most goods. Mechanization can handle many of the tasks formerly performed by cheap labour.

The new TNC is motivated by the need to service particular markets irrespective of national borders. Sometimes, investment is intended to ensure different product runs; sometimes it is to capitalize on the strengths of a particular location in a technology or skill. In each case, it is decreasingly true that finished products are assembled for sale in one market. Production is geared towards treating the whole of innovation, production, distribution and retail as one giant network.

Services are the new boom sector in FDI. Services accounted for about a quarter of the total world stock of FDI at the beginning of the 1970s; by the late 1980s, this share had doubled to fifty per cent. This undoubtedly reflected the importance of services worldwide in economies; and of the liberalization of markets in both host and home states. But it also reflected a change in the products themselves. Telecommunications is no longer a matter of switches and handsets; it is also a matter of advanced network services which knit together different markets, producers and consumers. The growth in FDI has been partly funded by the world expansion in service companies; while manufacturers can choose how to serve a market, either by trade or by production, many services need to be delivered at the point of sale.

This is one sense in which the world economy has become truly global and transnational, while remaining local. Instead of merely adapting to differences in comparative advantage and national peculiarities, it can weld them into its own formulation, create order out of chaos (and frequently, as with the investments mismanaged by many financial institutions during the 1980s, the reverse).

Managing this system is difficult enough for the corporations concerned; it is almost impossible for any one state, or even groups of states together. The flow of capital cannot be traced to any physical transfer across borders; nor can the flow of transborder information, be it via satellite television or the digitally coded faxes which buzz between the business centres of the world. Like air and water, modern communications recognize no frontier.

The transnational company expands the scope of national markets through its own needs and helps to create new companies with transnational links, albeit domestically located ones. It internationalizes existing competitors, suppliers and clients. The TNC needs transnational services, legal, financial, and technological. For this they require a growing network of such companies that can either accompany them worldwide or at least understand the problems they face. One group of TNCs – those that supply the infrastructure, services and machinery of commerce – does much of its business with other TNCs. Another group – which supplies consumer goods – does business with individuals. But for both, relationships with suppliers are of increasing importance: production runs are larger, flexibility is more important; and so is consistency.

Socialism in one country was difficult enough; capitalism in one country isn't even an option for most goods and services in the 1990s. In the process of change, companies that were once domestic champions have become TNCs – some of them formerly state-owned. The most obvious example is a company such as British Telecom, formerly the state-owned telephone corporation of the United Kingdom. It found itself in competition for international services with private-sector, global firms, which had far greater access to capital. Once privatized, it lost no time in seeking new overseas markets and products, forming links with overseas companies, and becoming a TNC, with controversially profitable consequences. It made some marriages in haste which it has repented at leisure.

Competition is part of the TNC economy; but it is competition that requires larger and larger scale, broader markets, and consequently leads to consolidation – mergers, takeovers, and joint ventures. In the case of telecommunications, the rapid changes in the sector have led to almost every market opening up, and to a decrease in the number of world players. Fifteen years ago, it was a national prerogative; now it is global.

Associated with the TNC's macroeconomic impact is a more complex interaction with the nation-state. TNCs play a crucial role as the transmission belt of modern international capitalism, not just at the political and macroeconomic level, but also at the microeconomic level. They transmit changes in technology; sometimes they bring it with them in the manufacturing process, and sometimes they bring it with them in the form of imported components. They speed the process of innovation. They promote research and development. They play a role in transmitting microeconomic change in other ways, too, through their attitude to the labour force, for instance. The TNC gets involved in the training and education of the workforce, creating skilled workers. It also imports techniques of labour management, and frequently plays a role in shaping the labour force's attitude to work.

The effect on the labour market is perhaps the most important. As Susan Strange wrote, 'in some ways it is arguable that the reshuffling of the pack in the production structure has affected class relations more directly than it has affected international relations . . . the fact that in many industries a transnational company can move its plant, or expand elsewhere, while the worker cannot move to another country has robbed labour unions in industrialized countries of some of their power to win concessions from management by the threat to strike.'[5] The changes in labour methods that they bring are often directly in opposition to the interests of local people, requiring changes to lifestyle, income and work practices that are resented. For the richest twenty per cent of the population, the opportunities delivered by globalization – travel, wider experience, promotion, and increased status – may be considerable; for the poorest twenty per cent, the access to these benefits is negligible; the consequent disruptions may be obvious, painful and costly.

Because TNCs have a set of functional needs, there is thus a homogenizing factor in their very expansion. The traditional national company is typified by the geographical integration of its production, distribution, management and financial structures within one country. It is only necessary to it that internal arrangements within that country are satisfactory; thus did US companies seek the reduction of interstate barriers in the nineteenth century, creating a single, relatively homogeneous market for many goods and services. This national confinement results in differing national solutions to the same problems. It also results in duplication of efforts.

The TNC thus places a certain degree of limitation upon the state by virtue of its political needs. Since it is tightly linked into the world economy as an exporter of goods and services, and as exporter and importer of capital, it is sensitive to changes that go beyond the national economy. A subsidiary of an American company in Quito is more likely to react to interest rate changes in New York than in Ecuador. The levers of national macroeconomic policy are less effective. The TNC may increase or decrease employment based on shifting patterns of comparative advantage, making employment less stable. The TNC will certainly bring with it a set of assumptions about the way business is carried out, and these will have to be accommodated. The growth of the Euromarkets, for instance, meant that 'national exchange restrictions and capital controls were doomed to failure even before they started'.[6]

Security, stability and efficiency are the resources which the host state provides to the transnational corporation, above and beyond the existence of resources which it exploits. The state provides them and the corporation pays for them in one way or another, although there are complaints that the TNC does not pay a fair price for the services which it receives: that it pays too little in tax. The TNC also demands a constant, secure environment and local politics may not provide this. In the extreme if they are not getting the environment they require they may import, to put it euphemistically, security: through requesting military intervention from their home country. 'Multinational corporations have posed real or perceived threats to the autonomy of Southern political processes.'[7] They may also become involved in lobbying for policy changes, which again is an activity that raises little concern when conducted by domestic corporations; but much more when the lobbying company is foreign.

The impact of the globalization of production is most obvious to us as consumers. For consumers, the spread of a global economy means that products from a much wider range of sources are available; but it means that some localized production may be driven out of existence. Pricing may bring down the cost of some complex, technology- and information-intensive products such as electronic home products or financial services; but for more simple products – food, shelter and transport – the demands of a global economy may make little difference, or even raise prices in some cases.

It is especially as consumers of information that we are brought into daily contact with the realities of the emerging global economy. At that individual level, we are now able to know a great deal more about one another than our ancestors ever could. We can test the success of our political systems and our economic well-being against those in other countries. As Susan Strange writes, 'the revolution in communications, and thus in the whole global knowledge structure, helped to reveal the widening gap between standards of living for similar groups under global capitalism and under socialism.'[8]

It is often argued that the communications revolution is the basis of an emerging international culture, ultimately reducing the differences between us and eroding the exclusionary character of nationalism. Technology could beget a communications utopia – non-confrontational, homogenizing and efficient; or a communications nightmare – centralizing, dehumanizing, intolerant. But the effect has been quite different from either of these extremes. To begin with, cultural communications are still heavily regulated by the state in most parts of the world. Defenders of national culture in France, Spain, Canada, India and many developing countries regulate (admittedly with varying degrees of success) access to 'foreign' material. Likewise, local communications networks cater to existing nationalist-inspired desires by focusing on discrete linguistic and ethnic groups within nations.

Indeed, this might be considered a new battleground of nationalism. Turkish television is beaming eighty-three hours of programmes a week into the six Muslim republics of the former Soviet Union. Muzaffer Baca, producer of television news in Ankara, has said: 'It could be that this is the foundation for a Turkish commonwealth.'[9]

More fundamentally, the wiring of the global village has not in fact proceeded as many expected it might in the 1950s. The argument that economies of scale and standardization of technology would lead to a few sources – perhaps one single source – of information, beamed from the centre to many spokes, has not been proven. There has been, instead, a multiplication of communications sources: the individual can pick and choose (at least pick and choose from what is available), and in a sense construct his own 'knowledge'. With the marriage of telecommunications, television and computers, the sources multiply endlessly. Indeed, such atomized communications networks might be seen as one basis for a post-industrial society dependent on the consumption of ideas over goods.

But the room for propaganda by the state and business, while perhaps shrinking with the increased access to communication channels of individuals outside the corporate and state sectors, is still present. The 'production' of knowledge is still controlled within the current technological climate not by the consumer (who is confronted only by pre-determined choice) but by the 'producer'.

The producer may be the purveyor of several 'lines' of communication, as the concentration of media and information companies in recent decades attests. The integrated 'entertainment' companies produce not only the hardware but the software as well. Large manufacturing concerns such as Sony now own film studios and record companies to supply the 'product' that feeds their range of hardware equipment (Walkmans, televisions, stereo systems, and so on). This vertical integration is matched by a trend toward cross-ownership of media, whereby a single company 'manufactures' newspapers and magazines, owns television stations, perhaps a television production company as well. News International, controlled by Rupert Murdoch, is one example: it owns Fox Broadcasting in the US, several publishing houses (including the British publisher of this book), a satellite network in Europe and five national newspaper titles in Britain.

Ownership on this level concentrates communicative power in fewer and fewer hands.

The consumerization of ideas, communicated across borders and targeting not classes but individuals, has wrought a transformation in the relationship of the consumer to economic power. His relationship to the economy is personalized, atomized. His interaction with the products he consumes is rendered particular. This transformation has exercised the minds of contemporary Marxists above all. Fredric Jameson writes: 'Theories of the post-modern – whether celebratory or couched in the language of moral revulsion and denunciation – bear a strong resemblance to all those more ambitious sociological generalizations which, at much the same time, bring us the news of the arrival and inauguration of a whole new type of society, most famously baptized "post-industrial society" (Daniel Bell) but often also designated consumer society, media society, information society, electronic society, or high tech, and the like. Such theories have the obvious ideological mission of demonstrating, to their own relief, that the new social formation in question no longer obeys the laws of classical capitalism, namely the primacy of industrial production and the omnipresence of class struggle.'[10] The consumerization of ideas and images undercuts the territorial limits of the nation-state. The form of the 'product' may still relate to 'national' character and taste: but the focus is the group (Muslim, 'youth', high-income-earners) or the individual; the political border, certainly for many marketing purposes, ceases to count.

But the consequences of this erosion of demarcations – or their redefinition – have been both more complex and often more negative than foreseen. Even as the revolution in communications and economics helped make borders obsolete, the political structures of the nation-state system retained their formal power. Only with the rapid changes since 1989 have the underpinnings of that world system been seen to have weakened fundamentally. For the end of the Cold War in Europe only served to crystallize the changes in territoriality that had been building up for decades. Eastern European borders were frozen in illogical, immutable lines which kept in populations, economies and societies while aiming to exclude trade, investment and inter-action with the outside world. The key factor in its collapse was the inability of East Germany to hold in its own people, who, given the opportunity, fled in large numbers to the affluent West. But it was also the inability of the DDR state to keep out the news of changes in other East European countries, to stem the flow of information about the West, to plug the gaps in a porous border. The revolutions in eastern Europe were relentlessly modern: they owed much of their success to the power of the televised image, to the free flow of information across borders.

Still, the end of the Wall also demonstrated the convenience of such large-scale territorial divisions. Because Europe is not an undifferentiated land mass, the dangers of the breach of the Wall were quickly apparent. Firstly, West Germany was forced into precipitate action to stem the flow of refugees from the DDR, through monetary union, then through political union. Secondly, the danger of additional incursions of refugees from farther east quickly monopolized political attention in Bonn. Without the Wall, what was to hold them back? The formation of a united German state also raised widespread concern elsewhere about German aspirations and German minorities; German communities became once more a tricky issue in relations between Germany and some of its neighbours.

The division of Germany had been, on the one hand, a denial of the national principle. On the other, it had been the bluntest statement of the importance of territorial considerations. Borders in the former Yugoslavia are likewise an example of how fraught the concept of nationality can be when tied to territoriality. Where does Serbia begin and end? What must be done by and with the Serbian minority in Croatia or in Bosnia-Herzegovina?

Yet western Europe is on its way to erasing borders. What was becoming evident in the 1950s – the waning importance of territoriality – is now concrete in the West, where its reduced salience has meant the virtual erasure of the frontiers between some western European countries. This results more than anything else from the end of military tensions. It is simply unnecessary to pretend any more that the border between France and Germany has any military significance. The two countries are as unlikely to go to war as are, say, Burgundy and Picardy. Nor, even if the threat came from farther afield, would there be any point in preserving the fiction that invaders from the east could be held at the French frontier if they came that far.

Secondly, the Franco-German border means less and less in economic terms. With the increase in trade between the two countries and the regular daily economic interactions has come Europe's desire to standardize, remove trade barriers and create a single economic space. This will eventually remove the need for customs posts. With the creation of European passports, the need to stop people from flowing across the border is fast removed.

But this very ease of mobility has led to calls for tighter controls at the edges of the emerging European superstate. As it becomes easier to move within the countries of Europe, it is likely to become harder to move between Europe and the outside world. The tightening of immigration policy in Europe is an obvious reaction to concerns about the unimpeded flow of eastern Europeans and economically disadvantaged people from the Third World.

The result is a sharp shift in the definition of the migrant. The 'jet set' of the 1970s was the archetype of a new international class: wealthy, mobile and leisure-oriented, they flitted from country to country. In the 1980s, this was broadened to include the international business class which seeks profit where it finds it: in Mexico, in Spain, or in eastern Europe. But this form of mobility is a pale reflection of the massive movements of population that have typified the Third World in the last decade, and which are set to increase. South–North migration has exploded as a result of regional conflicts, political repression, environmental degradation, economic collapse and the desire to seek affluence; East–West migration, a new phenomenon, has shocked European governments into action since the fall of the Berlin Wall; and South–South migration continues apace. As efforts to close the door to immigrants in North America and Europe intensify, more arriving foreign nationals are claiming asylum rather than applying for a dwindling number of immigrant places. From only thirty thousand a year in North America and Europe in 1975, the number of asylum-seekers reached seven hundred thousand in 1992 and is spiralling ever upward.[11]

Immigrants prompt new problems: cultural assimilation, racist reactions, a rise in the power of extremist groups, new demands upon the welfare state. Preserving social stability is rapidly becoming a priority that supersedes liberal assumptions about the revitalizing role of incoming communities and the duty to provide asylum. This shift in priorities is obvious not only in Europe, but also in the US, Canada, Australia and other nations that have traditionally welcomed immigrants. Germany moved to tighten its liberal asylum laws in 1993, in the wake of attacks on immigrants in several cities. Germany had accepted by far the greatest number of refugees from battle-torn Bosnia. But this huge influx, at a time of grim economic prospects under the heavy burden imposed by the costs of unification, convinced German leaders that new controls had to be imposed on migrants – even those fleeing chaos in their homelands. France, under its rightist majority, refined its nationality laws in mid-1993 to deny citizenship to some French-born children of foreigners, thereby compromising an ideal that had been for decades part of the very essence of French nationalism: rights of citizenship based on birth.

Building fences against immigrants raises the hackles of, among others, those liberals who believe that citizens of former colonies have basic rights to migrate to former occupying countries. But this enlightened view is not shared by those buffeted by economic dislocation in the West, as a result in part of increasing competition from the developing world.

As Harold Isaacs writes, 'A . . . fallout of the post-imperial experience has been the migration to the former mother countries of sizeable numbers of their ex-children: Indians, Pakistanis, Africans, and West Indians to Great Britain; Algerians to France; and Indonesian Eurasians and Amboinese to Holland. These are not, as in the past, small numbers of selected individuals come for schooling in the process of being co-opted by the colonial system, but large numbers of poor working people come to make their way down those gold-paved streets to some better condition of life. The collapse of the old authority relationship in which the lesser breeds knew their place, the class of newcomers and their status as permanent immigrants instead of tolerated visitors, and their larger numbers have led to new internal tensions, conflicts, and riots in the streets in each of these countries.'[12]

This presents western governments with a problem. The West may feel inclined to regard the world as being divided into two halves – one developed, civilized and safe in its borders, the other insecure, warring and predatory. But the erosion of the territorial state has not just made it easier to disregard frontiers within, for instance, Europe, it has also made it more difficult to ignore the frontier with the rest of the world. Turkey, for instance, has one foot in Europe, one in the Middle East. What happens on its borders is a matter of pressing concern for Brussels and for every EU capital.

The distance between core and periphery has shrunk as surely as that between the states of the core; it is just that the differences – primarily economic – have not; indeed, they have increased. The closer one moves to the periphery, the more this is the case. At the extreme, as the recent civil wars in Ethiopia and Somalia prove, there are still liberation movements devoted to national partition through guerrilla warfare. More to the point, the periphery cannot be separated from the core precisely because of the declining significance of the territoriality of states. Refugee migrations, environmental threats, regional violence, commodities trade, nuclear proliferation, and the international structure of production itself are too bound up in a global system without clear distinctions to allow disruptions.

The conclusion for the West may well be that it is no longer that strong fences make good neighbours; but that strong neighbours make good fences. A world of have and have nots may be inherently unstable; with porous borders, that instability may prove even more threatening to the economic system than organized communism and the Soviet threat could ever be.

For the lesson of the past twenty-five years is clear. Where borders are erased or eroded, both internal and external geography change. If the main direction of communication within states is between the centre and the periphery, the centre becomes much less easy to define and the periphery less easy to demote. Among the main functions of a border is the prevention, or channelling, of communication. When this function is removed, the lines of travel and trade will change. Canada's domestic communications network is built upon an east–west axis. But as the border with the US becomes less significant, the direction of travel is increasingly north–south. New infrastructure, new habits and new communities inevitably develop. Effortless communications across boundaries undermine the nation-state's control; increased mobility, and the increased willingness of people to migrate, undermine its cohesiveness. Business abhors borders, and seeks to circumvent them. Information travels across borders and nation-states are hard-pressed to control the flow. People burst across borders, seeking new or better opportunities.

The nation-state in its traditional form is increasingly powerless to withstand these pressures. This conclusion has become all but inescapable with the end of the Cold War, and with it the end of bipolar certainty. For if the erosion of borders has been at times a slow process, slow enough indeed to have been ignored by many, the breaching of the Berlin Wall and the subsequent disintegration of the Soviet Union has laid bare the nature of the challenges facing the nation-state.

PART TWO

New World Orders

INTRODUCTION

The End of The Cold War

'It is . . . not merely legal and political opinion within
the state system which has attempted to freeze the
territorial map; this outcome also corresponds to the
interests and policies of the two major powers.'

JAMES MAYALL[1]

It takes time to redraw maps, to re-imagine geography. For more than
forty years, the world order was based on the opposition of two armed
and stubborn camps. The Berlin airlift, the Cuban missile crisis, wars
in Korea and Vietnam, conflicts in the Middle East, *détente*, arms-
reduction talks, Reagan's inveighing against the 'evil empire' and his
promotion of the Strategic Defense Initiative: all these episodes were
played out against a permanent backdrop – the persistence of
bipolarity, the solidity of the Iron Curtain, the implacability of a battle
between two world-views.

The seeming immutability of this world explains why the year of
insensibly radical change, 1989, surprised Soviet generals, American
policy-makers, surprised even the protesters in the streets. It has still
not really sunk in, as the subsequent years, and faltering events, have
shown. The new geography is not yet fully imagined; the map is
flecked with alterations, half-erased lines, tentative pencil marks.

But what can be said for certain is that the world order based on
the Cold War geography was gone for good. In security terms, in
political terms, in economic terms, the clarifying proposals that underpinned forty years of history were no longer of much use. What new

geography then? How would the map of the post-Cold War world be drawn? The question became pressing with startling rapidity. And yet the answers given, with few exceptions, were based on the ortho-doxies of the past. The actions of policy makers in the post-Cold War era showed that they had failed to grasp how much the world had changed and how fast.

The changes we chart throughout this book – namely a shift in the nature and reach of international capitalism, underpinned by advances in technology, particularly in the area of communications – affected the Soviet Union and its satellite states radically, despite the Soviet bloc's relative isolation from the global capitalist economy. The decision to seek western credits on a systematic basis in the 1970s opened the domestic economy to specifically financial influences from outside. At the same time, the USSR continued to match – and in some areas exceed – military spending by the West, thereby diverting resources from basic foodstuffs, civilian industry and consumer-product manufacturing. The near-impossibility of running a centrally planned economy wherein every good and service would be produced according to five-year projections was made manifest. The Soviet Union could mount a space programme and arm itself with strategic nuclear weapons, but it could not ensure the availability of a full range of consumer products on store shelves, nor was it ever likely to match the high-tech challenge of the US SDI.

The Soviet Union and its eastern European satellites, in short, could not rely on the Stalinist system. Based as it was on the concept of a 'war' economy[2] wherein all productive capacity was directed to achiev-ing a narrow set of goals (industrial self-sufficiency, strong defence, adequate food supplies through collectivization), Stalinism concen-trated on heavy industry to the detriment of the consumer-goods sector. It required heavy bureaucratic planning and eschewed the market mechanism. Minor attempts to reform the system in the 1950s and 1960s, primarily by granting greater autonomy to state-owned enterprises and allowing small-scale private enterprise to develop, largely in the service sector, ultimately foundered on the rock of bureaucratic intransigence. A burst of openness in the 1970s, when countries of the eastern bloc were allowed to buy western goods and technology to offset shortages at home, was equally unable to endure. A slowdown in growth in the western economies and the rise in the exports of competing goods from less developed countries in the mid-1970s limited the market for Soviet-bloc manufactures in the West, and made it harder and harder for the Soviet bloc to pay for imports out of export earnings. By the mid-1980s, most eastern European governments, by now heavily indebted, were forced to cut back on the very programmes that had become the lynchpin of stability under Stalinism: cheap housing, cheap transport, cheap food.

Even so, the results might have been containable for a little longer had not those living in the satellite nations of eastern Europe been increasingly able to view images from the West – notably of consumer goods on full-to-brimming shelves – and to communicate with sympathizers in the West. Human rights activists could convince most Soviet citizens that the harsh treatment meeted out by the state – and particularly the restrictions on the freedoms of speech, faith and movement – did not have to last. East Germans could watch West German television, and could know how their cousins lived. The relatively more open Hungarian economy had already in the 1970s begun to encourage joint-ventures with western companies, thereby fomenting contacts between western and domestic companies. At the same time, two fears were fast fading, one of attack from the West, the other of violent repression from Moscow. Eastern bloc nationals no longer believed (US President Ronald Reagan's sabre-rattling notwithstanding) that the West was prepared to launch a war; and many dissidents were prepared to test Moscow's commitment to keeping control of its satellites at all costs. The prospect of another 1956 (the crushing of the Hungarian Revolution) or 1968 (the suppression of the Prague Spring) was discounted.

It required only tentative moves from the leadership in Moscow towards limited reforms to unleash pent-up frustration among those who believed that the West had a higher standard of living and greater freedom and that eastern Europe should, and could, have its share. When Soviet President Mikhail Gorbachev made it clear in 1989 that the Soviet Union would not sponsor intervention even as East Germans headed west via Hungary and later Czechoslovakia and even as demonstrations, at the Berlin Wall and in Leipzig particularly, grew larger by the day, the eastern-bloc revolutions were launched. The satellites were free to 'do it their way'.[3] The Soviet Union itself followed, when it became clear that order could not be reimposed on the country's republics, which were already withholding tax receipts from Moscow and demanding further autonomy. A hardline coup could not succeed in the face of popular anger.

The end of the Cold War posed intense challenges to the existing world order. These related to international security; to the prospects for economic reform and democracy in the transformed Soviet bloc; to Europe's existing political structures; and to the position of Third World states tied to the superpowers.

The end of the Soviet bloc seemed to promise to deliver the decisive transformation in international relations. It was achieved without international conflict; it involved the dissolution of the Warsaw Pact and Comecon; and it meant that their members were absorbed into the West's network of economic interactions. The dream of a safer, more co-operative world seemed briefly within reach in 1989, the *annus mirabilis* of political change in the Soviet Union, Europe and the world. The premature birth of the twenty-first century was welcomed by every world leader – even those, like Mikhail Gorbachev, whom it was set to claim as victims. 'We are only at the beginning of a new world order,' he said in 1990.[4] Later that year, as the US geared up for its intervention in Iraq, President Bush told both houses of Congress the same thing: 'out of these troubled times . . . a new world order . . . can emerge. A new era – freer from the threat of terror, stronger in the pursuit of justice, and more secure in the quest for peace, an era in which the nations of the world, East and West, North and South, can prosper and live in harmony.'[5]

If the end of the post-war world promised anything, it was a better functioning international system. President Bush specifically mentioned 'a world where the rule of law supplants the rule of the jungle, a world in which nations recognize the shared responsibility for freedom and justice, a world where the strong respect the rights of the weak'. This would be, as he said, 'A world very different from the one we have known.' The economic prospects seemed brighter than ever: the peace dividend, representing the sums of money liberated by reduced defence spending, was one aspect of this. But greater still were the possibilities for enhanced trade and economic expansion brought about by the creation of new markets, new resources and new producers. After the events of 1989, the existence and strength of the global economy were the surest proof to advocates of liberal capitalism that a defining point had been reached. With its institutions, its money and its values, liberal capitalism had triumphed: a rubicon had been crossed.

External security was the most pressing challenge. The end of bipolarity and the Cold War created a security vacuum. Some claimed that the US was strong enough to act alone in imposing a security system on the rest of the world. We witnessed, they believed, the launch of a unipolar era, in which the US would be the single sponsoring superpower, even if, as in the Gulf War, it sought international support and financial burden-sharing, and even if it relied on the UN Security Council to spearhead policy. A Pentagon analysis leaked to newspapers in 1992 – and subsequently toned down – reflected this view. According to the first draft, Russia was to be closely watched for signs that it might again threaten the West, while Japan and Europe were to be 'pre-empted' from competing with the US in security terms: they were to be deterred 'from even aspiring to a larger regional or global role'.[6] But since then it has become clear that the end of the Cold War presents the US with a dilemma of epic proportions. The centrepiece of American foreign policy since the end of the Second World War – the containment of communism – has dissolved, and with it any sense of certainty about the US role in the world. Without a clear-cut enemy, the US is left feeling its way case by case. It must do so without the fixed alliances on which it could rely when superpower confrontation helped 'freeze' the world map. It must do so as well without the overwhelming economic strength that once put the US far ahead of all potential competitors.

Policy makers are bound to accept these constraints, whatever the Pentagon advises. One response might be to pull back from traditional roles – in Europe probably, perhaps in the Far East as well. The initial decision to stay largely on the sidelines in the Yugoslav conflagration was an early sign of this. But the US will be unable to retreat completely. The end of the Cold War left a legacy of nuclear capability within the Soviet bloc and may embolden Third World countries to act in regions where Cold War politics had once kept them in check. As a nuclear superpower, if not an economic one, the US will be obliged to fashion new policies to respond to these less precise threats.

Meanwhile, there is next to no hope that the bigger ex-Soviet states – Russia and Ukraine – can inherit the superpower mantle formerly held by the Soviet Union. For a start, they are squabbling amongst themselves, and no single state, not even huge Russia, is in any condition to underwrite an expanding defence budget. Indeed, the pressures are pushing in the opposite direction. Even if Russia and Ukraine want to retain a measure of military independence, they will be hard-pressed to pay for it. The issue has become how to reduce the nuclear assets of the former Soviet Union, not how to maintain them.

Dismantling the nuclear armaments in the East will be complicated by rivalries within the old Soviet bloc and persistent calls from within the Nato bureaucratic structure and from within Nato member countries for the retention of an 'adequate' level of force. Weapons are the subject of intense jockeying, as the battle between the Ukraine and Russia over control of the Black Sea fleet attested. Tensions between the two threaten to undermine the joint defence programme – and associated arms reduction agreed with the US – that many former Soviet republics hoped to establish in the aftermath of the collapse of the empire.

For if the problems of external security, particularly the fate of the Soviet nuclear and conventional capability, are acute, the squabbling within the Commonwealth of Independent States suggests internal tensions may be even greater. Heavily armed states such as Russia and Ukraine, led by administrations with a large number of domestic critics, have already turned toward extremism and violence. Russia has already moved to reassert a hegemonic role, and the rise of ultra-nationalists such as Vladimir Zhirinovsky shows the danger of a reversal of reform. Transforming the economies of the former Soviet bloc comes at a high price, one that local populations may prove hesitant to pay. An appeal to nationalist pride, whipped up in a battle with neighbouring states, could be a diversion that republican leaders will find difficult to resist. Already, ethnic battles in Georgia and Azerbaijan threaten further to splinter the successor states, while the patchwork of internal borders bequeathed by the Soviet era are bound to exacerbate ethnic and economic tensions.[7]

The room for armed conflict is by no means limited to the republics of the former Soviet Union, or even to their multiplicity of ethnic minorities. In eastern Europe, the end of the Cold War has unleashed anew nationalist tensions that more than forty years of Communist Party rule had managed, just, to contain. The battles in Yugoslavia have pitted first Serbs against Croats in Croatia, then Serbs against the Croats and Muslims of Bosnia-Herzegovina, and last, Bosnian Croats against Bosnian Muslims. Kosovo and Macedonia, untouched at the time of writing by full-scale war, are unlikely to remain immune unless a solution is found to the border conflicts throughout the former Yugoslavia and adjacent regions. Four neighbouring countries lay claim to an interest in the future of an independent Macedonia, namely Serbia, Greece, Turkey, and Albania: that is a measure of the potential for regional conflict. Other eastern European countries, notably Hungary, Slovakia and Romania, possess the ingredients for similar chaos. The Baltic states face problems with their Russian minorities. Czechoslovakia has already succumbed to peaceful fragmentation, although perhaps more quickly and more decisively than the population might have preferred.

These nationalist tensions are long-standing and heartfelt – though not as long-standing as propagandists claim. The end of the Cold War has allowed them to blossom anew. In Lawrence Freedman's words: 'A long-locked cupboard, packed full of old, worn ideologies and prejudices, has suddenly burst open.'[8] Put simply, the ethnic volatility of eastern Europe that could not be contained by the Hapsburg and Ottoman Empires was in the end equally resistant to Soviet control. As Hugh Seton-Watson has written: 'as long as more than 100 million Europeans were kept in unwilling vassalage to the Soviet empire, national resentment would remain a dangerous explosive material.'[9]

Alongside the debate over a new security order that could fill the vacuum left by the evaporation of the Soviet Union went efforts to reform the states of eastern Europe, the former USSR, and its satellites outside Europe. Western advice and western models of development were freely on offer; western money less so. The pain of adapting to capitalism, the difficulties of creating democratic institutions and the lack of any deep-seated preference for liberal solutions meant that early expectations were quickly scaled down. The social and political systems that the states of the former Soviet bloc choose for themselves will not be, necessarily, a form of the 'universal homogeneous state . . . liberal democracy in the political sphere combined with easy access to VCRs and stereos in the economic', as Francis Fukuyama has written.[10] ('Some people mistakenly believe that eastern Europe will turn into some sort of Social-Democratic Hapsburg Empire,' a British Foreign Office official said recently.[11]) In the state of flux that characterizes the former Soviet bloc, there are a range of possible outcomes, few of them optimistic.

Manifestly, there is, *pace* Fukuyama, no end of history, that curious notion – based on a selective, highly idiosyncratic, sometimes tongue-in-cheek reading of Hegel – that humankind has developed the inevitable and final form of socio-economic organization, typified by liberal democracy and market economics. Indeed, as one particularly intelligent critic of the end-of-history theory has pointed out, 'it won't do to lump all regimes other than centrally planned communist dictatorships together and call them liberal democracies. It is only from an

altitude so great that most of human life is invisible that Japan and
the United States could be passed off as examples of the same socio-
political system.'[12]

Nevertheless, if the nations of eastern Europe want to be part of
the global system, they have to accept certain ground-rules concerning
the functioning of their domestic economies. They will need tradeable
currencies, central-bank apparatuses, transparent rules concerning
investment and trade, functioning commodities and stock exchanges,
and transparent accounting rules. Institutional reform will need to be
coupled with massive infrastructure development – road, rail and
communications networks – and modernization of production and
distribution techniques. Former Soviet bloc countries will also need
to develop modern computer networks. The government of the Soviet
Union restricted the use of advanced technology – computers, photo-
copiers and the like – for fear of losing control over the dissemination
of potentially seditious ideas.[13] Money from the G7 countries (US$24
billion promised in 1992, of which only some was actually delivered;
another $3.4 billion in 1993 from the US, and perhaps as much as $38
billion more from other G7 countries, albeit with strings – particularly
economic targets – attached) will help Russia at least to move toward
establishing these ground-rules. Technical advice and aid from the
EU, Japan, the US and Canada may also prove useful.

The costs of transforming the giant Russian economy are far higher
than the funds on offer from the West. Germany may end up spending in excess of $500 billion in its eastern *Länder* by the end of the
decade, to help a population of only seventeen million. That makes
the G7 offer look paltry. And there are still two hundred million more
people living in former Warsaw Pact countries; how much will it cost
to bring their economies into line?

The republics will not be required to introduce pure capitalism, of
course, which in any event hardly exists in the West today. The state
can – probably will – retain direct ownership of parts of the economy,
although widespread privatization programmes are underway in the
former East Germany and in Hungary, Poland, and in both parts of
the former Czechoslovakia. The key measurement of the reforms'
success, at least as far as citizens of eastern Europe are concerned, will
be the availability of consumer goods of adequate quality at affordable
prices. But there is less imperative to accompany these reforms with
the kind of liberal democracy that exists in the US, nor even the range
of corporatist-democratic systems that operate in Japan, elsewhere in

the Far East, or in much of western Europe. Autocratic traditions in Russia and Ukraine and the unstable nature of the statehood achieved by other former republics of the Soviet Union will together make it difficult to forge liberal democracies on the nineteenth-century model.

The nations of the eastern bloc will have to recognize the demands of their citizens nonetheless, in whatever form these views are put. By embracing capitalism – in the form in which it now operates world-wide – governments in the eastern bloc have yet to come fully to terms with the aspirations of a restive populace, just as concerned about crime, food, and decent working hours as about the perceived need to replace one economic and political system with another. Polish output dropped forty per cent within months of the introduction of the first serious market reforms in late 1989,[14] and only by 1993, with industrial output rising again by an annual rate of about five per cent, did the economy appear headed toward reasonably healthy growth. Hungary and the Czech Republic have also seen dislocation as they push through market reforms. Over all, eastern European economies have shrunk by twenty-five per cent since 1990, and inflation is still high – at a monthly rate of twenty-five per cent in Russia in the spring of 1993, for instance. The difficulty of finding new markets to replace traditional buyers in the Soviet bloc remains chronic.[15]

Cost-of-living increases and cuts in subsidies have fuelled frustration and even some defiance in the eastern bloc countries. Market reforms in Russia have helped fill shelves but prices have soared beyond the reach of many consumers. As journalist John Gray notes, 'the economic revolution has not created more food. It has meant only that the same amount of food is selling much more slowly because it is selling at prices most people cannot afford to pay. Thus there is no miracle.'[16]

Popular perceptions that the elites of the communist era are ben-efiting from the market reforms have heightened tensions.[17] Mean-while, mistrust of 'carpet-baggers' from the West is rife in several eastern bloc countries: as one official in the Czech Republic put it, 'Our two biggest problems are, one, false expectations on our side and, two, the great danger of gold-diggers from the West. I prefer the long-term investors, who see the potential for good, reliable markets.'[18] Extremism, local violence, ethnic disputes – these are the possible vehicles of popular dissatisfaction. The rise of right-wing nationalists and former communists, and the decline in support for centrist parties in 1993, are one symptom of this.

In western Europe, the twelve states of the European Union had already embarked on their own path to greater unity by the time of the eastern revolutions. The single market programme was intended to remove all barriers to the movement of people, goods, services and capital. Negotiations to forge a deeper European union were set in train as the Berlin Wall came down. The aim was to cement into place the achievements of thirty years of co-operation, in particular the Franco–German axis, and to demonstrate that in the New World Order there was a place for a new, more vital and powerful Europe. The European Union put itself forward as a potential brake on the violence in eastern Europe, seeking an increased role in determining the security agenda in its own neighbourhood, despite US resistance to an independent European defence policy. Many Europeans (among them senior officials of the European Commission in Brussels) believed that the EU could replace the US in Europe as a guarantor of stability, probably by investing the once-moribund Western European Union with the power to orchestrate a common military programme. "This is the hour of Europe," said Jacques Poos, Luxembourg's foreign minister in 1991 as the Yugoslav war raged. Yet the first real test of European resolve in this regard – the outbreak of war in the former Yugoslavia – proved that the EU remains far from being effective in policing its own backyard. Its peacemongering efforts, coupled with discussions within the Conference for Security and Co-operation in Europe (of which the US, Canada, and several eastern bloc nations are members), were unequal to the task of taming hostilities between Serbs, Croats and Bosnian Muslims; only United Nations intervention secured a series of strained ceasefires, invariably broken within hours.

Efforts to forge a common market by the end of 1992 and an economic and political union perhaps by the end of the century were given added impetus by the sudden collapse of Soviet control in eastern Europe. Some member countries – notably France – were concerned that the work of welcoming eastern European countries into the EU would divert attention away from European Political Union and European Monetary Union. France had linked her European policy to success in the talks leading to the Maastricht Summit in late 1991; anything less than full agreement on a deadline for the introduction of a single currency and on a framework for the creation of common political structures in coming decades would have been seen by France as a failure. Its concern was fuelled particularly by growing alarm at the preoccupation of Germany with its new *Länder* to the east. To make European integration work, the Franco-German alliance needed to remain intact.

The first Danish referendum decision against the treaty slowed the pace of integration in western Europe and gave a serious blow to the treaty ratification process. A razor-thin majority 'yes' vote on Maastricht was posted in France, followed by a slightly more resounding 'yes' in the second Danish referendum in mid-1993. Britain only approved the document after a long battle. The high costs of unification led to massive contradictions in European monetary policy, sparking the near-collapse of the European Monetary System. The result of a turbulent five years has been a change of mood, a return to Euro-pessimism. Economic and political union may not be at hand, and a common currency for all twelve EU members is out of reach this century. EU countries are moving toward greater and greater integration, but fitfully, and at times despairingly.

The ability of the European Union to act as a bulwark of stability has been tested in other ways, too. The prospect of the ultimate implementation of the Maastricht treaty – or something like it – emboldened regions within Europe to clamour for a greater degree of independence within nation-states, under EU sponsorship. By agreeing to pool sovereignty on key issues such as monetary policy and labour legislation, EU members would reduce the number of decisions taken by national governments. Independent-minded Scots, Flemish, and others see no reason why they cannot exercise more of the functions of nation-state governments, provided they remain under the umbrella of the EU. Indeed, as we shall argue later, the fact that so many decisions are now taken in Brussels has given regional governments a strong argument for insisting on greater devolution of the powers remaining to the central government.

The state of flux presented by the disintegration of the Soviet empire (and the rise in immigration from east to west and from south to north) has also created social uncertainty in countries of the European Union. The break-up of the Soviet Union presents particular challenges for Germany, which, despite public-sector strikes, a recession and persistent worries about the costs of reunification, is still the EU's most important economy. Throughout its modern history, Germany has traditionally looked east rather than west. If its commitment to EU integration wanes, fears that Germany will again seek to dominate '*Mitteleuropa*' are likely to grow. Without the organizing principle of east–west tensions and a defence structure based on containing the Soviet threat, the policy preoccupations that underwrote forty years of German history look bound to change. Already, Germany has signed friendship agreements with its eastern neighbours, and has offered more financial support to the states of the former Soviet Union and its satellites than any other single country.

In the Third World, the effects of the recent geopolitical changes have been extreme. Even before the dissolution of the Soviet bloc, states accustomed to being on the front line between two ideologies were increasingly unable to rely on the sponsorship of the Soviet Union, and had been left with little choice but to orient policies toward the West. They have now definitively lost the ability to use one superpower as a lever to extract benefits from the other. Syria, which had been close to the Soviet Union, learned this lesson early, and moved quickly in the aftermath of the Gulf War to strengthen ties with the US. Other Middle Eastern nations swiftly followed suit.

Turning to the West has required increased democratization in Africa and Latin America (although the record is far from even) and crash programmes in privatization, budget-balancing and austerity. A handful of outlaw states aside, market reforms are being instituted to varying degrees in nearly every Third World country. But the range of success will be broad: popular unrest is likely to curb the excesses of radical market reformers, while the relatively low level of political and economic development in some regions will make a transition toward democracy difficult to achieve. At the very least, rivalries among elites are now far more likely to escalate into violence, unchecked by the dictates of bipolarity. Fundamentalism in countries with large Islamic populations will also serve to slow any progress toward even rudimentary forms of liberal democracy. In much of the Third World, partitions, border skirmishes and secessionist movements are now far more likely to proliferate.

These historic developments have huge and sometimes troubling implications for the nation-state and the international nation-state system. The end of the Cold War undercuts a prime justification for the basis on which global security was maintained: no longer can the world rely on a balance of power under two sponsoring superpowers. The mutual fear engendered by the Cold War helped freeze borders that had been fixed in many cases at the end of the First World War. Their artificiality is now laid bare, and the fissure points made obvious anew. In the post-Cold War era, countries can – and will – break up.

Such instability is already prompting a transformation in the character of international diplomacy. Instances of superpower inter-ference (Vietnam, Afghanistan, Nicaragua, Panama) notwithstanding, the nation-state system was based, broadly, on mutual recognition of sovereignty and the principle of non-intervention. Countries, in theory, were free to do what they liked within their own borders. And above all, those borders were not to be changed. Indeed, in the last act of the old world order, the Gulf War, the US-led coalition stopped short of removing Saddam Hussein from power; the goal was to liberate Kuwait, not to interfere with Saddam's rule in Iraq. The coalition was only able to unite liberal and anti-western Arab nations because of a shared fear that Iraq's annexation of Kuwait would throw into question all the borders of the post-colonial Middle East. That view underlined initial US reluctance to intercede on behalf of the Kurds in northern Iraq. The battle between Saddam's forces and the Kurdish rebels was a civil war, Bush claimed. Few of Iraq's neighbours were keen to see the Kurds establish their own state – certainly not Turkey, Syria and Iran, each of which has sizeable Kurdish minorities of its own.[19]

But since the Gulf War the Soviet Union has dissolved, and with it even the fiction of a bipolar global security system. Washington and the European capitals are rethinking the inviolability of the sovereignty principle in instances where governments bully their own citizens. Western willingness to recognize the independence of the Baltic states and of Croatia, Slovenia, and Bosnia-Herzegovina suggests that the centrifugal forces at work appear too strong not to be accepted internationally, even if, so far, the West has evinced no will to help preserve newly independent countries in the former Yugoslavia. Elsewhere, a new round of intervention has been attempted, most not-ably, of course, in Somalia. As well, Britain and France gave public support to the US demand that Iraq cease mobilizing forces in the Kurdish enclave, and the US imposed its no-fly zone in Iraq.

For forty years, frontiers were frozen; even the unnatural borders of colonial Africa were retained following independence, notwith-standing ethnic divisions. There is as yet no adequate international political and security structure to manage these changes in any system-atic way. Nato is of little use in its current state, the organization is structured to respond to threats from the east, not to internecine strife in the Balkans, and only recently was accorded the right to act as a peace-keeping force outside the alliance territories. It has been slow to reform, although the Brussels summit of 1994 took some positive steps. The CSCE is hampered by its unwieldy size (fifty-two nations) and by the fact that all decisions must be taken unanimously.[20] The UN is still far from tested as a forum for global security decision making: the Gulf War was a specific case that promises little in the way of precedent for action in trickier situations.

The instability that has followed the Cold War has sat uncomfortably with efforts to continue the creation of a wider, more open world market place. The emergence of a truly global economy can be a brake on regional violence; states have to avoid political chaos if they hope to attract investment and trade. But the brake is far from automatic, nor is it a guarantee that stability and equity will be achieved together. Indeed, the response to integration on an economic level is fragmentation on a political level. Far from engendering a world government to match a world economy, economic change is helping to send people scurrying for the comfort of their communities. The spectre of tribalism is haunting not just eastern Europe, but much of the developed and developing worlds.

The challenges of the post-Cold War era are the subject of this section. We look first at the explosive new nationalisms of the developing and developed worlds; then at efforts to manage the world economy in a time of increasing political fragmention and economic integration. In Chapter Three, we consider the role of the US – the West's hegemonic power – after the Cold War. Europe's efforts to remake itself for a modern age are treated in detail in Chapter Four. Finally, we look at the prospects for the Third World in its relations with economies in the developed world, and at attempts to provide an adequate structure – a New World Order that works – in the aftermath of the Cold War.

1

The Return of the Nation: Tribalism Triumphant?

'And you German alone, returning from abroad,
Wouldst greet your mother in French?
O spew it out, before your door
Spew out the ugly slime of the Seine
Speak German, O you German!'
JOHANN GOTTFRIED VON HERDER[1]

The resurgence of nationalism in the 1980s and early 1990s, most obvious in the battles for autonomy in the former Soviet bloc but noticeable too in western Europe, the US and elsewhere, has confounded those analysts for whom the post-war era heralded greater international co-operation, the triumph of liberalism and the steady erosion of nation-state sovereignty. Why are we now witnessing the return of the nation, and with it intense outbursts of xenophobia, despite the weakening of the nation-state as an autonomous power, the declining importance of sovereignty, and the apparent redundancy of ethnicity?

Put another way, how is it that so eminent a scholar of nationalism as Eric Hobsbawm seems to have got it so wrong? He wrote, as recently as 1990, that 'the idea of "the nation", once extracted, like the mollusc, from the apparently hard shell of the "nation-state", emerges in distinctly wobbly shape'.[2] The 'nation' is certainly on the way towards being extracted from the nation-state, on any objective measure: the pact between the citizen and the state is undergoing a fundamental transformation, and governments can no longer fulfil their share of the bargain. Yet how 'wobbly' are the battles in Bosnia,

77

in Nagorno-Karabakh, in Georgia, in Kurdistan? To say that the revival of nationalism is merely a self-deluding, irrational response to circumstance does not diminish the fact that it is a reality, and it is a dangerously misleading approach simply to demonize it.[3]

We need, at the outset, to remember how diverse and complicated nationalist claims are. The glib use of the blanket term nationalism obscures the range of factors – economic, historical, social – that vary from case to case. Economic dislocation can make populations ripe for the kind of scaremongering, scapegoating and xenophobia that some leaders employ in a bid to gain political power. But it is worth asking why nationalism seems now to be on the rise nearly everywhere, if for reasons that differ markedly from country to country. Is there, in other words, a 'new' nationalism, and if so, what are its origins and characteristics?

The recent explosion in the number of successful (and usually violent) secessionist movements around the world dates from the end of the Cold War, but has its foundations in earlier periods, as we have argued. Once the superpowers could no longer perpetuate the freezing of international borders on the grounds of security, demands for independence within nation-states could be voiced more persuasively. These demands have served myriad purposes: to safeguard the political prestige of leaders; to avenge perceived wrongs visited on a people in the past; to wrest economic power from communities believed to have benefited unduly; to sweep into power leaders canny enough to hitch their electoral success to growing popular dissatisfaction and a widespread need to assign blame. The terms remain familiar. Secessionists claim the right of independence, and irredentists the right of annexation, under the principle of national self-determination. That concept underlined attempts after the First World War to contain the effects of the unravelling of multinational empires. Subsequently, national self-determination emerged as the prime justification for anti-colonial agitation in the 1960s. It has now been pressed into service not only in the republics of the former Soviet Union, the last of the nineteenth-century empires, but by 'nations' formerly within the ambit of one or another of the superpowers, particularly in the eastern bloc but also among ethnic groups in Africa.

The terms of reference for such claims of national self-determination are broadly historical, but coloured by idiosyncratic, sometimes mythologizing, readings of the deep past. As a consequence, many 'tribes' find themselves claiming territory which is already the object of competing claims. Even 'nations' able to trace their history far into the past, and which have maintained strong cultural cohesion irrespective of the political structures erected above or imposed upon them, have no easy way of laying claim to specific borders. Given the turbulent history of the Balkans, for instance, borders have been changed so often as to give several cultural groups a reasonably legitimate historical claim to territories now in dispute. This is no less true of the Caucasus, where borders (and populations) have migrated numerous times in the past two hundred years.

In any event, as Hobsbawm has observed, 'the populations of large territorial nation-states are almost invariably too heterogeneous to claim a common ethnicity, even if we leave aside modern immigration, and . . . the demographic history of large parts of Europe has been such that we know how multifarious the origin of ethnic groups can be.'[4]

Indeed, there are precious few nation-states anywhere in Europe, east or west, where an overwhelming percentage of the total population is of one ethnic group. Only Austria, Denmark, Ireland, the Netherlands, Poland, and Portugal can claim that distinction, according to a recent study by the Oxford Research Group.[5] Far more common is the patchwork of ethnic intermingling that typifies the former Yugoslavia, or parts of the former Soviet Union.

Despite the obvious difficulties of creating ethnically based nation-states in the late twentieth century, there is no shortage of nationalists waiting to do just that. Flying in the face of the pluralism of the liberal nation-state ideal, whereby all residents in a given country are, or (once they meet naturalization requirements) can become, citizens, nationalists throughout eastern Europe are adamant that the state belongs to the 'nation', not the other way around. In Estonia, the government was prepared to limit 'citizenship' to Estonian ethnics, thereby disenfranchising forty per cent of the population, most of them Russians who moved to the republic following Soviet annexation in 1940. Latvia is heading in the same direction.

The chequered history of the Balkans and the Baltics particularly has meant that minority populations there make up a considerable percentage of the total. The superpower balance helped keep control in regions where ethnic hatreds might have erupted far earlier. But with the end of the Cold War, the wounds have been opened anew. Some of them are very old. Given the clarion strength of claims to history, it is perhaps unsurprising that the best examples of secessionism can be found in that part of Europe where the problems of multinationalism were never fully resolved earlier this century. Under the Ottoman and Austro-Hungarian empires, ethnic minorities were encouraged to express their identities through an explicit policy of 'divide-and-conquer' fashioned in the imperial capitals. The channels allowed for such expression were never political but rather bureaucratic (a number of places in the imperial civil service were set aside for members of distinct cultural groups) or religious. That the Orthodox, Roman Catholic and Muslim churches acted as representatives of the Serbs, Croats and Bosnians helps explain the importance of religious differences in the current battles in the former Yugoslavia. 'What can we do, as a handful, against billions of Catholics,' lamented a spokesman for the Serbian cause in 1992.[6]

The collapse of the nineteenth-century empires generated short-lived independence for a handful of eastern European countries, but most of these remained multinational despite efforts to create single-ethnicity nation-states at the end of the First World War. During and after the Second World War, massive migration in some cases strengthened the dominance of the majority in a given country; but just as often, the new borders contributed to even greater ethnic intermingling. The legacy is one of fragmentation, ethnic rivalry, and political jealousies, leavened often by mutually distrustful religious convictions.

The Soviet Union under Stalin saw one of the most ambitious attempts to overcome the effects of inter-ethnic rivalries and hatreds, through explicit government policy. Of all the goals the Soviet system set for itself, the eradication of nationalism was perhaps the most daring. But it is obvious that nationalism was far from eradicated; that the break-up of the last European empire has created tensions similar to those accompanying the dissolution of the Austro-Hungarian and Ottoman empires more than seventy years ago. The Soviet policy on nationalism, at least officially, was to deny it; the socialist state was to create 'homo Sovieticus'. But the USSR also created scores of autonomous regions that reflected ethnic patterns throughout the country, even as it encouraged the resettlement of non-Slavic regions with Russians from the centre. Dogma was put at the service of Russian nationalism to store up a multinational empire. In the Soviet bloc, similar policies were followed. Governments used central planning to integrate regions that had formerly been quite separate, increasing the dependence of countries and provinces on the centre and on each other. An example can be seen in Slovakia, where military production was concentrated in a formerly pastoral region in an effort to boost the industrial fortunes of the poorer partner in the Czecho-slovak federation. This has left the now-independent Slovakia struggling to diversify its economic base.

At the same time, Soviet policy in the Third World was explicitly linked to support for national liberation movements in the decoloniz-ation period. This strategic accommodation with nationalism by a government ostensibly opposed to it at home helped create a strong anti-nationalist tinge to US foreign policy, fed by a liberal mistrust of ethnocentricity in the US. That mistrust was born in the inter-war period, when from the vantage point taken by the isolationist US the national rivalries in Europe looked retrograde, dangerous and distinctly old-fashioned. In the Cold War battles of the 1960s and 1970s, nationalism became an important element in the confrontation between East and West with both sides exploiting nationalist griev-ances in pursuit of wider goals. The fuse was lit then for many of the nationalist conflicts of the 1990s.[7]

The end of Soviet rule is likely to be typified by yet more violence and insecurity. As the then Czechoslovak President Václav Havel told delegates to the Helsinki Summit of the Conference on Security and Co-operation in Europe in the summer of 1992: 'The sudden outburst of freedom has not only untied the straitjacket made by communism, it has also unveiled the centuries-old, often thorny history of nations. People are now remembering their past kings and emperors, the states they had formed far back in their past and the borders of those states . . . It is entirely understandable that such a situation becomes a breed-ing ground for nationalist fanaticism, xenophobia and intolerance.'[8]

Within the erstwhile lands of the Soviet Union, secessionism has been fuelled in, among other states, Ukraine, Georgia, and Azerbaijan. Some of these movements merge with the other major threat to exist-ing nation-states, namely irredentism. For example, Russian troops have interceded on behalf of Russians in Moldova, a republic domi-nated by Romanians, where the Slavic minority is attempting to establish the independent Trans-Dniester Republic. Russia itself has twenty-one ethnically based republics, and another sixty-seven territories, regions, and districts.[9] That leaves room for considerable jockeying, and poses serious challenges to the federal leadership. Else-where in the region, revived nationalism has nurtured purer forms of irredentism. Potential conflict has been avoided between Germany and Poland following their agreement to accept post-war borders and bury long-standing German claims on territories in Poland. But the former Yugoslav republic of Macedonia set off alarms in neighbouring Greece by insisting on using the name 'Macedonia' (rather than the Greek preference, Skopje), Macedonia being also the name of a northern Greek province, and of course having historically glorious connotations the Greeks wanted to secure for themselves alone. Further north, claims and counter-claims for territory have been voiced by radical minorities in Hungary and Romania. Optimists hope that such demands may be foiled if the principle of self-determination is rigorously applied. Only if a people want to be 'reunited' with the mother country will such a transfer occur. Unfortunately, the ethnic patchwork of eastern and central Europe – the result of centuries of jostling within empires – does not admit of easy recarvings, and the prospect for greater violence is acute. The Hungarian minority in Slovakia is unhappy about its place in the new Slovak state and in 1994 called for a self-governing province. Ethnic Russians in Georgia are no less unhappy to find themselves the minority in an independent republic rather than the members of the dominant cultural group, as they were in the Soviet Union. The neo-nationalism of eastern Europe is matched elsewhere in the world, even if the issues seem less intractable. The demise of single-party systems in Africa has encouraged the growth of political movements based explicitly on ethnic background. For example, the Nigerian elections in 1992 produced an assembly that mirrored the country's ethnic make-up region by region. The end of the Cold War has allowed various secessionist movements to gather speed. In Ethiopia, ethnic Oromos and Afars are separately fighting the government in Addis Ababa, even as the government reviews a plan to allow voting on an ethnic basis, and to grant limited autonomy in tribal areas. The Ethiopian province of Eritrea has achieved independence after a bloody and protracted civil war; while rival claimants in Somalia have only stopped fighting because of the presence of US troops and other UN-sponsored 'peace-makers'. Ethnic battles are complicated by hideous problems, including wholescale famine and epidemics. Meanwhile, civil war in the Sudan (pitting black Christians and Animists of the south against Arab Muslims of the north) continues, while Zanzibar and Tanzania are negotiating a new relationship that will extend greater autonomy to Zanzibar. In north Africa, Western Sahara's independence movement, Polisario, continues to claim rights of secession from Morocco, whose government continues to prove unwilling to countenance a division, and has repeatedly delayed the holding of a referendum on the issue.

But it is not only in eastern Europe and the Third World that secessionist and irredentist movements can be found. Culturally distinct groups within traditional nation-states have often demanded a greater measure of autonomy, and a minority has used violence to further its cause. For example, militants among the Basques in Spain and France and the Québécois in Canada have long argued for a measure of independence from the centre and have been prepared to mount terrorist operations to achieve it. Meanwhile, a wave of neo-ethnicity in the 1970s has helped secure limited concessions from central governments for the Welsh, the Scottish, the Bretons, the Catalans, and other groups within the EU. These demands are likely to be voiced with increasing vehemence as a result of the changes we describe. Moves to enhance the power of regions within the nation-states of Europe are already far advanced in France, Belgium, Spain, and in Germany; one effect has been to revive 'provincial' attachments that many believed had been long buried under the weight of national culture and politics.[10]

The fact of revived nationalism is one thing: the shape it gives to the world is another. The reassertion of ethnic identities does point to revisions of borders, the end of old states and the beginnings of new ones. But it has deeper ramifications. Attempts to square the circle of nationalist discontent within the current structure of international relations have so far produced scant results. Such tensions have encouraged debate at international level about ways to ensure fair treatment of minorities at a time of great geopolitical shift. Unfortunately, a truly effective policing of minority rights will often clash with the competing claims of state sovereignty. The world community has yet to create a framework in which ill-treatment of minorities can be remedied in those cases where moral suasion or economic sanctions are ineffective.

There is no shortage of solutions on offer. Most centre on the idea of establishing international standards on the protection of minorities, by codifying existing United Nations guidelines strengthening the role of the UN, the Council of Europe and the Conference on Security and Co-operation in Europe in imposing conformity to international law. At the Helsinki meeting of the CSCE in the summer of 1992, delegates agreed to establish a High Commission on National Minorities, explicitly to pre-empt ethnic conflicts. The response to the

Yugoslav conflagration has shown how difficult it is to mount action of this sort. As much as the Serbs have been blamed for the fighting, all parties involved in the strife – Croats, Serbs and Muslims – have to some degree been guilty of the 'ethnic cleansing' that is meant to allow one or another ethnic group to claim control of territory. Unless populations move, it is virtually impossible to create micro-states within Bosnia: Muslims, particularly, live in communities scattered throughout the region, even though they make up about forty-four per cent of the population. Serbs dominate two broad swatches of Bosnia-Herzegovina, separated by Muslim and Croat enclaves. Taking sides in such difficult situations is therefore not that simple.

Attempts to square this circle have dominated post-Cold War theorizing. Stanley Hoffmann, for instance, outlines four principles of world order: state sovereignty, self-determination, self-government, and human rights.[11] He rightly points out that state sovereignty is undermined by the limited powers of the nation-state to operate independently. Self-determination is thwarted by nationalist tensions within multi-ethnic states. Self-government is impossible to monitor effectively. Human rights within nation-states can only be protected in the face of totalitarianism by ignoring state sovereignty. Without a superpower willing and able to finance and police world order, the results lean toward the chaotic.

In areas where rights can be guaranteed, and political structures are more flexible, the results may be different. The growth of nationalist fervour is in part a response to the geopolitical shift engendered by the end of the Cold War. But it is also a function of the emerging global economy, and the effect of globalization on the autonomy of national governments. New countries will emerge, with flags, bureaucracies, currencies, central banks and a national museum filled to the brim with treasured objects and folklore. These new nation-states will not win true self-determination, if by this is meant political and economic autonomy on the model of the territorial nation-state. They may well win self-administration, and can offer a stronger sense of community to the regional groups under their sponsorship. There may no longer be any reason for such ethnic groups to seek a nation-state, at least not in its pure form as a structure that weds citizens to an all-powerful state, and links them in a national economy.

Self-administration may be a more achievable goal for many 'stateless' nations. Agitation by regional groups for greater independence within Spain, France, Britain, and elsewhere has its roots in a growing realization that as long as national governments continue to pool sovereignty in many policy areas, there is little to stop a concomitant devolution of powers down to smaller political units within states. The micro-states of Hong Kong and Singapore prove that, provided national economies are firmly incorporated into the international system, and provided political leaders accept the associated limits on sovereignty that such incorporation inevitably implies, then size is no longer a criteron of global commercial viability.

Not surprisingly, then, the end of the Cold War, and the growth in recent years in the number and extent of regional trading links, has emboldened cultural groups within existing nation-states to demand greater autonomy within a federal structure, while eschewing claims for outright independence. Negotiations between Flanders and Wallonia to grant further powers to state governments are likely to lead to a dilution of central government authority in Belgium, but will not necessarily lead to the creation of two separate states. Polls suggest that Scottish voters are more inclined to demand greater autonomy, although not outright independence, provided Scotland is able to maintain its ties to the rest of Europe.

In Canada, tensions between the provinces and the federal government have long been exacerbated by the difficulty of marrying the French and English nations within a single nation-state.[12] While the population of Quebec voted against a 'sovereignty-association' framework in 1980, recent polls have confirmed the persistence of desires among French Canadians to redraw their relationship to the rest of Canada. The end of the Cold War, and the renewed interest in the concept of national self-determination, have helped put the constitutional future of Canada to the fore. A reasonably amicable agreement to boost the autonomy of Quebec (and by extension other provinces) is perhaps the most likely outcome of future constitutional talks, despite the failure of the Charlottetown Accord in a national referendum in late 1992.[13]

What is striking about most of these movements for 'independence' is the speed with which most separatist leaders are prepared to apply to join one or another of the large trading associations. Quebec *'indépendantistes'* say they would negotiate a free-trade agreement with the US, just as Canada as a whole did in 1988. Both the Czech Republic and Slovakia will ask for a place within the European Union, and so begin the process of pooling much of the sovereignty they 'won' with separation. Slovenia, the first of the Yugoslav republics to bid for independence, wants to join the EU.

The availability of constitutional structures to contain nationalism does not mean, however, that this powerful force has been domesticated. Despite such evidence of the need to dilute sovereignty in various ways, recent events have proven that allegiance to the nation-state over and above any other political level remains strong. Citizens still desire to situate their nationalism within secure borders, however unlikely that prospect. In the oldest nation-states, where efforts to create wider allegiances have been pursued with the greatest zeal, many citizens retain their belief in the territorial nation, and are prepared to fight to defend it.

The right-wing movements in Germany, France and Italy, for example, are explicitly nationalist in tone, and trade on fears of economic dislocation, increased immigration and the loss of political power to the benefit of supranational structures such as the European Union. The nationalism on offer in Europe is explicitly nostalgic; its leaders bemoan the loss of the 'old' values which had served so well in the past. The human targets of the new nationalism are the obvious ones: those of different cultures, those who speak foreign languages. Nationalists demand tougher border controls at a time when borders are increasingly impossible to secure. They want protection for 'national industries' although the term has ceased to have any distinct meaning. They call on governments to act in the national interest at a time when the policy tools at the disposal of the nation-state are no longer up to the task. It is no coincidence that the virulence of anti-immigrant feeling has intensified at a time of major economic dislocation. In the West, with the economic slowdown of the early 1990s, and in the East, with the high-stakes marketization programmes, ethnic tensions owe at least some of their intensity to economic factors.

The constituency of radical nationalism may be expanding. In France, the National Front made significant inroads in regional elections in the spring of 1992 on an anti-immigrant platform, and confirmed its strength by winning thirteen per cent of the vote (but no seats) in the parliamentary elections in the spring of 1993. The party helped fill a vacuum left by the unravelling of French President François Mitterrand's painstakingly forged coalition of the left, which since 1983 has sought to maintain social democracy and to marginalize the Communists. Mitterrand depended on Europe to give France weight internationally, and staked his government's fortunes on moves within the EC to deepen economic and political co-operation. German unification and the subsequent break-up of the Soviet Union wrongfooted the French president completely. He held out for an intensification of German commitment to the EC as the price for supporting early unification and appeared to hesitate before condemning the hardline coup against Gorbachev in August 1991. For voters, concerned that Mitterrand had lost his way and that events were complicating France's prospects within Europe, the Front's patriotic, anti-foreign message looked comforting. Even mainstream politicians climbed on the Le Pen bandwagon: for example, Republican Party leader and presidential aspirant Jacques Chirac told an audience in Paris that he understood how unpleasant it was to have 'strange odours' wafting from a neighbouring immigrant household. The centre-right government formed in 1993 recruited Charles Pasqua as Interior Minister, and he moved quickly to demonstrate his patriotic credentials by tightening nationality laws.

German right-wing extremists won seats in Baden-Württemberg, one of the country's richest states, and in Schleswig-Holstein, during regional elections in March 1992. The costs of unification and the sudden influx of immigrants has fuelled dissatisfaction with Helmut Kohl's ruling Christian Democrats. Nearly 200,000 asylum-seekers arrived in Germany in 1990, 250,000 in 1991, and 450,000 in 1992.[14] Germany has taken in far more people fleeing the battleground of the former Yugoslavia than any other European nation. However, as we have mentioned, the government has moved to tighten liberal asylum laws considerably. Migration is set to continue, as the battles in Yugoslavia and elsewhere force ethnic minorities to flee. The pattern is reminiscent of the great migrations of the aftermath of the First World War, when attempts to create ethnically based nation-states were typified by population exchanges on a massive scale. Political leaders (Serbs and Croats aside) are unwilling to mandate such solutions but citizens are making their own decisions and moving on.

These right-wing movements run counter to the liberal nationalism of the nineteenth century, and place the 'nation' above the pluralistic nation-state. In this sense, the strident neo-nationalism in Europe has reopened wounds long considered healed. Consider the example of Italy, unified for over a hundred years. The Northern League in Italy won ten per cent of the vote in 1992's national election on a programme of dividing Italy into three parts, of which the rich north would comprise one. (Such radicalism is unlikely to survive electoral success. But supporters knew what kind of signal their votes would send.) The traditional ruling party, the Christian Democrats, had owed their longevity in power to a strict anti-communist stance; the end of the Cold War removed the party's prime claim to legitimacy, and produced a vacuum that extremists – seizing on the growing climate of crisis surrounding corrupt elected officials – have not been slow to exploit.

Some of western Europe's new nationalists target the European Union as the culprit. They are wary of the powers that have been ceded to Brussels, and concerned that European unity will reduce national sovereignty to an unacceptable degree. The Danish rejection of the Maastricht Treaty in the first referendum in 1992 was in part a reflection of fears about ceding national sovereignty to a supranational organization.

The lesson for policy-makers appears obvious: as much as the trend continues to be towards the pooling of sovereignty, citizens maintain – and perhaps are strengthening – ties to the nation that will not soon disappear. It is unlikely that European nation-states can withstand the trend towards greater co-operation, in areas ranging from environmental protection and social welfare to business regulations and macroeconomic policy. But many citizens have yet to be convinced that monetary and political union are the necessary way forward, and the road to the implementation of the Maastricht Treaty is bound to be long and bumpy.

The return to nationalism of various kinds, even in countries with settled borders, relative prosperity and stable political institutions, shows that the tribalist revival is more than simply the preserve of the fringes of civilization, and cannot be contained merely by constitutional fixes. Heightened xenophobia has been one of the most obvious results of the political changes sweeping the world, particularly since 1989. Not surprisingly, the prospect of greater immigration into developed countries from the Third World is a persistent source of concern. But the new nationalism, particularly the new economic nationalism so evident in both Europe and the US, is linked to changes in the global economy as much as to irrational fears of a wave of unwanted foreigners storming the borders. National governments find it difficult to respond to demands for greater protection against foreign imports or foreign investment, since such strictures would be harshly judged in the court of the international economy. But the dislocations provoked by economic changes – particularly deindustrialization in the developed world – have encouraged anti-foreign sentiment and so translated into the kind of economic nationalism found on both the left and right of the political spectrum in the US and elsewhere.[15]

It should come as no surprise that some citizens are prepared to vote self-described neo-liberals out of power. There is no reason why the disadvantaged should simply shrug their shoulders and accept the judgement of an international economy in which they have no formal political say. If jobs are lost in the automobile industry, someone is surely to blame, and someone should put it right. Because there is only the nation-state, they expect that structure to respond.

Economic nationalists are thus able to tap a growing frustration at the citizens' lack of influence over economic conditions. As unrealistic as these campaigns are – for example, the US economy is inextricably linked to the global economy, and studied isolationism would send the US system teetering – there is no doubt a powerful groundswell of popular dissatisfaction. The prospects for a third force in US politics, spearheaded by the independent presidential candidate Ross Perot in 1992, seem rosier than at any time since the progressivist heyday of the early twentieth century. President Clinton has shown he will be tough on trade in his early dealings with the European Union: he and his advisers talk of 'fair' trade not just free trade. But not for long could developed countries, even the richest ones, maintain an economic isolationism.

In the case of the US, nostalgia feeds the new economic nationalism. The 1960s and early 1970s were not only a period of vast US power internationally, but one of impressive economic growth domestically. Nationalists argue that 'unfair' trade practices are the reason for a decline in US economic might, and that retaliation against foreign exporters is the simple expedient. But economic nationalism is not limited to the US. Anti-foreign sentiment, focused on worries about economic competitiveness, is strong in France, the Nordic countries, and in Canada.

So the effect of the revival of tribalist sentiment goes beyond the reassertion of ethnic identity in eastern Europe and in the developing world; and its causes are more complex than simply the recalling of lost ethnic identities. The rising tide of nationalism has been swollen by the economic dislocations of the past decade, particularly in the leading industrialized countries but also in the liberalizing eastern bloc. Unemployment, rising prices, and declining living standards in many parts of the world have been an important source of the intense frustration felt both east and west. Citizens everywhere, who look to their nations and communities for comfort, require of their governments some protection from the effects of globalization and interdependence.

2

Going Global

'Fuck the lira.'
RICHARD NIXON

The 1992 meeting of the Group of Seven should, in theory, have been an occasion of great joy. The world was now open for capitalism's unimpeded progress. The seven largest industrialized countries were now supreme – the global directorate. Since they had last met, the Soviet Union had been dismantled, and the republics which had emerged, including Russia, had abandoned their resistance to capitalism, and instead were now eager to join the club: it was, after all, the only game in town.

But only three years after the Berlin Wall fell, when the heads of government of the US, Canada, Britain, Germany, Italy, France and Japan met in Munich for their annual shindig, the prevailing moods were gloom, helplessness and futility. Growth was down; unemployment was up; and the citizens were in revolt. France had seen demonstrations by farmers on the streets, where these were not blocked entirely by angry lorry drivers, and the government was only slowly recovering from a defeat in regional and municipal elections. In Canada, the government was registering record levels of unpopularity in the polls; in the US, George Bush was fighting for re-election and the memory of riots in Los Angeles was fresh in the public mind. Germany was fighting the rise of the far right and economic distress in the east. Italy had only formed a government a few days before, which had immediately put up interest rates and promised to slash public expenditure. Japan was promising to raise expenditure to combat a serious economic slump and a stock market plunge. Within two years, only two of the heads of government present in Munich would still be in power.

The collapse of the Soviet model brought loud celebration from the cheer-leaders of western capitalism. But the system to which the east was now seeking to tie its future was by no means as efficient and well organized, or as just and equitable, as its propagandists liked to think.

In particular, the economic and financial system seemed close to chaos. There was no clear vision of where the world economy was heading and little in the way of international consensus about the solutions to its problems. The 1970s and 1980s had seen a flurry of ideological revolutions that had each proved as troublesome to implement and as flawed in operation as the last. The result was a curious mismatch of state and market, of national and international elements, which survived mainly through the skill of the protagonists in keeping it alive. 'More than anything else, perhaps, the financial structure that has evolved over the past four decades – often by a series of non-decisions and failures of the political will more than by deliberate design – seems to lack both a political vision and, supporting it, an economic doctrine that is effectively convincing. There is a bankruptcy of ideas and theories in the profession of economics that is ominously reminiscent of the period 1929 to about 1934 to 1936.'[1]

At the national, international and transnational levels, the system for economic management that ushered in the new era in 1989 was demonstrating some clear signs of distress. What replaced national economic management were a variety of schemes that combined elements of Keynesianism, elements of the new monetarism, and bits of other theories, with varied and often contradictory assumptions tacked on. David Henderson, former chief economist at the OECD, referred to do-it-yourself economics; Phyllis Deane, in rather more straightforward fashion, talks of 'bastard' economics.[2] In the 1980s a variety of paths to economic salvation were embarked upon, most without much theoretical justification and few with much long-term success.

Discretionary fiscal policy had been all but discredited as an instrument of economic management. Expansion in one country was likely to be penalized by the financial markets. Government spending created inflation, crowded out the private sector, and was an inefficient use of resources: that was the lesson the 1970s had taught the predominantly right-wing politicians who held power in the 1980s. Tinkering with policy by using discretionary spending had malign effects; and in any case, the markets had absorbed the new orthodoxy so rapidly that an increase in borrowing would quickly be followed by a deflationary response, as markets discounted future inflation and interest rates rose.

But monetary policy was also problematic as an instrument of management. This was partially because the rapid changes in financial systems that followed liberalization in many countries, and partly because of its uncertain effects in a world typified by large and open capital markets. 'The close links of national production and financial structures ensure that a crisis of any kind (or a recovery) cannot be confined to the country in which it originates.'[3] In particular, rapid capital flows can offset, negate or subvert government policies. When the oil cartel, OPEC, increased prices dramatically in the 1970s, the effect was to worsen inflation throughout the industrialized world and further weaken economic co-operation, moving the world economy further towards the pole of market-driven policies. In the 1980s, it was primarily the inability of governments, especially in the US, to manage their own economies which led to frequent policy shocks.

The most prominent attempt to replace the Keynesian orthodoxy, and probably the most catastrophic in its implications, was the Reagan Administration's grab-bag of Keynesian, monetarist and other ideas, including the paradoxical notion that successive tax cuts would raise government revenue. They did not. The budget deficit continued to spiral, the dollar weakened and the trade deficit remained stubbornly high. George Bush, who ran against Ronald Reagan in the 1980 Republican selection contest, called it 'voodoo economics', presumably because the word 'bastard' would not go down well on the campaign trail. But the legacy of Reagan set the pace for Bush, who did not confront the implications of his predecessor's policies. The market was to be given free rein, whatever the consequences.

Managing an international economy in these circumstances was bound to be difficult. The structures of management that emerged from the wreckage of Bretton Woods were weak and leadership from Washington intermittent. 'In the pluralist system of the 1970s and 1980s, there was no dominant power to resolve the conflict, and the result was stalemate.'[4] In 1977 and 1978, the US tried to force the burden of adjustment onto Germany and Japan. In 1985, in an attempt to bring the dollar down, James Baker, then US Treasury Secretary, enlisted the support of his colleagues in Britain, Germany, Japan and France to encourage a fall in the dollar's value; but when they tried to come to more certain understandings later in the decade over managing currencies, there was little agreement.

As with the management of national economies, there were few attempts to challenge market responses to growing economic interdependence. The effects of integration were vividly obvious in the way in which national crises spread throughout the developed world. Policy responses could not be taken in isolation. This was evident in the synchronization of growth cycles that took place during the postwar era but became more obvious in the recessions of the early and late 1980s. 'In an open economic environment, fiscal and monetary convergence is the only way in which to avoid financial instability. The snag is that . . . if countries pursue identical short-term macroeconomic policies their business cycles will become synchronized, increasing greatly the size of cyclical fluctuations in the world economy.' The ability of states to determine economic conditions, together or apart, has been minimized by the growth of a global economy. 'Economic interdependence and integration reduce the effectiveness of national policies.'[5]

This is partly because of the interplay of national levels of demand and production. The increase in the amount of produce traded across borders, and in particular the growing international division of labour, means that reflation or deflation in one country is risky. 'If a number of major countries are experiencing demand expansion at the same time . . . the total effect can be unexpectedly large. Each country finds that, in addition to the expected expansion of its domestic demand components, its exports are growing sharply. Overheating of the world economy can then arise. The equivalent effect, of inducing a greater than intended downturn, can just as readily occur in times of synchronized deflation.'[6]

This interconnectedness led to increasing strains between the main G7 partners in the 1980s as each sought its own road to salvation. The US loosened fiscal policy, let the dollar slip and allowed monetary policy to ease. Germany maintained a commitment to low inflation and the Bundesbank retained its traditionally tight hold on monetary policy. This was wrenched from its control at the time of unification; but it quickly seized back the tiller and put on the brakes in 1991. Britain's relatively tight monetary policy was relaxed, and the Treasury flirted with shadowing the German currency before being forced into the tightening that created recession. Different instruments of policy, different objectives and different players were a recipe for chaos. When growth was relatively kind – from about 1982 until 1989 – this worked, more or less; when it was not, the tensions became only too evident. Hard-pressed politicians saw votes disappearing; central bankers watched policy commitments overridden; civil servants struggled to implement contradictory sets of policies.

The tensions that emerged over macroeconomic policy were equalled by growing trade tensions between the US, the EU and Japan. Technological change also brought new patterns of competition that increasingly pitted each against the other. The nature of international economic competition was changing: each country was producing the same products, for the same markets. The post-war miracles of Japan and Germany, for instance, had been built on catching up with the United States. By the end of the 1960s, each was producing cars, electronic goods, machine tools, for the same people. By the end of the 1980s, a large number of emerging industrial powers had joined them. The result was a clamour for protection in Europe and the US, accusations of unfair competition, and the adoption of measures to block or limit foreign access to domestic markets.

The rise of foreign direct investment (FDI) as a motor of economic growth also precipitated severe strains among the G7 partners. As well as the panoply of trade-distorting measures which the G7 have resorted to, they have all adopted a broad range of measures against foreign investors who are deemed to break the rules creating a new agenda for international competition and conflict.

One focus is on regulation. What level of domestic regulation is appropriate, and what level is protectionist? Who should be the regulatory authority for banks that do business everywhere? Should some industries be regulated at all? Secondly, there are conflicts over the degree to which states and corporations can lock out competitors. Few transnational corporations and few countries are committed to the mode of openness which American multinationals advocate. The types of openness required by a European firm is markedly less than that required by a US firm, though more than that required by a Japanese firm. No less contentious is the role of the state. Japanese companies are seen to be more tightly integrated with the national government than those of either the US or the EU. But at the same time, the US row with Europe over the Airbus is based on the level of subsidies which EU governments give to the project. The EU counter-attacks that Boeing receives what are in effect subsidies from the US government in its capacity as a large defence contractor.

Attempts to reach solutions to problems of trade, economics and investment through international organizations have been few, and unsuccessful, despite the plethora of fora. The principal Bretton Woods organizations, the IMF and World Bank, had never taken up their functions as guardians of the international financial system which remains fundamentally a national preserve. As Wendy Dobson, one of the officials charged with preparing the G7 meetings, has observed, there is a reluctance to draw in the IMF to G7 meetings. The OECD emerged as an important mechanism for consultation through its Working Party Three in the 1960s, but there was little success in extending its role: instead, it has emerged as more of a talking shop, useful but inadequate to the task of policy management.

International organizations have similarly played but a weak role in co-ordinating the tasks of managing transnational corporations. International policy co-ordination is 'more of a platitude than a panacea', says DeAnne Julius. 'In banking, after twelve years of negotiations through the Bank for International Settlements, the Cooke Committee achieved agreement on a common set of capital adequacy ratios to be applied by bank regulators in the major OECD countries. That such a large effort was required for such a relatively small issue demonstrates the difficulty of the process.' He concludes that the direction of policy *vis-à-vis* FDI is likely to be towards 'spreading liberalization and deregulation of domestic markets and reduc[ing] scope for national policy autonomy'.

There has been an attempt in the General Agreement on Tariffs and Trade, for instance, to reach agreement on freedom of establishment and intellectual property rights, key issues for the TNC, as well as trade in services. But the last round of the GATT, launched in Punte del Este, Uruguay, in 1986 to hasten liberalization of the global trading environment, was not the ideal place to negotiate. Talks so often foundered on the narrow, mutually exclusive national interests of members. In the end, the agreement reached in December 1993 was a somewhat messy compromise, and certainly did not constitute a comprehensive new basis for the regulation of TNC activity nor for the provision of a 'level playing field' for TNCs in different markets. The negotiations culminated in the creation of a World Trade Organization, which will begin to deal with the complex issues of investment and competition. However, it is only a start, and if previous negotiations are anything to go by, progress will be slow. The IMF, the World Bank and the UN play a role, but more in assessing trends than in making policy. The UNCTC, formerly a focus for Third World criticism of the transnational economy, has instead become a collecting house for information. Attempts to form a UN code of conduct have foundered; the equivalent issued by the OECD is meek and mild. Instead of being made multilaterally, rules for the conduct of investment and transnational operations are instead made bilaterally. This shouldn't be surprising, since increasingly there are only three players: the EU, the US and Japan are both the major sources and the major hosts of foreign investment. In the same way, though the GATT round finished with a flourish, removing trade barriers and strengthening the rules of world commerce, increasingly it is the unilateralism and bilateralism of Washington and Brussels that set the agenda.

The mixed reception to the 1993 GATT deal shows that the longer-term impact of the market turn of the 1980s is open to doubt. So did the uncertain results of many of the policy revolutions it generated. Privatization was certainly far-reaching; though, in many cases, state monopolies were turned into private monopolies. The extent to which the market could be allowed to dictate economic conditions was undermined by the recession of 1981–2; and the subsequent recession of 1991–3 put the theoretical underpinnings of the market creed still further into doubt. But what cannot be doubted is that the market continues to exert a strong discipline on those countries which step beyond its orthodoxies. The risks of a crisis are all too obvious to the protagonists. The example of France was the most noted of these, because it seemed to represent a crisis in socialism. No less marked however was the collapse in confidence in the Conservative-led British economy in the late 1980s; or in the United States. Japan had seemed invulnerable; but this bubble was pricked. The market has become a form of political authority, passing a judgement on policy which is not easily refuted.

But if the discipline of the markets is ever present, so are the political risks governments face by abandoning activism. The tasks which the state had taken up in the post-war period did not magically evaporate with the tools to achieve them. In the first place, many states were left with severe balance-of-payments problems or other structural macroeconomic problems which did not admit of easy solutions. Secondly, the expectations of the electorate certainly did not evaporate overnight. The deterioration in the welfare systems of the post-war era became increasingly evident in the 1980s as funding dried up and societies changed. Thirdly, the death of old industrial sectors left serious problems of unemployment, regional decay and industrial decline throughout the developed world. These led to political pressures from business, labour and voters for action – action which the state could not deliver.

Governments are thus trapped between Scylla and Charybdis, the market and the electorate. Given that the post-war economic system was so explicitly predicated on political principles – a secure international system, democracy, the eradication of the underclass – this has helped to generate a crisis of confidence in government. Voting for different administrations seemed increasingly irrelevant in the 1980s and 1990s. Economic choices were progressively narrowed and thus so were political choices. In these circumstances, the dangers of a political backlash were also all too obvious. Economically liberal governments in the United Kingdom, Canada, Australia and the United States all came under attack in the early 1990s. So did the Mitterrand government in France, which had stuck to a basically liberal set of policies since its disastrous dash for growth. The state, it seemed, was stuck. It could neither go forwards nor back. Its policy choices were strictly limited; so were its choices of levers and tools. This paralysis has been amply shown in the regular gatherings of the G7. The 1993 meeting in Tokyo also achieved little, beyond the beginnings of a trade pact that had already been seven years in the pipeline. The gatherings have become, in the words of one commentator, 'punchless pageants'. The *Financial Times* says the G7 'conforms to the Sinatra Doctrine – they meet, talk and then do it their way'.[7]

The nation-state remains economically sovereign, in the formal sense that powerful supranational bodies have not been erected over their heads, but the size of their realm is considerably diminished. Few governments would now hope to be able to manage the business cycle. Stability has been removed; the degree to which governments believe they can affect welfare through state intervention is strictly limited; and modernization is no longer a function of state control. The tools which the nation-state can use to achieve its ends in this diminished realm are also reduced. The result has been a dispersal of the power which the state accumulated in the post-war years; to the market and to different forms of international economic co-operation.

The price of an open global economy run by weak states has been very heavy for those at the bottom of the social scale. Taking account of inflation, in real terms US median family income declined in the 1970s, plummeted in the 1980s and did not return to 1973 levels until 1990. The wages of average workers are below 1979 levels; family incomes were often only sustained by both partners going to work. The trend towards a greater gap between rich and poor prevailed throughout the industrialized world; but the US was in 'ignominious isolation' in its failure to lift its citizens out of poverty, according to a 1991 study. According to its definition of poverty, the US experienced steadier growth and lower unemployment than most of western Europe during the 1980s but nonetheless its poverty rate was 18.1 per cent, compared to 12.5 per cent in Britain, 10 per cent in France and 7 per cent in Germany.

Unemployment soared in the 1980s in Europe in particular. In the OECD area, it rose from twenty-five million in 1990 to thirty million in 1992, and the OECD predicted that it would continue to increase, despite positive, albeit weak growth. In France alone, nearly a million people had been without a job for a year.[8] In Europe, the unemployment rate averaged more than 10 per cent, with youth unemployment even higher.[9] The EU's social affairs commissioner, Vasso Papandreou, admitted in 1992 that even with growth, the number of jobless might not fall. 'We could end up with very good indices and a lot of people in a desperate situation,' she said.[10]

Technological change was a potent force in creating new jobs in the 1980s. But it erased many of the lower paid, unskilled industrial jobs, and replaced them with what were often worse paid jobs in services, or worse still with no job at all. Industrial sectors such as mining, shipbuilding and steel have lost thousands of jobs in the 1980s as new technology, new competitors and new markets have changed the basis of employment. The EU, the OECD and other worthy bodies have urged a greater attention to education and training in the face of this challenge. But most of the states with high unemployment have not concentrated on developing new frameworks: instead, they have poured cash into unemployment schemes that are but a bandage on the gaping wound of joblessness. Older workers often slip out of the net completely: without the skills required to enter one of the new industries, their prospects are dismal.

Inequalities have also burgeoned on the global scale. Since 1960, the countries where the richest twenty per cent of the world's people live increased their share of gross world product from seventy per cent to over eighty per cent, according to the United Nations Development Programme.[11] The disparity of income between the world's richest billion and its poorest billion is probably more than 150 to one. Yet the prospects for mobilizing foreign aid are also grim. The OECD said that foreign aid rose to $133.4bn in 1991 from $130.6bn; after taking account of inflation, that was a fall of 1.2 per cent.[12] That compares with debt service payments of $141bn made by developing countries in the same period. Competition for that aid is going to increase dramatically, at a time when most states are still not meeting the 0.7 per cent of GDP target for foreign aid set by the United Nations.

The case for free trade is that by expanding the size of the cake, everybody gets more. That did not seem to happen in the 1980s. 'It is a standard finding in economics that trade-offs between efficiency and distribution can best be handled by maximizing efficiency and using some of the benefits generated to compensate the losers (for instance, through income and profits taxes). This works within a national context where transfers can be engineered through the political system. But there is no international mechanism for arranging such transfers.'[13] Quite the reverse; resources are being transferred from the Third to the First World. Third World attempts to find economic justice in the 1970s, fed by the apparent strength of their bargaining interest, failed conclusively. In the subsequent decade, little has been achieved; if something imaginative is not done, then the prospects for the countries on the periphery of the global economy are grim indeed. The massive increases in income in the newly industrializing countries have in most cases only created new inequities.

The political questions raised by these problems of economic management hark back to those of the 1930s about the ability of capitalism to co-exist with democracy and social order. Capitalist democracy has been sustained in all of the western nations; and indeed transplanted to many of the developing countries. It has been exported to eastern Europe, and perhaps will be to the former Soviet Union. It is the only available model. But the problems that arose in the 1970s and 1980s pinpointed the difficulty of yoking together capitalism and democracy in a highly interdependent world economy. If the lesson of the pre-war years was that unfettered capitalism could not sustain stable governments, the lesson of the post-war years was that the state proved inadequate to the task of managing capitalism. This is a lesson which eastern Europe, in particular, is having to learn very quickly.

Without the rapid growth of the European economies in the 1950s and 1960s, political disturbance on a much greater scale might have been the result. Prosperity has brought peace to Europe. It has also helped to sustain the growth of new states in the developing world through the post-independence period, and when prosperity disappeared the integrity of many of those states came into question again. But the scope of the nation-state and its underpinning in a community organized along largely irrational, historical and traditional lines has fitted inadequately with an economic system that recognizes no borders and which has little relationship to community.

The myriad crises of the global economy in the past twenty years also demonstrate another parallel with the inter-war years. The management of a global system of commerce and security, it was argued by those who analysed the collapse of order in this period, relied heavily on the presence of a sponsoring power; and that was lacking. In the same way, the US, which filled the gap in the post-war years, has found it increasingly difficult to sustain its role. This has been brought home by the end of bipolar certainty. America is already drifting from the centre of the international stage. At the 1992 meeting of the heads of government of the seven largest industrial democracies, a European official told the *Washington Post*: 'this is the first summit in which the Americans are just another player.'[14] Though a US official rejected this, saying that 'there is no military action without US military strength and no global economy without the United States', the point was that on many of the issues which the Group of Seven discussed the US was not pre-eminent. The Gulf War had not been the first act of a new world order; it had been the last act of the old. It had shown American leadership at its most forceful and its most alienating, as far as many of its partners were concerned. This was not, however, the kind of leadership appropriate for complex economic tasks, such as those that face the Group of Seven. Nor are America's assets so well matched to the task in hand. Indeed, as David Calleo wrote in 1988, 'The danger is not merely that America's lingering hegemony will collapse, but that the attempt to hang onto it will ruin the chances for stability in a more plural system.'

Yet there is no sign of any other country or bloc emerging to take the helm. There is a great shortage of what Charles Kindleberger has called followership. There is an increasing unwillingness amongst European and Japanese leaders to follow the US. Yet all of these leaders have their own problems which preclude them from taking effective action of their own. The G7 summits, the public face of international economic diplomacy, reveal the disturbing prospect of the leaders of seven of the world's foremost nations unable to take action to resolve the problems that face them, but determined to show that they are in charge in some unspecified sense. 'They are all jockeying for leadership,' said a British official after the 1992 meeting, 'or at least the appearance of leadership.'[15]

3

The Limits to Hegemony

'Great are the myths ... I too delight in them.'
WALT WHITMAN

In 1985, Frances Fitzgerald, an acute critic of US policy in Vietnam and Central America, looked forward to the next presidential election. 'The question is', she said, 'what any candidate can say about foreign affairs that will get him elected and be true at the same time.'[1] The question answered itself, as it turned out: the dramatic improvement in US-Soviet ties between that year, perhaps the nadir of US-Soviet relations, and 1988, was one important piece in the Republican victory that brought George Bush to the White House. But her question was a time-bomb: it came back to haunt Bush in 1992, the year in which being the 'foreign policy president' was a liability, when isolationism returned to the lexicon of American presidential politics, when being the sole superpower was not enough, or perhaps too much.

There has always been a unique and difficult relationship in the US between domestic politics and foreign affairs. The support and consensus of the American people have been required for Washington to conduct a global role since 1945, and much effort went into manufacturing that consensus in the rhetoric of anti-communism, the vicious Red-baiting, blackmail and propaganda of the Cold War period. But the consensus, carefully nurtured by successive administrations and government agencies, has been unravelling for twenty years under the force of circumstance. At the same time, the problems in fulfilling a global role have mounted. Just as the ability of the state to run the nation has declined, so has the ability of any one country

to run the international system of states which is its counterpart. The
United States of America, which has played that role since the end of
the Second World War, has found itself increasingly unable to carry
out its hegemonic task. More than that, it has found the pressures of
a global economy, which it had sponsored in the 1950s and 1960s,
increasingly hard to bear at home. America's role in the world is
changing. Though this is partly a question of the declining fortunes
of America, it has as much to do with the changes in the nature of
the global system, and with the aspirations of the other players.
Already there is a fracturing of American authority over the post-Cold
War alliance on key issues.

It is admittedly hard to set the decline of American fortunes against
the perception that, after the end of communism, the collapse of the
Soviet Union, and the US victory in the Gulf War, the US stands
triumphant. The international system which saw in the 1990s was still
predominantly an American construct, paid for, staffed, designed and
given its creative energy by the United States. Yet, in ten years' time
that will not be the case; the international system which was created
at the end of the Second World War was already unravelling by 1989
and the collapse of the USSR only hastened its demise. America's
estrangement[2] from the world was already well established by the time
Ronald Reagan entered the White House; the triumph of America
over the Soviet Union only served to fuel it, and to reopen old wounds.

It cannot be doubted that Washington runs the international
system. Though each part of it, each committee, each institution,
contains representatives of many other nations, and though the system
is relatively open to consensual and co-operative decision-making, no
other nation commands such an influence. This is primarily a question
of its political weight in the key agencies of the post-war world. It is
on the Security Council, and is the largest 'shareholder' in the UN.
It is the chief military power in Nato, and it is the chief economic
power in the international financial institutions, most of which are
housed in Washington.

First and foremost, the structural basis of American leadership is
its possession of enormous resources: it is a very rich country. It is
also a militarily powerful state. But the sources of American pre-
eminence are more than just material. The US is broadly perceived
as a legitimate leader of the international system because it is guided
by principles that have become accepted as fair, just and good. E.H.
Carr called this form of power 'power in the opinions of others';[3]

it is akin to the legitimacy that Weber posited as the basis of order in the national political unit. Carr quoted Hume: 'The Soldan of Egypt or the Emperor of Rome might drive his harmless subjects like brute beasts against their sentiments or inclinations. But he must at least have led his mamelukes or praetorian bands like men by their opinions.'[4]

America transforms economic and military resources into the ability to determine outcomes primarily through the consent and cooperation of its allies. It can apply leverage, through linkage of issues or through persuasion. Certain things can't happen without America, since it alone possesses access to the requisite resources. It has sought to establish its self-professed values – broadly, democracy and free enterprise – at the heart of the international system. This arrangement has rested on a bargain, a bargain between the US government and its people, but also a bargain between the US and the rest of the world.

America's hegemonic position has become simultaneously the greatest strength and the greatest weakness of an international system that has stood up to forty years of strain remarkably well. It is a strength because the United States, of all the western democracies, still possesses the greatest resources, and the most effective ability to harness them. Having a single country at the helm has its advantages when that country acts decisively and in the interests of the other players and the system as a whole; that is the basis of the hegemonic approach. The role it plays is not just to lead, but also to knit the stitches that keep the system together. America ties together countries which would not otherwise be allied: Germany and South Korea have little to do with each other most of the time, but both are key allies of the US. In particular, the US, because of its geographic location, ties together the Pacific and the European countries.

But the US is also the system's greatest weakness because its role is subject to doubt. Its resources are not as great as they were; those of others are vastly increased. The way in which its international challenges have been handled has, rather than inspiring respect for the US, undermined confidence in the continuing dominance of America. Increasingly its actions have *not* been perceived as in the interests of other players, and the bargain has been devalued.

The slow ebbing of confidence in the sanctity of America's role in the world began with the overseas adventures of the 1960s, in particular the Vietnam War. In the jungles of south-east Asia, Lyndon Johnson lost much of his political credibility, saw his domestic ambitions undermined, and ultimately lost the Presidency for the Democrats. In the 1970s, a series of Soviet advances in the Third World seemed to unravel much of what the US had set out to construct in the 1950s. Behind the military and international reversals lurked economic stagnation and a series of domestic political crises, from Watergate to the Carter years. The American growth record in the first four post-war decades was very strong; though by comparison, it was never as strong as that in western Europe and Japan. In the 1970s economic growth weakened; and though it picked up again in the 1980s, other nations – particularly Germany and Japan – amassed great wealth. Europe's growing political strength meant that decisions in Nato became increasingly complicated by differences of opinion over the means and ends. France's defection from the military component of the alliance was followed by deep splits over the Middle East, over commercial links between west and east Europe, the rearmament programmes of the 1980s and US adventures in Central America and elsewhere in the Third World.

Even before the end of the Cold War, this had triggered a series of debates over the US role in the world and its standing in relation to other nations. This came to a head in the late 1980s, in a movement that stressed 'declinism' and 'imperial overstretch.' America possessed more, and more effective, weapons than it had twenty years before; and it was richer. Externally, it faced a vastly decreased threat from the Soviet Union. Yet Japan was now richer than America and other countries had superseded the US in other key respects. The most comprehensive work on the subject, published in 1988, was Paul Kennedy's *The Rise and Fall of the Great Powers*. Kennedy wrote: 'It simply has not been given to any one society to remain *permanently* ahead of all the others, because that would imply a freezing of the differentiated patterns of growth rates, technological advance and military developments which has existed since time immemorial.[5] But did it have to decline so fast? asked Kennedy. 'Even in the heyday of the Pax Americana, its competitive position was already being eroded by a disturbingly low average annual rate of growth of output per capita.'[6] He emphasized that the speed, nature and direction of change could all be affected by political choices. Guns, butter and investment were all objects of desire, and it was the choice of government which came first.[7]

Kennedy did not assume a simplistic relationship between economic standing and political power. Since the source of American power was never superiority in any one index, relative economic decline does not present a crippling obstacle to leadership. US hegemony was based upon a clustering of resources, and their mutually beneficial relationship; and upon the ability of the US to translate these into political power.

But it was precisely the failure of this relationship that the critics frowned upon. The economic ills of the US have been exported to other countries and in the process have started to shake the foundations of the post-war structure. America's domestic financial problems – and the way it has sought to cope with them – have increasingly caused problems for the rest of the world. Its inflation in the late 1960s helped to undermine the Bretton Woods system for currency management, and made US monetary policy a source of uncertainty. The benign neglect of the dollar that began after the collapse of the Bretton Woods system was followed by a short-lived attempt to revive co-operation among the leading economies; and this was in turn succeeded by the 'domesticism' of US monetary policy in the 1980s.[8] American monetary policy was tied to several different objectives: domestic recovery, the solidity of the dollar, the health of US financial markets: keeping them in line was not always achievable, but the suspicion of its partners was that America did not try. Susan Strange argues that far from the decline of US power being responsible for this mismanagement, it was 'its misuse, exploiting the system rather than managing it . . . It was the pursuit of short-term instead of long-term national interest that sowed the seeds of monetary disorder and financial instability.' This was a perception common in Europe, in particular, where de Gaulle's aphorism was frequently quoted: 'The Americans used the atom bomb only twice. But they use the dollar against the world every day.' In the second half of 1980s, when large-scale dollar devaluation was used as a tool to reflate the US economy, bring the trade deficit down and reduce the value of US debt abroad, it seemed that it could also be a defensive weapon.

This is not to say that other countries have not damaged the system through their own short-sightedness, stupidity or greed. But the position of the US is pivotal. The rise of the US as a market for goods rather than a net exporter and as a host state for foreign investment instead of its principal source meant that regardless of the external effect of US economic policy, its own domestic rules for trade and investment became increasingly important.

The economic shifts of the 1980s helped to create a new set of concerns. The reduction in the value of the dollar gradually brought US imports down to a more manageable level; but it was also one factor in the surge of foreign investment in the US. While America's place in the world may have declined, the world's place in America has increased. Until the 1970s, the US had attracted little foreign investment; but between 1980 and 1988, $250 billion of foreign capital went into the US, doubling the share of foreign-owned firms in employment, investment, assets – and attention.[9] Public concern at Japanese acquisitions of real estate, high-technology firms, and service providers such as film studios was coupled with anger in some local communities over aggressive takeover tactics and the restructuring and job losses that often followed.

Opposition to the foreign 'assault' on the US economy (although the level of foreign ownership is still low when compared with many industrialized countries) combined with fears about the trend towards deindustrialization and de-skilling. The sectors in relative decline were those that policy makers wanted most to see succeed (particularly manufacturing); many faster-growing sectors (catering, for example) produced low-paying, often part-time jobs. Perhaps more importantly, the US ratio of exports to imports has declined in some key sectors – in some cases precipitously – over the last decade. Whereas exports of computers and 'peripherals' (modems, printers, and associated hardware), for instance, were more than four times as great as imports in 1979, exports and imports were nearly in balance in 1987.[10] In 1975, US firms dominated the semiconductor market; by 1989, four of the world's top five companies in the sector were Japanese.[11]

But the picture of decline was, as a critic of 'declinism' has pointed out, overstated. As the US share of world exports declined, the US multinationals' share of world trade of manufactured goods actually increased.[12] The success of US multinationals, Nye has argued, meant that they were much less dependent on US hegemony than had been assumed; they were prospering despite the problems of the US at home. The US in 1988 retained the highest share of world stock of outward foreign direct investment (FDI), at thirty-five per cent, though Europe, at thirty-four per cent, was catching up fast. Looking at FDI figures gives a much clearer idea of the integration of the US into the world economy than looking at its imports or exports. If the definition of the US economy is stretched to exclude foreign-owned firms in the US and include American-owned companies based abroad, the US trade balance in 1986, nominally in deficit of $144bn (net exports) would actually be in surplus to the tune of $57bn (net foreign sales).[13] This is splendid for American capitalism; perhaps less so for the American public; least so for the American government, which found itself facing a revolt.

The political agenda which these developments have created has been dominated by fears of loss of competitiveness, loss of jobs and the impact of foreign ownership. The White House, under three successive Republican administrations during 1980–92 focused on the national interest as defined by the international economic system – maintaining pressure for a free trade and payments system, but also co-ordinating macroeconomic policy more or less loosely with its main partners. However, Congress focuses overwhelmingly on the national interest as defined by an agglomeration of local issues. On trade policy, for instance, individual Congressmen are influenced by local industrial and agricultural lobbies, whereas the White House in theory constructs a broader national view, taking into account also the international effect of such interests. But the White House, too, has been guilty of a drift towards protectionism. It has flirted in the past with various attempts to create an industrial policy, if unsuccessfully, and has made increasing use of administrative restrictions on trade.

Under Republican administration, arguments about America's economy predictably intertwined in Congress with arguments over foreign policy. Both Ronald Reagan and George Bush put a high priority on foreign policy objectives. Because Congress lacks power over foreign policy, it turns naturally to areas where it has more control. As a result, some foreign policy issues became hostage to economic issues. Congress plays a vital role in the process of turning latent power into effective force: through decisions over funding military expenditure, over foreign aid, and over decisions on deploying troops. The annual budget battles turned into a predictable round of havering, with the Democrats in Congress arguing for checks on military expenditure, and the administration pushing for cuts in other spending. The rising costs of new technologies, doubts over the efficacy of new weaponry and persistent fears of being 'overtaken' by the Soviet Union led to a destabilizing debate. As the federal deficit mounted, there were also increasing calls for the allies – particularly the Europeans and the Japanese – to take on an increasing part of the burden of defending the West.

Questions over the costs of foreign policy became increasingly intertwined with a debate on America's own social problems. Between 1977 and 1987, the average after-tax income of the lowest ten per cent of American families fell by ten per cent. By contrast, the average family income of the top ten per cent rose by 24.4 per cent.[14] The upper echelons of American society made a pile out of the financial speculation of the Reagan years. 'What I want to see above all is that this remains a country where someone can always get rich,' said Ronald Reagan,[15] and some did; but many others got much poorer.

Urban poverty, violence, social decay and the problems of the average American became key topics again on the political agenda. George Bush had entered office pledging to usher in a kinder, gentler America; but all he did to achieve this was to establish the 'thousand points of light', a charitable initiative under which some of the wealth of America's upper tier would be given to the deserving poor on a voluntary basis. Attempts to mobilize wealth by government activity were stymied by the massive deficit, which required less expenditure or more taxation just to hold constant. Ultimately, the impact of the deficit was more political than economic: it froze the American political process at a time when it required maximum flexibility.

Such clashes between a Democratic Congress and a Republican White House over the costs of foreign policy and defence were just one facet of a growing disagreement over the terms and conditions of American involvement abroad. Economic issues were not the only area where domestic and international interests collided; the question of American hegemony in security affairs is still more fraught. Despite its undoubted military might, the US has had many problems translating this into political influence. This found expression in arguments over nuclear strategy, intervention in the Middle East and US backing for anti-communist rebels in Africa, Asia and the Americas. Containment was the underpinning of US security policy; but as John Lewis Gaddis has pointed out, there has never been agreement over what containment means in specific instances, and particularly where, when and how to intervene. The wrong decisions were made in Vietnam, and this conditioned the congressional response for most of the next two decades. It also led to the White House circumventing the law to get its way, and to covert wars orchestrated by the national security apparatus that had poorly defined objectives.

The wars between Congress and the President, the varying attitudes evinced by the White House over the last twenty years and the growing demands for more burden sharing in the alliance have all had an effect on the US allies. The unreliability of the US response and the apparently chaotic decision-making procedure had always perplexed foreigners, who were accustomed, in most cases, to a more autocratic polity. What one analyst calls 'the inevitable mild anti-hegemonial reaction' was evident from the beginning in France, which opted out of Nato's military arm under President Charles de Gaulle. From the late 1960s, America's European allies sought new ways of dealing with Moscow. But America, after the dissolution of *détente* became progressively more unilateral, and this led to greater pressure for European independence in policy making. The resurgence of other interests, in particular European, in the running of the alliance have come about not just because of the weakness of the US, or the growing strength of the rest of the world, but because of a change in the strategic environment. As early as 1968, Henry Kissinger was predicting a more multipolar world, and others were discussing the growing disparity between military power and political influence.

The collapse of the Soviet Union raised all of these debates in a new form. Without the Soviet Union, the nature of the Atlantic bargain was not just questionable: it was, in the military sphere, largely redundant. Anti-communism had been a strong cement for the alliance. The attempt to revive it in a more political style, long delayed, was finally agreed to at the London summit in 1990 and codified at the Rome summit in 1991. But the nature of that political settlement, despite communiqué language that papered over the cracks, was uncertain. The post-Cold War settlement meant trying new links with the USSR and later Russia; some of these were with the West as a whole, but others were bilateral – particularly in the form of economic agreements. There was open competition between US and European companies for some post-Cold War economic opportunities; in other areas, both competed to stay out of certain activities, and avoid responsibility. Questions of financial assistance divided the allies, as did strategy towards, first, the emergence of Boris Yeltsin and, later, the way to deal with Russia's re-emerging expansionist tendencies.

Bill Clinton's handling of foreign policy aroused concerns among the allies in his first year. The Bosnian war created a thinly veiled antagonism between the US and Europe. The one-off interventions in Somalia and Haiti seemed to demonstrate hesitancy. Democratic control of both the White House and Congress did not appear to deliver the decisive leadership that had been expected. The focus of policy in Washington seemed to swing away from Europe to Asia, before returning in 1994. Yet all these problems reflected more than the weakness of a new administration.

In one sense, the end of the Cold War meant a de-linking of security and economic issues. Leadership in one does not mean leadership in the other. Security issues are traditionally solved in ways that demand chains of authority and single solutions; economic issues more often involve slicing a cake – it must be decided how to angle the knife, not whether or not to use it. Thus the US-European relationship had been dominated by two themes: military protection, and the trade rows that have grown increasingly bitter since the 1960s. When security dominated, the US could always exercise authority, and this took pre-eminence over the 'cake-slicing' issues. The corollary was that Washington was always reluctant to allow trade disputes to damage the broader strategic relationship with Europe. As Clinton and Warren Christopher, his Secretary of State, repeatedly underlined in the last phases of the GATT talks, this no longer obtains: foreign policy starts at home, in the domestic economy. Before, the security threat had sufficed to calm most of the transatlantic rows; now it is largely absent, and the terms of discussion became notably more heated as the 1990s opened.

Solving security problems had been a question of paying any price and bearing any burden, as John F. Kennedy put it. That will not be the case any longer: Congress has already cast a critical eye over defence budgets; it will also want to know why, given the increasing divisibility of security issues, it should pay for installations that encircle the Soviet Union when that is no longer the main threat – when, indeed, it is no longer clear what the major threat is. In short, the supremacy of economic issues and the change in the nature of security issues both mitigate against American leadership.

Delivering stability had been one of the prime objectives of US leadership. Who was the enemy now? On Sunday 8 March 1992, the *New York Times* published the first tentative attempt at sketching out the future, a plan produced by the Pentagon. It presented seven illustrative scenarios for new wars, and the kind of forces that might be required to fight them. All nations should be prevented from 'even aspiring to a larger regional or global role', it said, referring to the 'resurgent/emergent global threat' as the defining factor in its calculations. (Resurgent being, of course, a renewed Soviet threat, and emergent any one of a number of potential rivals, from Europe to Japan, to, broadly, Islam). The Pentagon's estimated expenditures of

$1.2 trillion over five years was not acceptable to those who wanted a reduction in the deficit, or to those who wanted a shift towards domestic expenditure.

With the doubts over the aims and efficiency of US policy has come renewed questioning of the legitimacy of US leadership. If the debate over what the US was *against* had become difficult, what it was *for* had become even more obtuse. It is not a new debate. The cost, methods and justice of American foreign policy have been at issue ever since the US first assumed a world role. But the difficulty in assuming a new set of solutions shows that at least one thing has changed: there are fewer answers. Ronald Reagan won by asserting a new, more unilateral style of leadership, by talking not of containing the Soviet Union but of 'prevailing' over it, and by constantly stating the simple moral virtues upon which he believed US pre-eminence depended. George Bush honed this into a more traditional, co-operative style but maintained the accent on American ascendancy. The 1992 election and its aftermath, by contrast, showed Bill Clinton to be the advocate of a more multilateralist approach, but one that quickly found its limits when military intervention hit trouble. Once again, as with Reagan's challenge, the case for a decisive shift toward unilateralism came from the populist right.

The arguments over foreign policy were by no means limited to the election campaign. In *Foreign Policy* magazine in 1991, William G. Hyland, one of the foremost of the American foreign policy establishment thinkers, set out his view of the past forty years and some milestones for the future in an article entitled 'The Case for Pragmatism'. 'The world of the 1990s will resemble nothing in America's previous experience,' he argued. 'The United States will be required to conduct a foreign policy for which there is almost no historical precedent, and to do so with limited resources in an increasingly competitive world in which the threat that held together the various American alliances will have vanished.'[16] But he concludes by saying: '"Put America first" is a dangerous old slogan, but in light of this decade's realities it is not altogether wrong.' Writing in the same edition of *Foreign Policy* magazine, David Gergen, Reagan's spokesman and then Clinton's says: 'the events of 1991 suggest that to a far larger extent than during the Cold War, political dynamics within the nation will determine its foreign policy.'[17]

What the populist rhetoric of the 1992 election and the analysis of the foreign policy nabobs revealed was a similar diagnosis: that

America's problems had started, and must be resolved, at home. There was a prevalent sense that America had built up a series of problems which needed to be addressed before it could turn to those of the rest if the world. The decay of America's inner cities, the recession and questions over the basic direction of the nation seemed to require a more urgent analysis than did the European security structure. One way of looking at the end of the Cold War is that a huge peace dividend has been delivered to, above all, the American people. But equally, this means that the military infrastructure that has been developed at great cost must now be junked in favour of something else. The problem that remains is: can successful leadership abroad be combined with an accent on domestic activism? Or is it the case, as Clinton has argued persuasively, that America's international role will founder all the quicker if the country does not resolve its social and economic problems?

The political attempt to resolve this problem is one that is likely to occupy American time and attention for some years. The US government is a huge ship, and it does not turn easily – despite the fact that many of the basic arguments have been around for two decades. Indeed, a common assessment over the past ten years has been to argue that the root of America's problem is in the American political system. It is slow to react to challenges and too insulated from overseas pressures. The presidency has come in for particular criticism as an institution, after the failure of Johnson, Nixon and Carter to make it work, and Clinton works under this shadow.

Kennedy suggests that 'the very unstructured, laissez-faire nature of American society (while not without its weaknesses) probably gives it a better chance of readjusting to changing circumstances than a rigid and dirigiste power would have'.[18] However, he also reminds us of 'the uncanny similarities between the growing mood of anxiety among thoughtful circles in the United States today and that which pervaded all political parties in Edwardian Britain and led to what has been called the "national efficiency" movement: that is a broad-based debate within the nation's decision-making, business and educational elites over the various measures which could reverse what was seen to be a growing uncompetitiveness as compared with other advanced societies'.[19] Both of these views reflect schools of thought in the United States. They are not easily reconciled, and in many ways reflect opposite assessments of the spiritual health of American society.

A fixation on domestic issues troubles some of Washington's allies, who believe that a resurgence of American nationalism, particularly in the economic field, has been the outcome. The revival of the politics of national economic security, for instance, has been a slow rumble in the US since the explosion of the US trade deficit in the early 1980s. But it would be misleading to see the America First movement, and the populist politicians who advocate domestic concerns, as representing a simple monolithic nationalist backlash. The opposition to 'mainstream' internationalism to American problems comes from the Republican right, the Democratic left, and a myriad other viewpoints. It is united only on what it sees as the problems: not on the solutions. If America's global role is the target, then that is partly because it relied upon an unstable alliance of interests ranged against a weaker coalition. The shifts in America's economic position have damaged that alliance. It should be remembered, moreover, that America First does not necessarily mean isolationism. Polls taken by the Potomac Associates in Washington suggest fifty-four per cent of Americans in October 1991 could be considered 'internationalist' in outlook. However, over sixty per cent of those polled in the same month in a CBS-*New York Times* survey indicated their support for the United Nations as the primary forum for international political decision-making. Analysing these and other poll results, David Gergen concluded: 'Clearly Americans want to shed their role as chief and almost sole protector of international order, but they recognize that the world still has problems – terrorism, thuggery, environmental degradation – and they are more prepared than in the past to co-operate in multi-lateral solutions.'[20] What has changed is the price Americans are willing to pay.

The new nationalism exists in uncomfortable harmony with the new localism, the politics of community that has reasserted itself in the 1980s. Whereas the crusade led by Ross Perot was a nation-wide phenomenon, it brought together many groups of people who at local level had already begun campaigning for change in towns, state assemblies or city wards. The two movements differ to the extent that one focuses on defending distinct local interests; the other is essentially a way of gaining control of a national agenda. Sometimes, they are in harmony, when the local interest can be effectively represented in Washington. At other times they are in conflict, when the particular interests of local communities demand the safeguarding of jobs, for instance. The emphasis on economic nationalism has returned to both. Resistance to hostile takeovers became one part of the revolt in the 1980s, but this manifested itself in – among other things – local anti-takeover rules, local measures to attract investment, and the expansion of state offices abroad, in competition.

The political fragmentation is mirrored in the differing reactions of US businesses to the competitive threat they face. Some businesses react by moving abroad; others by changing production techniques at home. Some lobby for protection, others for changes in external policy. Robert Reich, the Harvard economist who became President Clinton's Secretary of Labor, said: 'Rather than increase the profitability of corporations flying its flag, or enlarge the worldwide holdings of its citizens, a nation's economic role is to improve its citizens' standard of living by enhancing the value of what they contribute to the world economy.'[21] He argues for a 'positive' economic nationalism that favours intervention, but keeps markets open and treats any company as American that employs Americans. Lester Thurow, a liberal academic at MIT holds a contradictory view: companies are painted in the colours of their national flags, and a Japanese company in the US is still Japanese. His communitarian capitalism envisages a future that is definitely zero sum: if a Japanese-owned company is successful, then US corporate rivals suffer.[22] These are more than nitpicking differences. They help to determine policy outcomes. As Clinton has discovered, creating a national economic consensus brings its own problems. It is a question, as Reich put it, of Who is Us.

In this respect, there is not so much an *assertion* as a *crisis* of American nationalism: of the nationalism that was integrative, progressive and even radical in its time. In many respects, its interpretation of nationalism is the most perplexing aspect of this society, the 'One nation under God' that has always been a complex of ethnicities, identities and communities. American nationalism must always be reinvented, reimagined each day, symbolized by daily patriotic rituals. American nationalism is not the essentialist nationalism of nineteenth-century Germany; America is not eternal. It has to be reconstructed in ways that other countries, with historical claims to legitimacy that go back centuries, find inconceivable. The growth of new ethno-identities in the 1980s has coexisted uneasily with this. "National" goals and symbols have been reserved exclusively for the All-American political community and its culture,' which in the long run has weakened their hold.[23] The crisis in nationalism has fed the sickness of American internationalism, always a fragile creature. American nationalism, internationalism and localism have always moved in a strange dance. In this immigrant society, no one dimension to nationalism has ever sufficed: instead, nationalism in the sense of belonging has combined ethnic identity, related to another place, with an involvement in local community. In the same way, when projected abroad, nationalism has rarely taken on the manner of the great European empires. It has been justified by appeal to universal values, to the grievances of peoples suffering under foreign tyrannies, and to appeals to the decency of the American people, from Roosevelt's 'arsenal of democracy' to Ronald Reagan's equating the Nicaraguan Contras and the Founding Fathers.

The loss of idealism behind America's foreign policy that accompanied the failed adventures of the 1960s and 1970s thus found its mark in the evaporation of the last crusade in 1989. What was left seemed to some to be purely the pursuit of commercial advantage. 'If truths that once were self-evident now have to be sold like used cars, there must be something very wrong,' wrote one author, seven years before George Bush's disastrous trip to Japan with executives of US automobile firms concluded with his vomiting into the lap of the Japanese Prime Minister. At the same time, a neutral pursuit of stability is also unpopular, which is one reason why Bush's attempts to create a more pragmatic vision of American leadership were not well received. As one British diplomat said in 1989, 'The biggest challenge is to learn to think of America as just another country.'[24]

The result of the structural problems in the US economy, the failure of the political system to resolve them and the destabilizing impact of the return to domestic issues has been to weaken the consensus behind American leadership still further. The 'bargain' that underlay internationalism has been undone. George Bush tried valiantly to re-cement it during the dismemberment of the Soviet Union, by his role in the Gulf War, and by getting tough with Japan over trade issues. Bill Clinton, in 1993, began the process of renegotiating it both with the American people and with US allies. But it will be a long process and its success is by no means guaranteed. Frances Fitzgerald's question, and the ghost of the Vietnam War, had finally come home to roost. 'Peace and political legitimacy were becoming hard enough to attain at home; America hardly had the moral qualifications or the physical capacity to establish peace and project its power around the world anymore.'[25]

4

Europe: *La Grande République*

'Some form of association must be found as a result
of which the whole strength of the community will be
enlisted for the protection of the person and property
of each constituent member, in such a way that each,
when united to his fellows, renders obedience to his
own will, and remains as free as he was before.'

JEAN-JACQUES ROUSSEAU[1]

The shift from optimism to pessimism was much more rapid and
acute in Europe than in America. From dream to nightmare was a
journey that took only two years. The dream, fixed in the popular
imagination as in November 1989, initially seemed solid enough. The
nightmare crept up on us, from the first grim realization of the scale
and complexity of the task of rebuilding the former East Germany
through the disintegration of Yugoslavia, the destruction of Sarajevo,
ethnic cleansing, racist attacks and murdered Turkish immigrants, and
the more faceless political and monetary disasters that laid low many
of the European Union's cherished dreams. Nothing was what it
seemed to be.

Europe faces a twin crisis. On the one hand, structures for managing
the economy, security and society are crumbling, both in national
capitals and in the European Union. On the other hand, there is a
rising tide of agitation from citizens, often expressed in nationalist
and regionalist terms and directed angrily at the centres of power, for
representation, protection and jobs.

State and nation, nation and state: nowhere in the world has the relationship between the two been so problematic, so probed, so exhaustively experimented upon as in Europe. Yet until 1989, the idea of the nation lay half buried, a colossus that was of historical interest and which was assumed to be an atavistic relic. The question of the role of the state seemed to have been resolved in favour of a blend of capitalism, liberalism and democracy, differently expressed in each European country but crafted using similar tools to achieve convergent goals. In the West, the optimism of 1989 was partially influenced, it is true, by the prevalent belief that liberal values would prevail in the former eastern bloc as a result of the collapse of Soviet hegemony. But it also had much to do with a faith in the political and social structures that had emerged from the carnage of two world wars, and a belief that these could now be shared between the two halves of the continent.

Sheltered behind the Iron Curtain that was built by its adversary, western Europe's cautious peace was the most concrete result of the Cold War, and this was the framework for building a more lasting settlement within the borders of post-war Europe. The result was dense networks of political and economic contacts and co-operation and the growth of interdependence and efforts to manage it through political integration. The Council of Europe, the European Union and its precursors, the Western European Union and Nato, the alliance that tied Europe to America – all pulled the western half of the continent together. No comparable structures emerged in eastern Europe. Comecon, the system for managing the economies of eastern Europe and the Soviet Union (and their partners in Vietnam and Cuba) never approached the same degree of interaction; never fostered the same degree of joint political decision making. The Warsaw Pact and the associated political fora sponsored by the eastern bloc were always far more directly adjuncts of Soviet power, as was shown by the periodic interventions to assure Moscow's dominance.

The dream that seemed within reach in 1989 was that the structures of management that had emerged in the West would form the basis of a new partnership across the continent. The 1970s and early 1980s had been a time of great problems for the EU but by 1989 it was in a phase of confident expansion. The European Monetary System, an attempt to create a 'zone of monetary stability' in the destabilizing environment that followed the collapse of US monetary hegemony, was followed by a grand programme for economic integration, the single market, due to be completed by the end of 1992. The result was strong economic growth in the 1980s, economic expansion abroad by EU transnationals, and an explosion of trading relationships and investment within the EU's border. The 1992 programme brought about, even before it was completed, a wealth of new links within, between and across states. The accumulation of economic and financial integration led, by 1991, to an attempt to realize the dreams of monetary union which had been circulating in the EU for decades, and to turn the EU's growing economic power into political power.

The nightmare began where the dream found its fondest expression and its most powerful image: the end of the Berlin Wall. By removing the weight of superpower dominance from the multi-ethnic states of eastern Europe, this triggered the revival of nationalism, in particular in Yugoslavia, where civil war began with Slovenian and Croatian secession then flared into the Bosnian battles, into conflicts that confounded every international agency forced to focus on them. The inability to resolve the impasse in the early days fed the later conflagration; the broad failure of the humanitarian effort stoked a crisis in surrounding countries, as well as a crisis of conscience in the West; the inability of multilateral organizations to cope, combined with the inadequacy of Nato, fed a fracturing of relations between the US and Europe.

The Yugoslav crisis, by precipitating a rush of refugees from the region to western and eastern Europe, helped to crystallize an existing crisis of racism and xenophobia. Partly because it was an island of prosperity, partly because it was a sanctuary from persecution, Europe switched in the mid-1970s from being a net sender of emigrants to being a net receiver of immigrants. The sudden rush of asylum seekers that followed the coming down of the Wall and the subsequent Yugoslav war led to a rapid rise in tensions between local communities and immigrants. Attacks on Turkish immigrants were the tip of an iceberg. The rise of the Vlaams Blok in Belgium, far-right parties in Germany and France, and attacks on immigrants in Italy, Spain, Britain and even liberal Denmark made a big impact on governments concerned with political stability. Right-wing parties made electoral gains, and centrist politicians found themselves under pressure.

Racism combined in an ugly cocktail with high unemployment. The 1980s boom had never paid off in terms of jobs; unemployment dipped but remained high. The recession of 1992, set off by high interest rates in Germany, had a lot to do with that country's faltering response to the pressures of reunification. But it also reflected Europe's inability to compete in the world against low-wage economies elsewhere, and the build-up of debt and instability from the financial liberalization of the 1980s. The combination of the recession, mismatched interest rates and poor co-ordination in turn sent the European Monetary System into a dive, leading to the exit of two currencies and the devaluation of others. By August 1993, the pressure for further reform had become inescapable and the limits for fluctuation within the system were loosened to the point where its disciplines almost disappeared.

The EU states had foreseen the need for change in the circumstances of the late 1980s; the blueprint they had drawn up, in the course of the intergovernmental conferences of 1991, was the Maastricht Treaty on European Union. After the Danish referendum of June 1992, the EU entered a profound crisis from which it was still struggling to emerge a year later. Denmark's rejection, reversed in a second vote in 1993, was half-echoed in France's 'petit oui', a referendum that approved ratification by the slimmest of margins. Britain saw a pitched battle take place as the Conservative and Labour parties both scurried to prove how little love they had for European political and monetary integration. Germany left the fate of the treaty open until the last, after a constitutional challenge.

The response to all these events was hesitant. The EU moved rapidly with ideas for renovating the EMS, but the events in the financial markets inevitably cast a shadow over plans drawn up in the conference room. The prospects for a single currency, the centrepiece of the Maastricht Treaty, were put in doubt, certainly in time for the first deadline of 1997. The idea of economic union seemed to mean little and economic convergence – the idea that economies would come into line over time – was also in trouble.

The international and economic crises were matched with an extraordinary implosion of the domestic political systems in western Europe. Politically, the post-Cold War years saw rumbling discontent emerge into open revolt in Britain, France, Germany, Italy and Spain, as voters and party members deserted old loyalties, often overthrowing large majorities and nearly everywhere reshaping the nature of national politics.

The revolution in Europe had evidently been badly misunderstood by those who believed that it simply meant a new open landscape. Just as America's political class underestimated the impact of the end of the Soviet Union upon their place in the world, Europe's political class was slow to grasp the political, economic and social impact of the end of the Berlin Wall. And just as the world's leaders had continued with the free market programmes of the 1980s even when the problems they caused for social cohesion were manifest, so Europe proceeded with its liberal strategies for expanding trade and commerce to promote growth, apparently without regard for the social consequences. The essentially conservative view of international relations in the new Europe – keeping the east at arm's length and promoting security ties before economic development – was similarly flawed.

Europe was handed a Toynbeean challenge and failed to respond. The external shocks of 1989 and the years that followed were unexpected and large-scale. It was the external shock of German unification upon the European Monetary System and the reaction by the Bundesbank – holding interest rates high while fiscal policy was relaxed – which confounded attempts to hold the exchange rate mechanism together in 1992 and 1993. The Yugoslav war was, despite predictions by experts, apparently unexpected by policy makers, or at least misunderstood. And it was external shocks – the opening of a border, then all borders – which precipitated a refugee and immigration crisis in Germany in 1992.

All too often, failures of co-operation by the key European powers exacerbated problems. The Yugoslav crisis took them unawares, and its inception saw several states – principally France and Britain – committed to holding the state together, with Germany increasingly dedicated to recognizing Croatia. Nor was there agreement on handling the refugee crisis, with Germany taking by far the largest number of migrants, and little burden sharing. Frequently the EU merely reiterated existing nostrums, and repeated its own convictions, no matter how distant from reality they seemed. The other face of the failure, in these terms, was the EU's commitment to over-ambitious new plans, and its intention to press on regardless with a single currency and political union. It reacted to assaults – by the market, by citizens, by politicians – by ignoring the crisis and pressing on.

The botched challenges of 1989–93 were more than just failures of vision, will and political leadership, however. They reflected deep problems in carrying through what had been already achieved in the circumstances of the 1990s, and in particular the idea of creating a political and economic 'space' with a set of institutions to supervise it. The European crisis was fed by the dramatic erasure of internal borders in the West and a failure to anticipate the pressures it would bring or to manage them. Borderlessness had been foreseen, designed and promoted by the Single European Act, which set out a blueprint for achieving the four freedoms of movement – for people, goods, capital and services. But the plan's architects and promoters did not foresee the end of the east–west division, and the consequent and sudden creation of a political vacuum to the east. The intended results of the SEA were unsettling enough. A growth in cross-border competition had, even before the Wall came down, unleashed new competitive forces that were stripping some regions of jobs and reallocating them elsewhere. Even official estimates of the effects of the Single Market programme show that the benefits were derived in part from job losses and reallocation of production.

However, the unintended consequences were more unsettling still. The EU states had always realized that 'bads' as well as goods could flow across borders: they had not made sufficient plans to do anything about this. The Mafia expanded from Italy into France, Spain and especially into Germany. In France, organized Italian crime, particularly the Neapolitan Mafia known as the Camorra, 'does not control the territory, but invests its dirty money, finds sanctuaries for its sought-after men, and moves drugs', according to Jacques Poinas, the head of the French anti-Mafia research unit. Between 1989 and 1991, the Mafia in Germany had revenues of about DM4 billion (or about $2.5 billion) through extortion, stolen goods, and drug trafficking.[1] With the rise of organized crime came new forms of trading – in illegal waste and in drugs particularly. In 1992, a scandal over dumped medical waste led to a spat between France and Germany. The war against drugs is becoming hard to fight in light of the decreasing salience of European borders. City officials in Brussels, the putative capital of the new Europe, admit that the town has a growing drug problem. Seizures of illegal drugs in the first half of 1992 were twice as large as the entire catch in 1991. Drug-related crimes climbed by sixty per cent in 1992 after two years of stagnation.[2] The 'compensatory measures' intended to counter these phenomena were slow to come into effect; consequently the ambitious Schengen project for a completely border-free zone was postponed due mainly to French concerns about drug trafficking, and similar objections from other countries – principally Britain – retarded the removal of passport checks at borders.[3]

The inability of the political system to cope with either the removal of borders or the fracturing of communities that came with it was not simply the contingent failure of a structure that had been overloaded. In the east of the continent, the lowering of the flood waters exposed the ugly realities of socialist rule, the cruelties, inequities and also the mechanisms of power. But in the West, too, the retreat of the socialist tide left strange structures on the beach – revealed, indeed, a whole new geography. The end of the Cold War caused enormous problems for the traditional alliances that had cemented the European Union, and in particular for the role of Germany. Its traditional alliance with France was threatened by disagreements over Yugoslavia, over trade and over currency management. The position of Germany in Europe was put in question by unification, which made it once more the dominating political power on the continent. France found itself once more in the uncomfortable position of junior partner, and it was partly this concern that led President François Mitterrand to press for rapid moves to European unity in 1991. The tensions between Germany's role in the West and its eastern destiny, its economic dominance and political weaknesses, the lack of any alternative alliance in the EC that could provide a foundation, had long been evident: they were crystallized in the events of November 1989.[4]

The economic problems of western Europe, similarly, reflected far more deep-seated failures which went back decades but which became apparent after the end of the Cold War. As the EU belatedly recognised in 1993, its job creation record compared pitifully with the US. Rising labour costs and falling competitiveness had caused a steadily deteriorating trade performance. The European Monetary System and its problems had been understood by economists: the debate over German leadership in the EMS and its asymmetry, its inability to handle external shock and the inadequacy of its arrangements to realignment were well known. Nothing had been done; indeed even a reappraisal of the EMS in early 1993 failed to make significant recommendations for reform.[5]

The crises of 1989–93 thus raised far more profound doubts about the foundations of European co-operation. The decisions that had to be made about new members, new agreements, new borders meant that the whole rationale of integration was increasingly called into question. Which Europe was being built, why and where? The questions of definition, of borders, were more than just bureaucratic necessities: they reflected basic uncertainties about the project. It was the European 'idea' itself, a construct that had legitimized construction of a political entity and not just a free trade zone, that was put in question.

The federal vision for Europe sought to promote the idea that even though Europe has been the home of the nation-state, it need not necessarily have been that way; there was a different type of state with a different type of legitimacy that was possible, desirable and necessary. There has always been another tradition – the Europe of Rome, of Charlemagne, of Napoleon. As we saw in the first section, the influence of the French Revolution – with its mixture of universalism and particularism, the balance between the empire of reason and the national spirit – was decisive in forming the nation-state over the next two centuries. But with its intellectual foundations in the Enlightenment, it also provided a different version of the future, a tension that has shaped Europe ever since. Voltaire in the eighteenth century called Europe 'une espèce de grande république',[6] while Gibbon claimed that 'a philosopher may be permitted to consider Europe as one great republic.'[7] It was this that the founding fathers of Europe sought to reimagine.

'The broad sweep of European history from the Romans, through the eras of Charlemagne and Napoleon, to the twentieth century shows the continual potency of a European wide concept' writes one commentator. 'Yet at the same time, Europe also has to be regarded as the home of the nation-state, each country jealous of its sovereignty, and unlikely to accept for long a unity imposed by force.'[8] The conflicts of the twentieth century once more empowered an alternative vision. Europe's place at the heart of the world system was comprehensively undone by the period between the end of the nineteenth century and the end of the Second World War. The cause lay partly in its inability to prevent the wholesale destruction of the two world wars and partly in the economic and political rise of the two superpowers, the US and the Soviet Union. Europe entered the second half of the twentieth century at a historic low, destroyed, discredited and decentred. The intellectual foundation of the European Community is deeply interconnected with both the earlier successes and failures. A vision of Europe's history was adduced to support a possible future, one that would remedy the weaknesses and imbalances that had soured the past. The European Idea referred backward to a Golden Age of Europe, and also to the crises of the twentieth century. This idealistic element was important in the European construction, a complex of ideas that took in Voltaire, Kant, and Locke, but also Briand,

Churchill, and those who had fought fascism and communism. Its emphasis on the European experience and European culture reacted against what some of the advocates of a stronger Europe considered the Americanization of global culture; but it also reacted, more strongly still, against the other uncomfortable neighbour, the Soviet Union.[9]

The twin pillars of European construction were the promise of stability and prosperity, greater than that which was on offer from the nation-state alone. Stability and security meant not just the minimal domestic order provided by the nation-state but freedom from the disturbing shifts in economic and political circumstances that had destroyed Europe during the Second World War. Stability was also defined in relation to the resurgent threat from the East. The threat of social disorder and communist subversion in the West was always overestimated, but it contributed powerfully to the attempt to rebuild social cohesion and order, and to support for Christian Democrat parties as bulwarks against the overthrow of the existing order.[10]

Prosperity meant preventing a replay of the damaging inter-state economic conflicts of the inter-war period, by co-operation – first over coal and steel, then over trade, agriculture and monetary affairs. And the pursuit of geopolitical – that is to say international – stability was explicitly linked, from the very beginning, with the concept of social justice. Greater equity to remedy the social divisions that had also contributed to turmoil was built into the design of the European Union. The ideology of Christian Democracy provided an ingredient, not only in its anti-communist stance but also in its opposition to unfettered free-market capitalism. So the pursuit of physical security and stability was matched with a concern for economic prosperity, fairly shared, not just because it was desirable as a means to the other two ends, but because it was important in and of itself. The European institutions sought to translate this into a form of transnational justice, achieved through national co-operation – resource transfers, subsidies and joint programmes.[11]

The crises that followed the end of the Cold War put all these objectives in doubt. The European Idea had in any case been of declining salience for those born and brought up after the end of the Second World War and the poverty that followed it. The end of the threat from the USSR meant that this could no longer be used as a prop for a system that had ceased to face an ideological enemy. But at the same time, the sense of instability and insecurity that came with the end of the Cold War was tangible. The rise in cross-border crime, immigration, and uncertainty as a result of the demise of the Iron Curtain was matched by the evidence of violent fragmentation to the east. The failure of the EU to confront the Yugoslav conflict – dismissed as being in an area that was not of vital importance, or as an unwinnable war, or as a civil conflict – thus undermined the European claim to being a zone of stability. Competition from eastern industry, the costs of German unification, recession and unemployment increasingly made prosperity look out of reach. Something had gone badly wrong.

The first solution, simply put, was to stick with it: everything would be fine if only everybody kept their heads. From the first indications of trouble (which came before the Maastricht negotiations were concluded) to the first explicit acknowledgement that the EU faced a crisis was a long time, too long. The second solution on offer was to go faster: to advance union, to press ahead. This came from those states preoccupied with the dangers of German unification, from the federalist camp and from the European Commission in Brussels. The third option was to slow down, rethink, patch up the problems and start dealing with the new agenda of change. It came from Britain first, a country that had not signed up for a single currency or for the treaty's social chapter. Britain insisted, after the Danish defeat, that the answer lay in clarifying how power was shared out in the EU – by a complex principle called subsidiarity – and that authority should remain with the nation-state. Integration had gone too far, too fast, and was threatening political stability.[12]

It was, in many senses, an old debate, one that had been going on in the EU virtually since its inception. Formal integration was to be the physical expression of the political vision of the founding fathers of Europe – the creation of new institutions to build unity.[13] One view of Europe's integration has always centred on the key importance of these new, federal institutions in overcoming the fragmented nature of European political and economic responses to modernity. Federal institutions were to be the vanguard of a new political order that would sublimate nationalist tensions. Another view of integration has always seen informal integration as the motor of change: the intensity of interaction across the continent, through trade, travel, business and social interchange will forge some kind of union. Informal integration has been accompanied by the growth of new patterns of international interdependence that are extra-European, and by the expansion of plurality in the international system. The informal integrationists thus viewed Europe as a far more contingent creation, but also one that had no logical outcome. Walter Hallstein argued that integration is like riding a bicycle: either you go forward, or you fall over. Margaret Thatcher often seemed determined to prove this, but not in the way that Hallstein, a vigorous advocate of integration, argued.

The result of these twin patterns of formal and informal integration has been a curious accumulation of energies and edifices in the Union. Thus, one aspect of the EU's development has certainly been its progressive accumulation of mechanisms for overriding sovereignty, albeit with the consent of the member states. What differentiates the EU from other attempts at regional solidarity or organization is above all its institutions and the way that they operate amongst themselves and with the member states. Supranationalism in the EU is represented by the Commission, the executive which proposes legislation, the Parliament, which has gradually accumulated powers, and the Court, which interprets the EU's laws. EU decision making has also become more supranational through the adoption of qualified majority voting for some issues between ministers of the Twelve, where the interests of one nation can be subordinated to those of others. It is rare that decisions are actually taken that override significant interests: it is the *style* of supranationalism that sets the pace. As Ernst Haas has commented, supranationalism is as much a style as a mechanism: it is the view that each can gain from submitting, on occasion, to the interests of others.[14]

But this has always been matched against intergovernmentalism, the principle of sovereign equality in the EU's institutions. The institutions that have emerged from the past three decades are marked by frequent clashes between different capitals and the Commission, in particular, but also among member-states, about how far supranationalism could be allowed to extend. The Commission proposes, the Council of Ministers disposes, as officials and ministers alike are prone to explain when pushed into a corner over a difficult issue. The Parliament's powers, as yet, are minimal: even after the Maastricht Treaty, they amount principally to an ability to kill legislation off. Equally, the Court of Justice has not yet asserted itself as a European Supreme Court.

It was towards intergovernmentalism that the EU's members moved, in pursuit of greater stability, after 1992. As the EU had always combined the two approaches, this was not a decisive shift, but it was a change of direction. The consensus, after the crisis peaked in late

1992, came down in favour of some return of powers to states, a weakening of the role of the Commission, a greater say for governments and national electorates in vetting new initiatives. It was a precarious balance, with the expansionist Commission President Jacques Delors still fighting his corner, if weakened. The fights are likely to go even after Delors' departure, but the weight of argument is certainly against any increase in Community integration. Indeed, it has started to pull in the opposite direction.

In the vacuum left by the old idea of the European Community, the instability of any solution based on returning the EU to being merely a 'free trade area', or allowing national governments tighter grip on the reins, or carving the EU up into twelve again, is starting to become apparent. Bringing Europe 'back where it belongs' – to the national capitals – is a dangerous strategy, based on poor information. For the European nation-states themselves are in trouble.

The resurgence of nationalism and the nation-state was a plausible theory to explain the emerging pattern of politics in Europe in 1993: the new states of the East, and the revival of national assertiveness in the West, certainly seemed to reflect a revived nationalist consciousness. The Flemish and the Walloons in Belgium, the Gaullists in France, and the Catalans in Spain voiced their nationalism with increasing fervour, albeit in very different ways. States appeared to see less virtue in the supranationalist routines of Brussels. Yet there is a potent argument for believing that the reverse was true and that the British answer to Europe's problems – a return to intergovernmentalism, to reliance on co-operation between states – was at the least inadequate. The crisis of 1989–93 revealed, more than anything else, the weaknesses of the nation-state.

There are practical reasons for doubting the durability of a system poised between the tight interdependence of states and their political separation. The structures of co-operation to which the advocates of a *'Europe des nations'* appealed were clearly inadequate to the task of mediating between and among European nation-states: the system was bound to be unstable. If the assertion of the importance and robustness of reborn nationalisms was one skein of the early 1990s, the risks this implied for world order were unavoidable. The effects of national management were particularly obvious in the currency crisis, in the sense that no government was capable of tackling the problems alone. In other words, even if the revival of nationalism, of the *nation*, seemed real, the role of the *state* was limited. The potential for any one government to dig itself out of its hole was poor, even if most seemed more eager to bury themselves.

Economically, most of the states of western Europe entered the 1990s in economically weak condition. Britain, after the *laisser-faire* reforms of Margaret Thatcher, was facing a continued trade deficit, a rising budget deficit and a recession. Spain faced the end of the boom years; Belgium was looking at a monstrous state debt. Socially, many faced huge challenges brought on not just by rising unemployment but also by attempts to handle the problems of multi-culturalism, immigration and rising extremism. Politically, many were in worse shape. The revolution of the 1980s proved just as pressing for some states in western Europe as for those in eastern Europe. Italy, its political system held together by corruption and violence, saw a complete regime shift as magistrates threw out the old order. The prosecution of politicians, officials and the industrialists who had oiled the system meant the cleansing of an entire political class, loathed by citizens for their cynicism, arrogance and lies. It was made possible by the removal of one of the system's key pillars: the threat of communism. France and Spain, too, saw a succession of scandals claim the heads of leading members of the establishment. Germany went through a paralysing search for those who had collaborated with the former East German secret service. It was not the best time to be a national politician, anywhere in Europe. The lack of stability in so many capitals mitigated against the idea that this was time to create a system based on the power and authority of nation-states: many possessed neither.[15]

A return to the nation-state also failed to tackle the key institutional problems that came with the European Union's new role. The slide away from tight co-ordination of Twelve towards 'picking and choos-ing' – what is called, in EU jargon, 'variable geometry' – was begun by the deals given to Britain and Denmark in the Maastricht Treaty, and subsequent debates over monetary and fiscal arrangements made it even clearer that some states were in different camps. Military and security arrangements always divided the neutrals from the Nato members. The promise of new members with significantly different interests promised to increase the variability of commitments. But the problem is that this simply serves to weaken the process of co-operation, not strengthen it. It leads to 'mini-Europes' in policy areas, where some states co-operate and others do not. And where it is essential that Europe speaks with one voice – on environmental or trade policy, for instance – the possibility is weakened. Subsidiarity, the notion introduced by Britain to regulate the accumulation of powers by the Commission, did not provide any very satisfactory answer to the question of how to handle the dilemmas of a more fragmented Union. Britain and France managed to provide a list of policy areas where legislation should be scrapped or reduced, but the basic question – who should do what and how – remains a question of interpretation. The renationalization of policy, which was what the British interpretation of subsidiarity implied, carried grave risks in issue areas like trade and agriculture policy, where some states simply started to carve out their own paths.[16]

The possibility for EU members to find their own roads to prosperity would be less worrying were it not for the fact that the states of western Europe are themselves increasingly open to challenge from regionalist and nationalist movements within their own borders, as a result of the rejection of traditional parties and power bases, and the reassertion of older identities. A formula which simply sought to re-establish the nation as the philosophical pivot of European co-operation had misunderstood the dangers of the citizens' revolt that characterized the early 1990s, just as it neglected the lessons of the inter-war years.

The ugly face of European fascism reasserted itself in the political vacuum left by the decline of long-standing political parties in Germany, France and Austria. Racist and xenophobic, neo-fascist parties set themselves against the rising tide of immigration – still very low for the most part – and pledged 'ethnic unity' instead. Nationalism had long been a potential source of instability in those states harbouring ethnic minorities, but in the late 1980s it crystallized into effective opposition. In Belgium, the Walloons and the Flemish came close to dismantling the state; in Spain the Basques and Catalans pushed for greater autonomy. Regionalism asserted itself in Italy, where the sense of nation has always been weaker and where unity itself is recent. The Northern League in Italy represents an attempt to undo that unity. As William Pfaff says, 'Lombardy is more populous than Switzerland or Sweden, and its people ask themselves why they should remain shackled to the Mafia-ridden south of Italy, subsidizing it while the central government in Rome remains incapable of providing the nation as a whole with the effective administration or a modern economic and social infrastructure.'[17] In most states of Western Europe, the fringe political forces found foot soldiers amongst those displaced by economic competition, ready to embrace protectionism, or facing the loss of a rural living. The result was a fragmentation of political systems in every European country. William Pfaff calls the situation in Italy a 'crisis of democracy'; it was also a crisis of liberalism, of the idea that Europe should be open to the world.

All of these problems – the weakening of nation-states, the rise of exclusive nationalisms and the inadequacies of simple co-operation – had their roots in the 1980s, and would have been powerful enough arguments against renationalizing policy in the EU under any circumstances. The difference was that these pressures were twisted in different directions by the end of the Cold War, ways that made a simple turn to the nation even more unrealistic. To the EU's own agenda of political and economic change were added the new problems stemming from the end of the Soviet Union. The remaking of Europe that took place after 1989 was the most immediate effect of the coming down of the Berlin Wall and the dissolution of the Soviet bloc. It affected the EU in virtually every aspect of its operations. The opening of the East meant that one geopolitical border that had existed as a bulwark of the EU's development was suddenly removed. The unification of Germany enlarged the Union at a stroke by seventeen million people; it also brought a new queue of entrants for the Community. The states that had previously stayed outside as neutrals – Austria, Sweden, Finland and Switzerland – were all forced to reconsider their stance, and all made applications to join the EU.

The new world reopened in dramatic form the long-running questions of Europe's place in the world that had first been formed a century before, with the rise of new powers that dwarfed it. No longer in the shadow of the Soviet Union, Europe nonetheless found itself faced with the threat of instability to the East. In the Bosnian conflict, it was repeatedly unable to achieve anything more than a minimal level of agreement on policy. The pressure to create a more durable security and defence identity was increased by the reduction in US forces and Washington's declining interest in European security, and by the fracturing of the Cold War alliances that had underpinned defence. At the same time, the rise of economic security as a factor in international relations underlined the need for Europe to play a more significant role, with a more coherent set of policies. The 1993 agreements that cemented the GATT accord were threatened almost until the end by discussion among the key players, and in particular by French demands.

The debate over Europe's external role is matched by an internal debate. The citizens' revolts of 1989–93 showed that the EU lacked the deep loyalties and ties it had long sought. Opinion polls showed its popularity waning as the recession deepened. It is remote and unknown, and positive programmes to redress this have had limited appeal or success. The EU focuses on those at work and on those who are likely to travel across borders. But this by no means accounts for the EU's total population. The Parliament has so far had an uncertain relationship as the sponsor of a democratic Europe and democracy has not evolved in step with economic integration. Most links to popular sentiment are directed through national capitals, but even then they are only indirect. The Maastricht treaty created the concept of European citizenship, but it carries little content. In balancing the needs of the 1992 liberalization against the needs of its citizens, the EU has developed social programmes. But these have done little to help the unemployed, the regions that are falling off the edge of the map, or the states that are struggling to keep up, let alone move ahead. The new Europe is most accessible to those rich and educated enough to derive benefit and feed their imagination. The underclass everywhere is far more likely to retreat into narrow-minded nationalism. European citizenship is currently an elite preserve.

The Union, in short, suffers a dual problem of identity: generating an internal sense of unity, or at least common purpose; and rethinking its relationship to the rest of the world. But it is doing this within an institutional framework that is weak and at risk from the nationalization of policy, while the member states are subject to fragmentation and political pressures for extremist solutions are rising. The self-confidence of the 1980s is waning. There is an alarming intellectual vacuum about the Union's future direction, and a sense of paralysis and drift crept into most of its institutions in the early 1990s. The ideas that informed the founding fathers no longer possess the intellectual power, even amongst federalists, that they did.[19] The idea of a European Union of states, open to the world, seems to be in some peril. There is a risk that what emerges from Europe's heart-searching will be distinctly unattractive.

It was no accident that Europe developed the types of institutional structure suited to the territorial nation-state: it is a crowded place with many identities jostling for space, and the prevention of conflict between them – by force if necessary – has always had an important role in government thinking. Those precautionary policies are by no means always liberal and attractive, as the inter-war experience shows. The strategies embarked on by some eastern European states – mobilizing the population through appeals to ethnic unity and opposition to 'outsiders' – have some appeal in western Europe, too. The threat of protectionism was a valuable weapon for the French centre-right in elections in 1993; they also exploited to the full the attractiveness of the anti-immigrant policies wielded by Charles Pasqua. Increased attention to problems like these can, and indeed often does, play a role in welding communities back together. Focus on the enemy, however defined: forget your own disunity.[20]

Are the identity-generating strategies of a nation-state possible or desirable for a set of institutions like the EU? Some authors have raised the possibility that the EU itself might seek to confirm its identity in opposition to its neighbours and by rallying support against other states – the US, perhaps, or its Muslim neighbours.[21] 'Japan-bashing' has always had its uses. The unifying factors in Europe can be used in positive ways to embrace new communities; or they can be projected as a weapon, to the exclusion of 'others'. Accentuating what divides us, undermining the legitimacy of common action, and rejecting any greater unity is potentially an extremely dangerous strategy for Europe to adopt.[22] But so is a unity built on the assertion of 'European' values that seeks to exclude: to lock out foreigners and to adopt anatagonistic attitudes toward other cultures.

If Europe is to continue to play a regional role, an international role and a role in welding together its states, it will have to find a different way of accommodating communities. The combination of fragmenting authority and rising unrest means that what Europe faces is not just a rerun of some rather tired, intellectually jejune arguments about sovereignty. The debate which began in Brussels in 1992 was more than just a reworking of the old questions about the rights of the nation-state, which had been the hallmark of the EU's difficult relations with both Margaret Thatcher and with General de Gaulle. The questions that are being asked now are about not just where authority lies in a political system, but about how it is used and who endows it. How can Europe stay liberal, capitalist and democratic, and on what terms? The debate over the Delors White Paper, proposed in 1993 at the Copenhagen summit, showed some of the fault lines. It brought the EU's liberal free traders – Britain, the Netherlands and Germany – into conflict with the more centralist states. France, for instance recommended an extension of the principle of Community preference, excluding other states from EU markets. It also fed arguments about social protection, about the role of government spending and about accommodating the unemployed, which threatened to dominate the agenda.[23]

There are some similarities between the position of the US, sketched in the previous chapter, and Europe. Both show an increasing preoccupation with domestic, as opposed to international, concerns. Both in the US and the EU there are sections of public and elite opinion questioning the terms of engagement in the traditional international order. There is, in both the US and the EU, an inability to generate consensus over the key political and economic questions, which is hampering progress in any particular direction. The debate over European competitiveness reproduces very closely that which the US has staged at regular intervals for the last ten years.[24]

This raises questions about the likelihood of an international system based upon the old Atlantic institutions surviving in a recognizable form as an essentially liberal, open structure that can manage international security and a global economy. Doubts over the idea of a 'joint hegemonial concert' between two powers as thoroughly uncertain of the world as the US and the EU stems from more than their frequent, and usually amicably settled, trade disputes. They arise from questions about whether the two are simply up to forgetting their differences, and can find enough common ground. In Brussels, officials of the EU Commission followed the twists and turns of the Clinton Administration's trade policy in 1992 with scepticism, and in national capitals, many criticized – in the open – US reluctance to commit ground troops to Bosnia while threatening air strikes. Doubts about the idea of joint global leadership also arise from the apparent isolationism of the two main partners in the relationship, both pushed towards limiting immigration, restricting trade and resisting any implication in conflicts outside their immediate areas. They also arise from the apparent crisis of liberal internationalism in both the US and the EU, faced as they are by ever more insistent demands for protectionism from within.[25]

The stability of a 'global directorate' of Japan, the US and the EU looks still more questionable when examined from the perspective of those countries outside the privileged circle. Many have little reason to accept the continuing domination of these states; some will actively resist it. Others already find themselves in open competition over economic, financial and investment issues, or have carved out their own regional roles. The lack of a global community reflects not just the inability of the main players to lead, but the transformation of their relationship with those countries who will be expected to follow.

5

The Politics of the Periphery

'European administrative methods ... centralized, impersonal, uniform, undiscriminating in their incidence, had a levelling and pulverizing effect on traditional hierarchies and loyalties.' ELIE KEDOURIE[1]

Just as there are haves and have-nots within the economies of the developed world, there is a broad division between rich and poor countries globally. The trends we are describing have had a particular and peculiar effect on the Third World, whose role will emerge as one of the key determinants of the global system's ability to withstand change peacefully.

Only for reasons of analytical convention can one talk about the Third World as a monolithic bloc. The formulation owes its strength to the Cold War era, when countries of the poor 'South' either joined forces in the Non-Aligned Movement, tenuously balanced between the US and the Soviet Union, or tied their fortunes to one or other superpower, sometimes in alternation. Economically, the term marked a bifurcation between the developed and developing nations, and usually between enormous extremes of wealth. With the collapse of the Soviet bloc, and the end of bipolar certainty, Third World nations have been brought irrevocably into the sphere of the international economy.

The points of difference among the less developed countries, particularly their relative economic strengths, are far more significant than the points in common. The relationship between the North and the South existed on three axes, those of ideology, security and economics. Starting with the post-war independence struggles of

Africa, Asia and the Middle East, states found it convenient to move into the camp of one or other superpower, not just for material advantage but for reasons of state. Marxist socialism or US-directed conservatism were powerful motivating concepts for new regimes. Militarily, both the US and its allies on the one hand and the Soviet Union on the other sustained governments through military assistance and the provision of troops. Economically, foreign aid, trade concessions and technical advice were dispensed to build alliances and deter enemies. Attempts to secure an independent position – principally through the Non-Aligned Movement – were defined in relation to bipolarity. Few states sought or obtained complete exclusion from superpower rivalry, and the NAM's weakness resulted from the growing tendency of members to form alignments of a weaker or stronger nature. The commodity cartels of the 1970s, the New International Economic Order and the search for unity amongst debtor nations never came to anything. The end of the Cold War left these states as divided as ever.

Rather than view the Third World as a single entity, John Ravenhill sees five distinct categories: high-income, oil-exporting countries; industrializing economies with strong states and low debt; industrializing economies with weak states and/or debt problems; potential newly industrializing countries; and primary commodity exporters.[2] Common cause is difficult to achieve among nations with such varying profiles and prospects. Some would like to see commodity prices increase; others want lower costs for inputs. Some want the West to lower barriers for textiles; others are far more interested in market access for coffee, tea, or bananas. Some face hostile neighbours in regions of minimal security, where borders are contested and old, pre-colonial rivalries still hold sway. Others are in relatively secure neighbourhoods where regional co-operation and diplomacy have eased tensions. Many states, though not all, are authoritarian and corporatist; some are divided along religious or ethnic lines, others are homogeneous and yet riven by differences in income and status.

Commonalities, of course, do persist. The developing countries, even the richer ones, operate on the periphery of the world economy in the sense that they represent a small share of world manufacturing and trade. They largely depend on the markets of the rich nations, even if they are often denied full access for the goods they produce. In most cases, elites dominate the domestic economy and the majority of the population lives in poverty.

The nations of the developing world largely share, too, a history of imperial subjugation at the hands of the West, and this has had a profound effect not only on their economies but on their political institutions as well. Modern nationalism in much of the Third World was largely a function of anti-colonialism. The battles for independence in the Middle East in the first decades of the twentieth century, and in Africa and the Far East since the Second World War, routinely took as their point of departure the theories of nationalism developed in the traditional nation-states of Europe, even if many then sought to overlay theories of state socialism along the Soviet model. As country after country won autonomy from former colonial masters, old tensions – ethnic, religious and economic – may have returned. But on the whole, the potential for chaos was (at times uneasily) contained by the assertion of state power and the periodic influence and occasional military interference of the US or USSR.

The major exceptions to this Third World decolonization model were the countries of Latin America, where the Spanish and Portuguese settlers, rather than colonized indigenous peoples, led the battle for independence early in the nineteenth century, and China, which had never been genuinely colonized, despite the trading concessions extracted by Europe and the US in the nineteenth century.

But even these exceptions to the imperialist experience were influenced by the western ideas and experience of nationalism and the nation-state. Latin American revolutionary leader Simón Bolívar was unable to convince independence fighters in South America to forge a continental union; the borders established by the departing colonial powers were retained despite their obvious meaninglessness. Argentinians, Bolivians and Ecuadoreans – the native populations aside – were, in the early days of independence, indistinguishable.

The glue of anti-colonialism united internal opposition to overseas control. Political elites trained in the ruling country returned to demand independence in their own nations, but on terms dictated by the lessons learned in the 'metropole'. Leaders of nationalist movements in Africa and Asia were influenced by Marxist thinking above all. This is hardly surprising, given that demands for independence in the Third World were supported – financially as well as politically – by the Soviet Union, which saw colonialism as one of the nastier faces of international capitalism, and decolonization as a way of welcoming new nations into the communist orbit.

Elie Kedourie points out how influential western models were for the independence movement in India. In his view, western influence goes a fair way toward explaining why Indian leaders resolutely sought to contain Hindu and Muslim populations within a unitary state. 'Modern India, we may say, was impaled on the horns of a dilemma which no man could surmount, a dilemma consisting of two propositions, one that India was two nations and the other that India was one nation. This dilemma dominated Indian politics because Indian politicians came to speak a western political idiom. It was not, to be sure, the only western idiom of politics; but it happened to be influential and widespread in Europe at a time when Indians were much impressed with all things European and hence they came speak it. In this way they were like many other Asians and Africans who also picked up the idiom.'[3]

For much of the world, the relationship between the imperial powers and the colonized was a tense one. It was to lead, in the period of rapid decolonization after the Second World War, to an explosion in the number of nation-states. For even if the independence fighters sought to eject their foreign occupiers, they were intent on retaining the structures imposed by colonialism: a state, fixed borders, a national economy. Most states in the Third World were (and are) far from democratic, nor was the social contract as sacrosanct as scores of written constitutions in Africa and Asia implied. Tribal coercion, caste systems, and barely concealed slavery existed in countries with all the trappings of modern nationhood (state bureaucracies, courts, constitutions, national anthems and flags). But by retaining the basic model of the European nation-state, Third World independence leaders helped create the conditions to socialize their citizens, at least those forming part of the educated elite. Through western-style schools, libraries, museums, state-financed training, even the rudimentary structures of modern market economies (central banks and state bureaucracies), Third World nations soon created their own cultural and power elites with a vested interest in retaining the nation-state model.

As Hugh Seton-Watson writes, 'In African as in Asian lands occupied by European rulers, the traditional political and religious elites complied with the policies of their new masters while basically resenting them. As in Asia also, the new masters' policies soon created incentives and mechanisms for the formation, from among their subjects, of new cultural elites, through the development of European types of training and education. Inevitably these new elites became familiar with European ideas, and began to judge European rule by European standards and find it wanting.'[4]

As much as it has been disadvantaged, the Third World has played an important role in the emergence of a global economy in the years following the Second World War. It was, variously, the source of commodities, the site of cheap labour, the sponsor of lucrative public-sector contracts for large construction companies from the West. But with the exception of India, parts of Latin America and some nations of the Far East, countries of the Third World did not develop anything like consumer economies along western lines. Their economies were strictly peripheral even in this regard: they remained relatively untouched by the social implications of consumerization that have revolutionized the West.

This peripheral status has helped perpetuate the huge divisions in most Third World countries between the rich, westernized elite and the poor, under-educated majority. A politics of dependence has enriched a minority whose wealth and power are buttressed by their links to the international economy. The strategic importance of some Third World countries during the Cold War had, moreover, made it nearly impossible to alter the status quo through radical policies, and helped keep in power odious strongmen with little or no commitment to social justice or participatory democracy.

Ironically, the end of the Cold War has limited the choices of Third World governments yet further. They have accepted that they must play by the rules of international capitalism, whatever their level of economic development, and that means co-operating with trans-national companies, reforming domestic markets and lowering trade barriers. As Peter Calvocoressi writes pungently, countries of the developing world 'have become areas of opportunity; opportunity spells competition; competition has an aggressive edge; at the cutting edge is not a sword but money, not men in uniforms but men in suits. The "No trespassers" signs have gone and there is now no place where men bearing gifts may not go.'[5]

If material wealth, judged by consumption levels, is any indication, the integration of developing countries into the global economy has done little to improve the lot of their populations. The debt crisis of 1981–2 was sparked by a combination of rising interest rates and falling prices for the commodities exported by debtor countries to finance their loan repayments.[6] In the course of the 1980s, as the waning influence of the Soviet Union helped push Third World countries towards accommodation with the market-economy model, poor nations had little choice but to accept western-backed solutions to the crisis. Between 1983 and 1987, the total outflow from developing countries to the West was $100 billion, according to the IMF. In 1988, Latin American countries made net repayments of $18 billion on outstanding loans. In the same period, foreign aid from the developed to the developing world rose not at all.

Although the less-developed countries as a whole posted average growth in GNP of 3.6 per cent in the period 1983–9, dynamic Asian countries accounted for most of it. African economies grew only 1.8 per cent annually, while those of Latin America posted an average of only 1.7 per cent. In both cases, population growth exceeded economic growth.[7] By every economic measure, the 1980s were truly 'the lost decade' for many developing countries. The example of Latin America is particularly apposite: twice as wealthy as the newly-industrializing nations of the Far East in the 1970s, Latin American nations are on average only half as rich today.

A significant part of the Third World has yet to be industrialized, let alone consumerized to any noticeable degree, and this accounts above all for the major differences between, say, African political and social development and that of the dynamic economies of south-east Asia. The basis for the spread of consumerism – an adequate level of economic development based on profitable exports – may now be unreachable in much of the developing world, certainly sub-Saharan Africa (not counting South Africa). The two greatest advantages enjoyed by some poor nations – cheap unskilled labour and plentiful commodities – are not currently key factors in the international economy. International production is decreasingly reliant on cheap unskilled labour, while many commodity prices are in cyclical, probably secular, decline. Gearing domestic economies to the export of raw materials is unlikely to produce adequate profits to finance further development, certainly not when debt levels are so high. But making the leap to manufacturing, in the way pioneered by Japan and imitated by the NICs, may no longer be an option for the poorest nations, starved of direct investment. Markets in the West are far from fully open to Third World exports.

At the same time, population growth shows no signs of slowing in the poorest countries. Conservative estimates see the world's population topping eight billion by 2025, with fully ninety-five per cent of the increase coming in the developing world.[8] Based on these figures, it will take only forty-one years for the world's population to double. Significantly, however, it will take Europe 338 years to double, but only twenty-three years for Africa. Overpopulation impedes efforts to raise standards of living, and imposes huge costs on the natural environment. According to the United Nations, population growth is the main culprit in the galloping rate of deforestation in the Third World.

Because many nations have yet to develop 'modern' economies, forms of allegiance beyond ethnicity have failed to materialize. As we have seen, industrialization and the emergence of the nation-state system led to a multiplicity of social ties beyond ethnic background – class and citizenship above all. The lack of social development accounts for some of the virulence of tribal battles in Africa, where the work of creating citizens out of diverse ethnic groups has yet to be effectively undertaken. Persistent tribalist tensions are, indeed, exacerbated by those leaders whose positions of power are owed to the nation-state structure. While paying lip-service to the concept of nation-building, dictators such as Kenya's Daniel arap Moi routinely played one 'tribe' off against another. As Michael Chege has written: 'Even as they denounce [tribalism], incumbent African leaders back-handedly indulged in ethnic patronage to bolster their own authoritarianism or to distribute power and resources and maintain political stability.'[9]

There is a growing, if guarded, optimism in some quarters that the changing geopolitical realities may yet allow the Third World to escape the dependency trap that has hitherto limited its scope for economic progress. For thirty years, the superpowers surveyed the landscape for signs of intervention from the other camp, and rushed to bolster client states notwithstanding the relevant government's record on human rights and political freedom. Now, the first steps towards encouraging democracy in traditionally hierarchical and turbulent political systems have appeared throughout the developing world. The differences between developing countries, just as they prevent any coherent unity that would constitute a 'Third World', militate against the emergence of any single ordered relationship with the developed world at the end of the Cold War. One group of countries has moved closer to the old 'core' of the First World – those with accelerating growth rates, a sound base for economic reform and a high propensity to export manufactured goods. Singapore, Hong Kong, South Korea, and Taiwan are all in this category; so, increasingly, is Mexico, bound to the US by trade and finance if not by culture or politics. At the furthest extreme, another group of countries has detached itself into a 'Fourth World' by virtue of complete political and social collapse. Somalia, Chad and Sudan are the best examples.

The majority of states, however, are in yet another category, neither striving to enter the First World nor dropping into the Fourth. Strong regional military and economic powers exist; small, weak micro-states; countries with stable authoritarian governments, weak new democracies; federations that preserve unity only at the cost of slow development. To speak of these countries as being either in the core or the periphery is misleading. Some are at the centre of new regional arrangements, and tied to the West militarily, such as Turkey or Egypt; others are of increasing economic importance, such as Vietnam, the Philippines and Indonesia, while not yet in the category of the NICs. All of them combine social, political and economic progress with strong elements of economic inequality, instability and financial risk.

The 'little tigers' of the Far East have developed export-oriented economies, usually under authoritarian regimes, and have only recently toyed with the introduction of a measure of democracy. Hong Kong and Singapore have per capita incomes on a par with that of Israel, while an average South Korean earns almost as much as a Portuguese; but it would stretch credulity to term these thriving countries pluralistic democracies.

For it is a fact that while the Asian economies have certainly outperformed the Third World average (and indeed have grown far faster than the developed world in the past ten years), political development has been slow and sometimes chaotic. As the crackdown on opposition movements in Burma (1988), China (1990) and Thailand (1992) suggests, economic dynamism has yet to be matched by the introduction of true political pluralism. The military is strong in Indonesia, Thailand, Burma and the Philippines, while the outlines of civil society (a free press, independent churches, trade unions) have yet to be confirmed. In parts of Asia, the rapid economic growth has produced a middle class endowed with the right to make money but not to make politics. As George Hicks writes, 'They are not civil societies in the making. There are few intermediate organizations – opposition parties, trade unions, independent churches, media groups, intellectuals – that could form a basis for a pluralistic political marketplace.'[10]

In the communist countries of south-east Asia, a rapid move towards democracy is even more unlikely.

The lack of political freedom is not merely the result of the overweening influence and power of the military. The civilian regimes in the region have little more legitimacy than the juntas with which they have often shared power. Bribes are commonplace; civilian leaders are routinely and suspiciously wealthier than their constituents; electoral fraud and violence too often mar national votes. Thailand and the Philippines are two obvious examples. The military coup in Thailand in 1991 was launched in part to end the apparent self-enrichment of civilian cabinet ministers at public expense. In the Philippines, Corazón Aquino oversaw six years of notably corrupt and inefficient government, even if she herself was never inextricably implicated in financial scandal.

The consequences of such limited democratic accountability are an impetus toward greater political fragmentation and the prospect of more violence. Some of this will occur along tribal lines, particularly in countries where ethnic tension already runs high or threatens to ignite anew, such as Indonesia and Malaysia. A more immediate fear is a clash between authoritarian governments and nascent democracy movements. Ruthless efforts in Thailand in 1992 to crack down on dissidents may have forced the military government from power, but bode ill for stability in the medium term. China is set for further confrontations between the old guard in Beijing and intellectuals, students and an emerging middle class. Such crackdowns could poison domestic politics in neighbouring countries such as Hong Kong, due to be handed over to China by Britain in 1997, and could temper experiments in economic liberalization particularly the government's encouragement of Guangdong province's fast-growth, open economy.

The presence of China in the region, given the decline in Russia's influence, is dangerously destabilizing for other Asian nations. Increasing intra-economic links have failed to remove fears about confrontation over maritime and border conflicts, such as that over the Spratly Islands. US promises of a continued nuclear and military presence reassure but do not convince; and the growth in bilateral and multilateral diplomacy has served to underline rather than remove fears about Chinese ambitions. China, meanwhile, is growing steadily more powerful economically. This has not yet translated into greater political freedoms, nor have the benefits of superior economic performance been spread evenly throughout the country. The south, particularly the provinces adjacent to Hong Kong, is growing quickly; the hinterland is less affected by the regulatory changes and market reforms of the past fifteen years. Nonetheless, a greater reliance on the market mechanism, as well as the introduction of private ownership and a reduction in the direct role of the state in key sectors such as financial services, have helped put China at the top of the growth tables in Asia. As a consequence, there is greater interest in China than has been the case in decades. As the APEC meeting in Seattle in late 1993 attested, the US is increasingly preoccupied by the prospects for greater competition from Pacific Rim nations in Asia.

All the same, the domestic political challenges in China remain acute. Anti-reformers retain strength in Beijing, while local party officials and the army are both wild cards – especially in light of Deng's prospective exit from the scene within the next few years. Nor, as elsewhere in Asia, has pluralistic democracy flourished. In short, considerable economic progress – the little tigers are expanding sharply, while China's GNP is rising by fifteen per cent a year, and its economy is already the world's third biggest in brute terms – has not been balanced, in Asia, by greater security and democracy.

Latin America presents a similarly mixed picture of economic reform and political weakness and instability. Governments in the 1960s and 1970s pursued policies of import substitution, encouraging local companies to grow behind high tariff barriers. Although Latin America is nominally democratic in most instances, true, stable democracy has yet to flower anywhere in the region. As most of Latin America moves to create functioning free-market economies – privatizing and reforming avidly in recent years – little effort has been made to ensure a more equitable distribution of wealth. The huge underclass in Brazil, Argentina and Venezuela has seen little improvement in the five years since the continent introduced the beginnings of a programme of economic reform.

Politically, most of Latin America is now run by centre-right governments; and here, too, the end of the Cold War has helped contain some of the right–left tensions that dogged the region in the 1970s and 1980s (although civil war in Guatemala is still raging, an uneasy truce between the government and the Sandinistas may yet fail in Nicaragua, belligerents remain armed in El Salvador, and Peru's constitution has been suspended). The relative calm has made it easier to meet western demands for reforms in return for renegotiated terms on outstanding sovereign-country debt. Optimistic officials at the IMF believe the reforms will be successful provided efforts are made to address social inequities. Indeed, some believe that Latin American economies may have a brighter future than has been the case at any time since the 1960s, the decade when Brazil, particularly, was meant to escape Third World status at last. Certainly the continent's manufacturing sector has grown impressively even in a decade of relative stagnation, the 1980s.

In the matter of economic reform, Chile and Mexico are farthest along, but Peru, Argentina, and several small Central American nations have cut public-sector deficits, privatized state-owned companies, and introduced anti-inflationary monetary policy in recent years. They have been rewarded with an increase in investment, some of it repatriated by local elites from the Swiss bank accounts in which funds had been deposited in previous decades. The reform programme has encouraged the unleashing of additional funds from the Inter-American Development Bank: the bank may even be allowed in the future to lend directly to the private sector, thereby bypassing profligate and badly managed governments. The ultimate prize for right-thinking Latin American countries may be membership in a pan-American free trade area, under the accession clause of the North American Free Trade Agreement, signed by the US, Canada, and Mexico.[11]

Unhappily, social tensions remain extreme. Inner-city poverty is matched by horrendous conditions in the countryside. Unhappiness with the austerity programmes imposed as a condition of international aid and debt relief has taken the form of public-sector strikes, burgeoning crime rates and sporadic outbreaks of violence. The uprising in the south of Mexico in early 1994 was one symptom. The modernizing, westernizing Mexican government cannot yet rule out resistance to its ever-closer integration with the US. Significantly, the rebels launched their attack on the very day the NAFTA trade deal came into effect. Governments throughout Latin America cannot be assured of public support in the short term, unless the benefits of liberalization become widespread. At the same time, the US continues to view the region as key to its strategic and economic interests, and covert involvement in the political process there is unlikely to wane, despite protestations to the contrary in Washington.

In the neighbouring Caribbean region, for the most part poor and dependent on agriculture and tourism, market reforms have also picked up speed. Governments have begun to sell state assets to help cut budget deficits. For example, the Jamaican government sold its thirty-nine per cent stake in a commercial bank, Puerto Rico sold its long-distance telecommunications carrier to a Spanish company, while Guyana, Trinidad and Tobago and the Dominican Republic have also leapt aboard the privatization bandwagon. But here, too, the benefits of market reform have accrued largely to the elites, while the bulk of the population continues to suffer a poor standard of living.

Surprisingly, some of the more hopeful political changes are occurring in Africa, the least developed region on the globe and the site of some of the longest-running battles of the Cold War. The end of the era of superpower confrontation has hastened the collapse of one-party systems on the African continent. Particularly in the frontline states, authoritarian leaders formerly able to rely on superpower sponsorship have been forced to promise some measure of democratization in order to secure aid from the West and to silence demands from below for a more equitable division of economic wealth. Kenya is allowing the registration of political parties and has not yet silenced a more vocal and critical domestic media. Former Liberian dictator Samuel K. Doe has been killed and new leaders are promising pluralism. Elections in Zambia saw the departure of Kenneth Kaunda after twenty-seven years in power in favour of Frederick Chiluba, a trade-union activist. Even war-torn Angola (formerly a hardline Marxist state) and Ghana may yet introduce multi-party politics.

But poor economic prospects in Africa make it likely that further development towards secular, liberal and democratic systems will be slow. Most states in Africa are highly centralized and their economies state-controlled, whatever the political colour of their leaders. Without widespread reform, aid money is likely to be squandered as in the past, although optimists hope that democratically accountable leaders will be less able to line their pockets with diverted funds from the West.

In more troubling vein, the trappings of nationhood extend hardly at all below the stratum of the dominant social elite, where all political decisions continue to be taken. One-party systems may be harder to maintain now, as is evidenced by the departure of strongmen and the jockeying for position among various political leaders from the erstwhile opposition. However, low levels of economic development, the fitful commitment to market reform, and the lack of a middle class and a civic ethos make an early transition to modern democracy highly unlikely in many states.

Tribal differences – far from being subdued with the introduction of embryonic democracy – will be enhanced at the political level. Without the discipline imposed by single parties, with their control of the state apparatus and their monopoly on the exercise of military power, the leaders of various political parties and cliques find it easier to gain support on ethnic grounds.

More generally, even if political development has been varied and slow in the poorer nations, the changing role of the nation-state worldwide will have an influence in the Third World just as surely as in the First. The integration of the Third World into the global economy, coupled with the inheritance of the western nation-state model, has meant that even the poorest nations are witnessing political fragmentation similar to developments in eastern Europe, and for many of the same reasons.

These events worry many African leaders. The sanctity of borders has been a basic tenet of the Organization of African Unity, which sought to limit ethnic tensions by safeguarding the artificial frontiers inherited from the European colonial powers. Many separatists understand this fear, and are looking at ways of limiting the fragmenting effects of redrawing borders. For example, political leaders in favour of breaking the union between Zanzibar and Tanzania say they want the moribund East African Community to be revived as an effective basis for economic co-operation among newly constituted African states.

Political fragmentation in Africa will be difficult to contain unless the regional economy shows signs of improvement, and this is likely to require further market reforms. While there has undoubtedly been some movement toward liberalization, the level of political development is low enough to ensure that the benefits will accrue largely to elites. That leaves open the possibility of yet more violence, pitting ethnic groups against one another within the unnatural borders inherited by post-colonial Africa.

Most fragile and unstable is the near east, a region that can be taken to extend from the Maghreb states through the Levant, the Arabian peninsula, through Iran and Iraq, almost to the borders of China. Regional instability focused on the Israeli–Arab conflict always seemed most likely to tip the world into war during the 1960s and 1970s and even the agreement between the PLO and Israel is likely to be dogged still by disruptions from within and from neighbouring countries. To this source of uncertainty has been added resurgent

Islamic fundamentalism in Iran, Sudan and Algeria. Border conflicts in the Arab world involving Iraq and Kuwait, but also Iran and the Gulf states, Egypt and Sudan, and Saudi Arabia and Yemen have either caused or threaten to cause armed conflict. The new-found independence of states in what was Soviet-controlled central Asia and the Caucasus precipitated new wars that continually threaten to involve the rest of the region. Disputes over water match those over oil as sources of tension.

Few states in this region can claim to be democratic. Those that have tried – Algeria, Egypt, Yemen, Jordan, Kuwait – have either been forced to suspend democracy or have found the experiment destabilizingly difficult. Most have poor human rights records, little experience of peaceful transition between regimes and few of the liberal institutions of civil society. Many are authoritarian regimes led by ruling, dynastic families (the Gulf states and Saudi Arabia for instance) or praetorian regimes backed by force (Syria, Iraq and some of the states of central Asia).

Equally, it is these states that have achieved the least in economic reform. Resource-dependent and lacking any industrial base, many exist on remittances from expatriate labour. Rising oil prices only ever enriched an elite; falling oil prices have impoverished those who never fully shared in the good times. The presence of poor urban communities, swollen by rural deprivation and immigration from neighbouring states, cheek by jowl with wealthy middle-class suburbs, is an invitation to social unrest. Islamic fundamentalism has exploited poverty but also mistrust of western intervention and the inroads made by consumerism, liberalism and secularism.

The challenge posed by the Third World continues to be immense. Although developing countries have introduced a measure of market reform, many are strait-jacketed by high debt, pitifully substandard education, low levels of political development, endemic violence, and continued dependency on drip-feeding from the West. With the end of the Cold War, pressures are building to integrate the nations of the developing world into the global system as partners rather than dependants. But the West continues to deny meaningful access to goods from the Third World, and maintains and is indeed strengthening barriers to immigration from poor and overpopulated regions.

As the global economy subsumes even the former communist economies, and as sponsorship for anti-market policies in the Third World evaporates with the demise of the Soviet superpower, governments in the developing world are left with little choice but to accept the terms of the global economic system. Yet their internal development holds out little hope that stable, humane political and economic systems are achievable without steady and large-scale help from the West.

The attention of both western governments and international business has been diverted from the Third World periphery to the emerging economies of the eastern bloc. Much of the developing world is being ignored, except as the site of ethnic violence, the source of unwanted immigration, or the locus of ecological mismanagement. Western aid levels overall have remained constant but calls for more money have fallen on deaf ears.

The prospects for advancement in the Third World vary greatly. The Far East, despite the slow development of political pluralism and the likelihood of civil unrest, is economically robust enough to take its place in the inner 'suburbs' adjacent to the western-dominated economic centre. An indicator of its success can be found in the large share of total trade – forty-five per cent – that is intraregional. The Far East is less dependent on bilateral trade with First World countries than Africa or Latin America. Much of Latin America hopes to join the dynamic Asian economies in that select group, largely through closer free-trading ties with the US. Many Middle Eastern countries are, of course, blessed with oil reserves and are consequently an integral part of the international economy. But Africa is at the extreme of the periphery, and is unlikely to match any time soon the economic growth of Asia or even Latin America. As Lawrence Freedman has argued: 'A number of regions lie outside the immediate influence of a western pole. Some of these are generally well-ordered and fully integrated into the international community but others, such as the bulk of Africa, are not. These disconnected areas represent the major losers in the new order, because their appeal to the West has to be made largely on the basis of altruism rather than self-interest. They can no longer play the superpowers off each other.'[12]

Despite this range, much of the developing world shares at least one fate: barring the exercise of firm political will in the West, poor nations will remain peripheral and quite probably dangerous and unstable.[13] The challenge will be to involve the Third World in decisions affecting the emerging world order. The West will need to open its markets, perhaps even open its doors to greater immigration from poor nations. It will need to encourage the development of democracy and be sure that economic benefits accrue not just to elites but to the masses too. It will need to contain regional conflagrations that may result from the forced integration of erstwhile closed economies into the international system. The prospect for greater violence will test the makeshift international order that has supplanted bipolarity. Nowhere will that violence be as intractable and as destabilizing as in the stratified and beleaguered nations of the Third World.

The fact that the zones of greater instability – the Middle East, Africa and parts of Asia – sit on the doorsteps of the world's industrialized nations is a powerful argument for building new co-operative structures, if only to ensure peace. Since 1989, however, little has been achieved. The Rio Summit in 1992 built up expectations in developing countries that were not subsequently met. Periodic decisions to reschedule or write off debt do not replace the need for new capital inflows. While the security structures of the United Nations have been a focus for reform, its mechanisms for improving welfare, health and education have been neglected. The only progress has been in bilateral initiatives, and on specific issues where a clear and direct western interest could be shown. The US, Britain and France, for instance, have all shown interest in arms sales, security arrangements and military co-operation with oil-rich Middle Eastern states. An emphasis on tying aid to good governance and economic reform has not substituted for more constructive assistance, and it has in many cases only been aimed at unseating dictators originally put in place by the West.

The other face of relations between the North and the South has been conflict. Where less developed countries show themselves to be moving into product areas where they might match output in Europe or America, the North's response has invariably been to impose trade barriers. Where states show an intention of building a position of regional military strength, they are to be kept within strict limits. Conflict has also characterized the bilateral ties made by the developed countries. Japan's formation of a 'yen bloc' stirs fears in Washington and Brussels just as US moves into Latin America concern European investors and politicians. In their efforts to forge greater regional co-operation, south-east Asian countries have in some cases deliberately sought to exclude the English-speaking nations of Australia, Canada, New Zealand and the US. The Gulf Co-operation Council has focused on European moves against its oil and oil-related exports. By no means all the regional integration of the past three years has been directed at trade restrictions and the replacement of ties with developed nations. However, much has taken place in the absence of multilateral action to create a global basis for co-operation. If Europe, Japan and North America want to create global structures, they will need to give co-operation on security, economics and aid a decisive boost, and fast.

The West will need to do all this at a time when its own stability is uncertain. For if conditions in the Third World are cause for concern, the post-Cold War era represents equally difficult challenges in the West as well. As we will see in greater detail, the legitimacy of nation-state governments and the scope for international co-operation are both at risk as the world lurches toward a radically new configuration. Containing the pressures of globalism and tribalism will test governments in rich regions just as surely as in poor ones, especially in those countries (the US for example) where the gap between the affluent and those living at or below the poverty line is not only wide but growing. Even as the Third World reimagines itself in the light of its links to the global economy, and seeks political change in the service of efficiency and modernization, the West is embarking on its own quest for new certainties – for a new world order that will provide the basis for stability, equity and efficiency. In short, the West has its reimagining to do as well.

6

Order and Change

'Dost thou not know, my son, with how little wisdom
the world is governed?' COUNT OXENSTIERNA,
SWEDISH STATESMAN, 1648

The resolution of the ideological conflict that divided Europe and the
world before 1989, in combination with the economic revolution that
had convulsed the West in the 1980s, seemed to many of those then
in power to set the stage for the creation of a new world system, one
based on liberal democracy, international co-operation and market
capitalism. It did not; and insofar as there are pressures toward ushering in this vision they can be highly problematic, creating a world
that is interdependent but also unmanageable and often riddled with
severe conflict. We are entering an age characterized, above all, by
the rapid growth of interconnections between states, and the inability
of any single body – or even any group – to manage those linkages
to their satisfaction. It is a tangle of networks, where actions rarely
produce the effects that are anticipated, where authority is highly
dispersed, and hence where the possibility of stability is greatly
reduced.

Order, a word that was bandied about so frequently in the months
and years after the end of the Cold War, seemed very absent from
the world after 1989. Indeed, it seemed in many ways an empty concept, given the violence of the conflicts that ensued in Africa, the
Middle East, eastern Europe and on the borders of Russia. Nor was
there much that seemed radically new; many of the conflicts sent
journalists and diplomats scurrying to old encyclopaedias, consulting

154

historians, pinning yellowed maps of pre-1914 Europe to their walls. The globalist pretensions of 1989 quickly evaporated: large parts of the world were all but forgotten as others disintegrated into chaos.

The methods which the West adopted to tackle these problems seemed equally to lack millennial fervour, and often appeared curiously antique. The cautious pessimism of a British official, speaking during the Gulf War, seemed amply justified, both by that conflict and those that followed: 'It's not about the world, it's about parts of the world. It's not new. It's tacking onto existing bits of machinery; and it's certainly not going to be orderly.'[1] This conservative view was taken to its utmost by those who feared that order was precisely what had collapsed with the Berlin Wall. A prolonged period of peace seemed to have come to an end, symbolized by the title of a glum article in the *Atlantic Monthly*, that paragon of right-thinking liberal thought: 'Why we will soon miss the Cold War'.[2]

George Bush, the man who typified New World Order thinking, paid for this reversal with his job. The common accusation that his crusade lacked a Jerusalem was justified: Charles Krauthammer, a right-wing foreign policy thinker, saw a vacuum. 'For Mr Bush, the new world order is principally about order,' he wrote. 'And order is indeed a high value. But maintaining order is a rather pinched version of America's vision of the world.' It could not 'command domestic support', he wrote. Nor did it attract favourable notices abroad.

Stability is an important goal of societies and of the international system as a whole. But as was shown by the groups that chose violence, protest or rejection of prevailing wisdom in the three years after 1989 – and there were many – the narrow preoccupation with stability that characterized the 'new world order' was not enough. It should not be forgotten that the sacrifices and the risks taken by those who brought down the Soviet Union were not in search of order; they were looking for other things, be it greater prosperity, or greater justice, or simply an end to tyranny. None could have foreseen the effect East Germans fleeing to the West through Hungary might have on the sclerotic post-war configuration: even if they could, how many would have stayed in Leipzig?

The deeper problem with this focus on maintaining or restoring order was that it failed to take into account how far, how fast, the world had changed. Like those who gathered in Vienna in 1815, or Versailles in 1919, the dignitaries who attended the great post-Cold

War conferences (the Nato summits in London and Brussels, the CSCE summit in Paris or the G7 meetings between 1989 and 1994) simply did not seem to heed the constant rumblings of trouble. They planned a continuation of what had gone on before, apparently unaware that the ground was shifting under their feet. Reconstituting a clear orderly pattern from the world of the early 1990s is simply not possible in the short term because of the strength of the forces that have been unleashed. But neither is it necessarily desirable if it is merely to impose a new stability. The system that existed from 1945 to 1989 provided order at the cost of many more desirable outcomes. Nor, as we have seen, is any process of stability going to come about purely as a result of the agreements struck between governments that seek to impose order. There are other forces at work now. Any stability is the result of complex arrangements involving governments, regional organizations and global organizations, but also corporations and citizens, minorities and majorities, markets and military force.

It is worth examining the idea of the New World Order to see why it was inadequate as a concept for the 1990s. In the first place, it relied on the continuation of an idea of American leadership that had run its course. It is unlikely, for the reasons sketched out above, that the United States will continue to be in a position to exercise unilateral leadership; or that the other major states would accept it in any case. The US, under George Bush, seemed intent on carrying out its old role, regardless of the stress it thereby induced; but his vision, if there was one, was not widely accepted either at home or abroad. The 1992 election sealed the case for making what Bill Clinton called 'a new covenant' with the American people; and within the international system. In Bosnia, Somalia and Haiti, this showed its limitations.

No single country presents itself as a candidate to replace the United States. Certainly the Soviet Union, the other former superpower, is no longer a candidate, nor Russia, its successor state, the heir to so many sorrows. The other two most powerful industrial states, Japan and Germany, lack the requisite political and military structures; nor would they be acceptable to large numbers of their neighbours, with wartime memories yet to fade; equally, neither has indicated a desire to fill the gap. The view that had emerged by 1994 was of a collective process, 'an arrangement and a mechanism that will give all of the states ... an important say is what the post-Cold War security order looks like', according to Strobe Talbott, US deputy Secretary of State,

with the president as 'chairman of the board'.[3] The emerging inter-
national system is to be led by a group of states, working together.
At the core of this system will be the United States, and the European
Union states, along with their partners in Canada, Scandinavia and
Japan.

If the alternative to single-power hegemony is a looser form of
hegemonial concert, the omens are not all bad. Pluralism in international relations has often been perceived as stronger, fairer and
more efficient than single-power hegemony. Drawing on his analysis
of the British experience, David Calleo says: 'Hegemony has a tendency to break down because of the absolute or relative weakening of
the hegemonic power itself. A hegemon in decline begins to exploit
the system in order to compensate for its progressing debility.'[4] A
pluralist system may provide greater durability; it also coincides more
closely with reality, in a multipolar world, where power is dispersed.

There is no reason to expect this to be a stable arrangement. There
are a number of serious problems in expecting the US, the EU and
Japan to stay together rather than hang apart. The economic hierarchy
that has emerged from the last forty years does not parallel the political
hierarchy; Japan and Germany do not have seats on the UN Security
Council, which has come to be the predominant organ of arbitration.
This can be justified on the grounds that neither Japan nor Germany
is a military – hence a security – power; and neither is a nuclear
power. Does this, however, mean that nuclear powers should be given
precedence? Or that military strength is the only criterion? The con-
tests between these states over political power are exacerbated by their
conflicts over economics: over trade and the conduct of monetary
policy, but also over the conditions of foreign direct investment, competition policy and the terms of access to third markets.

This focus on leadership was similarly misleading because it sought
to minimize the role of states outside the charmed circle, the regional
powers of Asia, Africa, Latin America and the Middle East. The place
of these states at the great power table is far from answered, as the
Gulf War, Bosnia and Somalia showed. Even Russia, the erstwhile
competitor-partner of the US in global power, has had to fight for
the right to appear at G7 summits. In this sense, the problem left by
the evaporation of bipolarity is not just about leadership: it is about
representation. The second element of the New World Order (as
initially conceived) was that the institutions of the past forty years
were sufficient, if carefully managed, to establish stability, with a little

mild reformism. Much of the framework for managing a plural system already existed from the Cold War years: a plethora of international groupings in the field of security and economics. Once again, the evidence of the past five years is of a numbing conservatism. These institutions had remained virtually unchanged throughout the Cold War. The subsequent attempts at reform have been halting and unspectacular, and have done little to remedy the faults that were apparent long before 1989.

International security was the scene of the most activist attempts to impose a new order after 1989 and the mixture of successes and failures was not encouraging. The old 'stability' seemed to last not much longer than the Berlin Wall. In many respects, what appeared to emerge was not so much any new conception of how to operate the security system, but rather the resurgence of an older, state-centred tradition of force, diplomatic manoeuvring and acceptance of power as the ultimate determinant of international relations. Many of the security issues which preoccupied world leaders were old issues in a new context – principally, those of disciplining aggressive states and protecting weak states, particularly in the Iraq–Kuwait conflict of 1990–1. Though the United Nations was used to ensure legitimacy for a collective effort, it was a fairly clear case of the manipulation of the institution by the more powerful states. 'International action and order were subordinated to a national purpose with consequences for the UN which were at best ambivalent.'[5] The aftermath of the Kuwait war was unsatisfactory to nearly everybody involved: Iraq was left in possession of a large armed force, the territorial dispute between it and Kuwait remained unresolved, and subsequent humanitarian abuses by Iraq of its Kurdish and Shiite minorities went largely unpunished. The regime in Baghdad remained in power, efforts to create a new security club in the Gulf failed, and the attempts to disarm Iraq were still going on at the time of writing.

The new issue on the agenda was the breakdown of states, which emerged rapidly after the collapse of the Soviet Union as a global problem. It presented a series of challenges, from handling the interests of minorities to the problems of compensating adjoining states forced to handle huge refugee crises. Few principles for dealing with these issues emerged: instead, a set of poorly thought-out responses largely based on maintaining state unity to preserve stability were offered. The dominance of the state framework was obvious during the Soviet crises of 1990–1, when the US, the UK and France all demonstrated a clear preference for the devil they knew – Mikhail Gorbachev – over Boris Yeltsin, and where the independence struggles of the Baltic states were all but ignored. Tackling the issue of minorities within states remained a highly contentious issue while so many countries had minority problems of their own.

The sternest test was the rapid disintegration of the Yugoslav state. Competing frameworks for handling the crisis – those of the European Union, the United Nations and the Conference on Security and Co-operation in Europe – became arenas for competing interests. The existence of regional frameworks for peace need not be an obstacle to a smoothly functioning international system, insofar as they are consistent with an overarching framework. But it quickly became obvious that the interests of the major players – in particular the US and Europe – clashed over the choice of regional frameworks and the appropriate military bodies for intervention; Nato, the EU, the UN and the US all found themselves in conflict. The lack of mechanisms for intervention and the preference of European powers for the preservation of state integrity both hampered action.

There was an inability to pull together the diverse elements of managing conflict. In the Middle East, for instance, an effort was made to compensate countries that suffered from sanctions against Iraq, and to share the burden of the war's costs amongst the 'coalition' states. This generated great controversy, and left few states satisfied. After the Bosnian collapse in July 1992, the refugee burden fell largely upon states that could ill afford it, in particular the former Yugoslav republics of Croatia and Slovenia themselves and Hungary. German efforts to share the burden were tentative and poorly received. The needs of humanitarian relief and peacekeeping clashed, and immigration policy was used to keep out asylum seekers and refugees.

This failure to manage complex tasks involving financial, social and political problems was even more evident in the fresh challenges dumped onto the world's lap. The 'new agenda' of international security which was heralded in the late 1980s included such diverse topics as the environment, drugs and nuclear safety. But progress on these was decidedly limited, and there is still no adequate structure by which to co-ordinate international action. This lack will likely hamper relations between the First and Third worlds, as we make clear in Part Three. The Rio summit in 1992 was a disaster; co-operation on drugs policy was minimal and the most significant element was the US attempt to unseat General Manuel Noriega in Panama, and the dispatch of US troops to Peru. Nuclear safety was the subject of an unseemly row at the 1992 Group of Seven summit when each country pushed its own companies' interests at the expense of a multilateral plan. The UN's security and social development arms seemed to operate as separate entities.

It was not just the ineffectiveness of the western response which undermined its claim to legitimate leadership: it was the apparent imbalances in the way the system operated. Far greater priority was given to problems which directly affected northern industrial states than those which affected poorer southern nations. In many areas of the world, the test of the New World Order was never even approached. When the government of Siad Barré was pushed out of office, Somalia was the scene of one of the worst disasters that Africa has seen. US intervention, late and poorly executed, gave the impression of being aimed against the inhabitants rather than in their interests. It was scaled down as soon as light casualties were sustained. In Angola, the United Nations failure to disarm rival factions led to a return to bloody civil war in 1992. In Haiti, a military dictatorship was left in power despite US pressure. The record of the New World Order and its institutions was especially poor in areas where poverty and underdevelopment already prevailed. The result was a grave blow to the idea that the world was being run on anything like a symmetrical basis. Northern isolation from this and other problems threatened to undermine the sense that the international security system was run for the benefit of everybody.

In the field of managing the international economy, many of the same problems of co-ordination and leadership emerged; but there were fewer attempts even to make a pretence of managing the process. The market set the measure of the way the West managed the transition, in eastern Europe as in the Soviet Union, from communism, and the existing international agencies continued pretty much as they had. The model that was pressed on eastern Europe, as on the Third World before it, relying on structural adjustment of the economy, stabilization policies, privatization and market access, and 'good governance', was effectively made a condition of aid. All of these impulses entailed reforms that were often socially painful. Yet the First World response was nugatory. No market opening was announced in the West to match that which the Third World had been forced into. The costs that these measures imposed were virtually ignored. Economic costs were quickly transformed into political backlash in many countries. Yet the IMF and World Bank, seemingly insulated from political pressure, continue on the same track.

In both the political and economic fields, reforms were thus limited, and in the main the presumption has been that the world can totter along with its institutions largely unchanged. In both fields, this approach bred common weaknesses. There was a lack of foresight and planning. This was dangerous enough with longer-term threats to security, but when – as in Yugoslavia – a situation deteriorated rapidly into bloodshed, it became murderous. The question of matching resources to capabilities was never satisfactorily resolved: organizations such as UNHCR repentedly complained of underfunding. Indeed, economic questions and those of security were separated as far as possible in the institutions that planned the new order. Dealing with problems as early as possible was a precondition for managing international security, yet far more resources were put into assembling armouries than were put into diplomatic efforts.

There is clearly a need for more effective leadership and co-ordination; for reforms of the structures to accommodate change; and it must be established that the costs and benefits of economic change are applicable to everyone. If the northern powers acting together are to create a new way of running the world that can be extended successfully to the states of the former communist bloc as well as to the Third World, they will have to lead together, persuade others that their goal is worthwhile, and show that their strategy is fair. Instead, there has been a presumption of the virtues of existing arrangements.

The international organizations which were set up during the last forty years should, in theory, be capable of carrying out some of these functions. Yet significant institutional change was never addressed, at least partly because of the inherent conservatism of the major states, and particularly the United States, Britain and France.

The weakness of multilateral institutions is hardly a new development, to be sure. The history of international co-operation on economic and security issues reveals deep-seated contradictions. On the one hand, there are examples where states acting together have achieved far more than they could acting alone. On the other hand, as James Mayall says, 'International co-operation is always and everywhere dependent on the prior recognition of the sovereignty principle.'[6] This generates what might be called the paradox of intergovernmental co-operation: states enter into international co-operation because in some sense there are problems that they cannot handle alone. Yet they retain their formal authority, remaining masters of their own, albeit declining, universes, and this puts serious limits on how far international organizations can help to serve as the instruments for imposing order let alone for facilitating change.

As one analyst of international organizations puts it, 'States retain all their prerogatives of ultimate decision-making and co-operate through international organizations when their perceived national interests are enhanced rather than diminished or threatened by such co-operation. International organizations become the convenient tools of foreign policy of the individual states. Most of the energies and resources of each state are reserved for bilateral not multilateral activities. As soon as a regional or global organization is perceived as taking an action or series of actions inimical to the internal interests of one or more members, the spirit of co-operation disappears and the vitality of the organization suffers.' [7] They are closely tied down by their constituent documents. 'Whereas states possess unrestricted international legal personality, that of international organizations is clearly circumscribed in terms of the express and implied power laid down in the constituent instruments.'[8]

Nowhere have these problems of matching the demands of sovereignty with those of an effective international system been more obvious than in the United Nations, the core of the set of institutions that were intended to sponsor a new world order. At the end of the Cold War, the UN was to have its place in the sun, now freed of the restrictions placed upon it by superpower vetoes. Even after the reforms of 1991–2, it was left gravely weakened by the remaining restrictions upon its actions, by underfunding and by lack of support from the northern states. It is often prevented from effectively enforcing decisions by restrictions on how far sovereignty may be overridden. In the United Nations charter, after the high-minded preamble and the lofty words of Article 1, Article 2 states: 'The Organization is based on the principle of the sovereign equality of all its members.' This limits the UN to being, at best, a 'weak confederation'.[9] The removal of the Soviet–US split helped to ease some of the obstacles to its application; but it quickly became clear that it was not just the Soviet veto which had caused the problem. 'The fact that the UN is an organization of sovereign states places drastic restrictions on the independent power of the organization. Sovereignty indicates that the members reserve the power of ultimate decision making for themselves and confer no real authority upon the international agency.'[10] The weak multilateralism of the past five years has put the UN in a double bind. It has created what Boutros-Boutros Ghali calls a 'surplus of credibility,' an assumption that all crises are susceptible to UN action; but it has failed to deliver the resources, commitment or tools to finish the job.

The third element of the New World Order was that there was an underlying belief in the growth of an international community under American sponsorship, with shared ideas about how the world operates. Bringing down borders and freeing trade would create a convergence of views among people. The concept of the advance of a global community of interests through the growth of human interchange is in many respects just new wine in old bottles. Capitalism and free trade have been linked together in international relations since the last century, by those who saw in both the prospect of prosperity and peace – and perhaps more than a little self-interest as well. Free trade underpinned prosperity, and thus would underpin international peace. This was part of the liberal ideology of Cordell Hull, the US Secretary of State who set up the post-war trade system; but also of Adam Smith and of the nineteenth-century thinkers who followed him. It is a view that has always proved popular with industrialists, particularly of the transnational variety. 'We now know that anything which is economically right is also morally right. There can be no conflict between good economics and good morals,' said Henry Ford in 1930[11] at a time of earlier bourgeois triumphalism.

The more modern versions of this essentially liberal thesis on the harmony of nations are in most respects far more compelling than Ford's simplistic reductions, because they take account of the transformation in the role of states which has been a facet of the post-war world. Because there is increased interchange between states, war between them is less likely. 'No age until the present one', writes one advocate, 'was marked by a set of conditions conducive to an increased emphasis on international co-operation.'[12] Because states live in each other's pockets, they are less able to take action against each other; and they are more likely to co-ordinate policy and action; and ultimately, they are more likely to agree. The evolution of international organizations and transnational contact has on this argument begun to lay the basis for a different kind of world order, one based on greater co-operation, the acceptance of interdependence and the limits that both impose. 'To predict an end to international conflict is unrealistic and naive, but the atmosphere in which interstate inter-actions occur may be ameliorated by the impact of the web of personal relationships.'[13]

But, as we have emphasized, interdependence is just as likely to generate conflict as co-operation. Living in each other's pockets brings severe problems for states that are adversely affected by the actions of others; and insofar as it limits states' autonomy, it may create the basis for greater misunderstanding and mistrust.

By bringing the world into one camp, rather than two, the end of the Cold War did help to lay the groundwork for an international community that is more than the sum of its parts. But it does not automatically entail any consensus over how that community is to be run. Interdependence means that there is a price to paid for acting unilaterally; but that price is not always paid by the state which decides to go out on its own. It may thus be that it creates a desire to reduce the linkages between states and preserve their autonomy of action.

Isolationism, like unilateralism, is also in theory more difficult when states are interdependent; but what goes for unilateralism also goes for isolationism. It is easier in larger groups, especially the regional structures that have emerged from the Cold War. Thus the European Union and Japan (as the leader of an emerging, if still informal, grouping of nations on the Pacific Rim) both have ample opportunity for withdrawing, or isolating themselves, from aspects of the security and defence system. Isolationism saps the power of the idea of an 'international community,' either by drawing key players out of it, or by segmenting areas of the world off as of no consequence to the system. The inter-war years showed that isolationism could be just as potent a threat to world order as unilateralism, particularly where an unstable or potentially unstable system requires support. American isolationism is the other side of the coin to its unilateralism. This became evident in the campaigns of Ross Perot and right-wing Repub-lican Patrick Buchanan against George Bush in the 1992 election; but also in the wider claims of Americans on the left and right of the political spectrum. Europe has equally found itself forced into a new set of roles for which it is inadequately prepared and, in some quarters, of which it is uncertain, at best. Its hesitancy in taking a role in the Bosnian conflict partly reflected an unwillingness to pay the price for intervention in a region where most states felt they had no vital interest.

The idea of an international community presumes the ability to make, and police, a set of rules. The restriction on the use of military force makes it very hard to impose discipline in the modern world. If unilateral action in an interdependent system is costly, so is punishing a rival state. This has long been noticed in terms of the use of economic sanctions to punish trading offences: if closing the market is the answer to a US–Japan trade row, this may penalize US companies as well as Japanese companies. Economic sanctions are also ineffective where several other states may well be willing to break them. The interdependent system relies very highly on states keeping to the rules because they see them as legitimate and beneficial. Where they do not, it has little to say.

Nor is a sense of legitimate international community likely to be manifest while there are such large-scale economic differences. The development of the global economy, it needs hardly be said, has not been made in single leaps, nor even in smooth, steady progression. The extent of international economic integration, though great, is not complete by any means; and it is still quite possible that its progress may even be temporarily reversed. The fact that there is a borderless world does not mean that there is a homogeneous world.

The market turn which affected the northern and southern states in the 1980s did not make for any broader community of interests. The degree to which each nation-state has embarked on marketization and democratization varies with their history and their location, as did the prior enterprise of state economic management. Putting the market first may have been the priority of most governments in the late 1980s and early 1990s but the reasons were diverse, as were the methods. What each programme had in common was a desire to substitute the private sector for the state's management of markets. Market forces in most cases simply meant removing state capital, state regulation and state direction and allowing in private capital, competition and management techniques. The diverse forms of private capital, as much as the diverse forms of public ownership, shaped different responses to the market turn.

There remain significant differences within nations – at the level of the region, but also at the level of social groupings and levels of education. The core–periphery relationship, in which terms some social scientists used to describe the north–south system, also applies within the developed countries. Not everybody can be, or will be, equally involved in the global economy. At the very least, then, there are significant degrees of differentiation between the market economies, and between them as a group and the developing countries.

Lastly, it is worth pointing out a fundamental flaw in the idea that some kind of international consensus, operating through US-led international organizations, could be the basis of a new world order. The values and ideas that the US and its liberal capitalist allies seek to promote simply are not shared by the vast majority of the world's population. It is not neceassary to go as far as Samuel P. Huntington in his article in *Foreign Affairs*, 'The Clash of Civilizations' and predict a rupture along religious lines. The evidence from six years of failed attempts to install human rights, democracy and capitalism as universal values shows that each of these concepts can be applied differently, even where they are accepted; where they are not, many other traditions exist to legitimize state practices.

Under these circumstances, the role of international organizations in promoting order will continue to be strictly limited, though a shifting balance of power is likely to be evident. 'They will continue to be dependent on governments for funds and legal powers; but the relevant agencies of governments may be dependent on them for information and for the policy co-ordination by a legitimate system-wide actor, which is required to achieve their own objectives.'[14] Individual states, too, will find that their independence is limited.

A form of international community is emerging, but it is not the consensual, ordered one that we might have hoped for. What may now be developing is a system where states, regions, international organizations and transnational companies vie more equally for power. None would have an automatic claim to pre-eminence, nor is there any universal set of values and ideas to legitimize and order that community. This all sounds very post-modern. But it is equally redolent of the pre-modern, where spheres of responsibility overlapped and overrode according to the occasion. Adam Roberts points out that, in many respects, the world as it looked in the aftermath of the Cold War takes us back in time, to models of state systems in the nineteenth century. And, he argued, 'Perhaps the new era is taking us back further still, to an international society bearing resemblances to that of the Middle Ages, where there are different hierarchies of authority for different purposes, rather than a parcelling out of the world into sovereign states with claims to the exclusive loyalty of their subjects.'[15]

The impact of a system under diffuse leadership operating with so many different actors will have uncertain results. Hegemonic systems dominated by one power are associated with stability, with a degree of order imposed from above but accepted from below, even though that hegemony may be coercive. The lack of a single power in charge is compounded by the complications of a world bound so tightly together, a world that has been slowly changing for several decades. Writing as early as the 1970s, Keohane and Nye described an emerging international order 'in which actors other than states participate directly in world politics, in which a clear hierarchy of issues does not exist, and in which force is an ineffective instrument of policy'.[16] Multiple channels would connect societies; multiple issues would be on the agenda, and hence not just a different kind of order, but a different kind of leadership would emerge. Stasis is unlikely to be the outcome; but change is going to be hard to manage.

It is misleading to argue either that what is emerging is world government, at one extreme, or a return to atomized nation-states at the other. Neither is practical: states are not likely, *en masse*, to give up their sovereignty; but nor are the pressures for integration – and consequently for pooling or devolving sovereignty – likely to disappear. The search for a new stable point from which to lead the international system is a fundamentally mistaken one. What is needed, in short, is not a new geographical centre – another Washington, another Moscow, another Byzantium or Rome; nor indeed a new single philosophical pivot – the citizen, the state, the market. There is a need, rather, for a way of combining the existing, and proliferating, power centres, a way that does not engender chaos. There is a need to find a new set of principles by which to assess where decisions should be taken, on what basis and by whom. What we face is not a crisis of power, but a crisis of authority.

PART THREE

Reimagining the Nation

INTRODUCTION

Breaking Up the Communities

'A multitude is strong while it holds together, but so
soon as each of those who compose it begins to think
of his own private danger, it becomes weak and con-
temptible.'   NICCOLÒ MACHIAVELLI[1]

Los Angeles burned in 1992. Not all of it; just the parts where the
nice people never went, the parts where the poorest and most desperate were concentrated. Military units which, months before, had
swept across Iraq, were now patrolling the streets at home. It was
another element in the death of George Bush's presidency; but it was
also a sign of the changes that America was undergoing. The Gulf
War enterprise and its ramifications were brought home in other
ways, too: a popular bumper sticker read: 'Saddam Hussein still has
a job. Do you?'

The years that followed the coming down of the Berlin Wall were
years of political and economic tumult. In eastern Europe and the
Soviet Union, the consequences were all too obvious: but in the West,
too, a political price had to be paid. Not just the price of the disappearance of the Berlin Wall, but the price of years of economic change
that could no longer be put off. As Robert Louis Stevenson once
wrote, 'sooner or later we sit down to a banquet of consequences.' The
consequence of the global opening which characterized the 1980s, the
breaking down of borders across the world, was the weakening of
the communities that had sustained political structures.

The new world order that saw in the 1990s was top-heavy and

heavily institutional. Its proponents believed that the system could still be managed on the old terms: that the US would be at the helm, that the post-Second World War structures would remain largely intact, and that an 'international community' could be readily defined and achieved.

The challenge is to reformulate questions about power, authority and accountability, not only within polities but also in international affairs and the global economic system. This must be done in an age where familiar signposts have disappeared. The old way posited a leading role for the nation-state, not only in balancing interests within countries but in managing the international system as well. That way is now blocked. We must reimagine the links between and among citizens, their governments and the global system. This is partly about reimagining the connections between liberalism, capitalism and democracy, the modernist triumvirate. It may, indeed, be about reinventing all three.

The liberal western economic order of the post-war era, sustained for forty years by US sponsorship and managed through the linkages established by international organizations, finds itself in difficulty at the very moment its 'triumph' seemed assured. This is partly because, as we have argued, the global capitalist system increasingly operates on bases other than national, and effective means of asserting political control over the transnational economy and of requiring TNCs to be accountable to political institutions have yet to be developed. But it is also because democracy, an easy fellow traveller of liberalism, is faced with equally formidable challenges.

The decline in nation-state autonomy has compromised the pact between citizens and the nation-state. It has made it difficult for governments to mediate between their citizens and the rest of the world, and to manage the relationship of the individual to the global economy of which he is a part. Any solution will require ways of managing the multiple links between and among the citizen, the state, regional and international organizations, and the global economy. It will require a rethinking of communities and their rights and responsibilities. The effort is made doubly difficult by the retracing of borders – political, social, cultural and economic – the defining characteristic of the age.

For the process of globalization does not eliminate community: but it does undermine the types of community we have inherited, and in particular the nation-state. Other forms of community can be manufactured, synthesized, invented and imagined, some of them larger, some smaller, but on different bases. It is not just physical boundaries that are redrawn as a result; it is also social boundaries. Drawing boundaries and distinctions is at the heart of the enterprise of all social science, and most linguistic practice. From the question of boundaries, 'all others flow. To draw a boundary around anything is to define, to analyse and reconstruct it, in this case select, indeed adopt, a philosophy of history.'[2]

In southern California in 1989, there were borders. In the misty haze of a Pacific morning, the chain link fences that separated it from Mexico, its former colonial master, were in plain view. The border that winds its way along the rivers and valleys from one coast to another is sometimes invisible; sometimes cut deep by natural boundaries; and sometimes marked by man-made obstacles, like the fence that cuts off San Diego from Tijuana. It is supposedly an unbreachable fence. But in the evenings, as the Border Guard makes its daily patrol, the holes are all too evident.

On the other side, hundreds, thousands of Mexicans are gathered, as if for some great game. But it is no game. The wage differentials are enormous: the gap between southern expectations and northern realities even larger. Yet that border is fading. One Californian in five is of Mexican heritage, compared with fewer than one in ten in 1970. By the turn of the century, Latinos are expected to make up thirty per cent of California's population, and they already account for thirty-eight per cent of the residents of Los Angeles County. 'Five hundred years after Christopher Columbus first brought the New World to Europe's attention ... the distinction between North America and Latin America is eroding,'[3] and it is the Anglo-Saxon culture of the north which is being diluted – even if it is still the more powerful politically. It is not just in California that the United States is trying to cope with new patterns of immigration. Miami has two daily newspapers in Spanish, two Spanish-language TV channels, and half of Dade County's two million residents are Latino.[4] Here the predominant influence is Cuban, making for very different politics and cultural influences; but other Central American and Caribbean communities are also becoming important.

The relationship between California and Mexico runs deeper than merely the migration of people. There is a two-way flow of goods and services across the border, and the volume of such traffic is set to expand with the free trade pact. At the beginning of the 1980s, some policy experts had assumed that Latin America was about to fall off the map, faced as it was by debt, drugs and a dearth of democracy. 'Instead of falling off the map, Latin Americans are helping to redraw it,' wrote Abraham F. Lowenthal, one of the few experts in the US who have consistently called for dialogue with Latin America.[5]

It was against the Koreans who ran corner grocery shops that much of the anger of the Los Angeles riots was directed. In Los Angeles you will find more Koreans than in any city but Seoul; more Filipinos than in any city but Manila. America is in the process of enormous social change. By 2005, one-third of all Americans will be non-white. 'It is not that American society is disintegrating, but that it is being transformed into something quite different, with all the attendant violence and loss of orientation which the transmutation of any society brings in its wake.'[6]

It was not just in the United States that riots and civil disturbances convulsed the West. In France, outbreaks of strikes and demonstrations culminated in the blocking of roads throughout the country, in demonstrations by farmers and the wave of violent suburban riots of the summer of 1992. A handful of farmers held French foreign policy hostage, and their dogged stand was the dramatic foreground to the showdown in the shadows between the EU and the US over the issue of farm subsidy reform. In Britain, a growing tide of urban unrest brought violence to the streets once more, with petrol bombs, barricades and the appearance of armed policemen. Germany faced an unprecedented wave of strikes and the disturbing attacks on refugee hostels.

There was a strong ethnic element to many of the disturbances, as there had been in earlier waves of unrest in the previous decade. But there was a difference. As one British sociologist pointed out: 'In the eighties, it would have been possible to pinpoint the sites of rioting in this country by marking on the map where there were concentrations of blacks and Asians. Brixton, Tottenham, Handsworth, Toxteth all fit this pattern,' wrote Jock Young, Professor of Criminology at Middlesex University.[7] 'In the nineties, the dots on the map are much more widespread ... As the recession has spread, the white population of depressed areas has joined the ranks of the violently disaffected.'

'Riots are the politics of despair,' wrote Professor Young, 'the collective bargaining of the dispossessed.' Eldridge Cleaver, who spoke to Stanford students in 1969, had long ago understood this: 'There are rumours going around today that people have lost their spirit, that they can no longer deal with the problems confronting society, that it's necessary to throw up both hands, and allow the professionals like Nixon, Reagan and Georgie-boy Wallace to come in and rescue us and to save us and to offer salvation to the people. We think this is another lie, a part of the tissue of lies that everyone in this country's been fed all of their lives, all of the history of this country, and we say that people don't have to submit to such lies, that you don't have to tuck tail, when a fool like Ronald Reagan screams at you; that you don't have to do a thing like that. There is such a thing as free will, and it is possible for you to stand up, to let your voice be heard, if you're willing to suffer the consequences.'[8] By the late 1980s, it was not only California's black population who understood.

This was the era of the televised riot, the era of instant exposure: 'To see their estate on television is quite exciting,' said a politician from northern England of the conflict in one urban backwater. This was, in a way, a perversion of the effect that had been seen in earlier civil disturbances: television offered new opportunities. The Los Angeles riots were sparked by video film of a black motorist being kicked and beaten by four LAPD policemen. Gil Scott-Heron had once famously sung 'The revolution will *not* be televised,' – social upheaval could not be packaged, commodified. But, he was wrong: television footage was used to convict rioters; but it also helped rioters to co-ordinate action.

The early 1990s were marked out not just by violence but also by political change and unrest. Voters deserted established parties, for right-wing, populist or regionalist parties. In the United States, Ross Perot's populist campaign disrupted the election and helped to produce the swing that brought Bill Clinton to power. In France and Germany, both the traditional right and the left lost out to far-right candidates. In Italy, the Christian Democrats and Socialists who had ruled in cosy proximity for forty years were miraculously and swiftly discomfited and destabilized by a judicial onslaught and a consequent shift away from the old politics.

And urban communities have not been the only ones to experience change. There has been a fresh exodus from the countryside in the West, as farm prices have fallen and structures of protectionism have become less effective. In Britain, one politician estimated that nineteen farmers were quitting the land every day and that farmers' fixed assets were half the level of ten years before.[9] In south-west Britain, some farmers had seen a fifty per cent decline in income; some had committed suicide. In France a similar pattern precipitated roadblocks, riots and attacks on politicians. Even when these blocked the flow of British produce through France, some farmers and their representatives secretly confessed to admiration for the French: 'If we had done this, perhaps things would be better here,' said one.[10] 'We should put up some roadblocks. But we lack their solidarity.'

Changes in the global economy are at the root of this dislocation. Governments can no longer manage national economies in isolation; they cannot protect their citizens from the effects of financial deregulation; they cannot prevent unemployment when transnational corporations decide to move operations or to find new supplies elsewhere.

TNCs have been the prime authors of economic change in the post-war era. They look to the cheapest sources of raw materials wherever they are found, manufacture their products where labour costs are at their lowest (subject to the standards of local infrastructure and the security of investment), and sell where the intersection of supply and demand generates a price at which an acceptable return can be made. Even smaller firms, traditionally fixated on their home market, are finding that the costs of competing – particularly those associated with the introduction of new technology – have risen so sharply on a relative basis as to make offshore sourcing, low-cost labour and high-price markets the *sine qua non* of commercial success.[11] This globalization is matched by a revolution in communications technology that has helped make borders irrelevant. Information is now a key commodity, and it can travel, like money, without hindrance. Change is nothing new; the industrial revolution was as earthshaking as trends in our present era. What is truly new is the speed of change, the speed with which it is communicated from one point to the next.

In the last decade, states have for the most part ceased to resist these tumultuous changes and have sought, instead, ways of managing them. The areas of policy where they can act autonomously have been reduced. The predominant reaction to economic change has been to allow the market to take its course.

The international economic pressures have also helped determine the course of post-liberation politics in eastern Europe. By accepting the consensus on the liberal economy, countries such as Hungary, Poland, and the states of the former Soviet Union are attempting to liberalize and deregulate just as those political structures which managed (with difficulty) to contain nationalism disintegrate. Citizens east of the former Iron Curtain are being consumerized at a rapid rate;[12] but the political stability that might underpin these changes is not yet in sight. Attempts to forge regional trading agreements along the lines of the 'associate membership' deals reached with the EU have intensified throughout the Soviet bloc, but these elicit little commitment from frustrated and confused consumers more open to tribalist propaganda than to the wonders of economic co-operation.

In Germany, aside from the economic and political effects of the coming down of the wall, the reunification of the country brought new social challenges. Crime soared in the east, in states that were not used to it. Car thieves stole an estimated eighty thousand vehicles in 1992 to smuggle across the border.[13]

If it is undeniably true that the world economy is becoming increasingly integrated, it is similarly a fact that populations throughout the world are retreating into tribalism of an exclusionary, often violent nature. Is today's nationalism merely a variant of the nineteenth-century phenomenon? Clearly not, or at least not altogether, given the declining autonomy of the nation-state, the primary vehicle for the empowerment and dissemination of nationalist feeling in the past. Claims to specific territory, whose borders are fixed and penetrable only with the acquiescence of the country's rulers, are difficult to justify at a time when the border itself is in many senses indefensible. Today's tribalism matches nineteenth-century nationalism's fervour, certainly. To a large extent, it shares traditional nationalism's vocabulary; many tribalists extol the virtues of 'national' sovereignty and cultural commonality with as much commitment as any proponent of national self-determination in the early 1900s. But it is becoming increasingly obvious that the nation-state lacks the autonomous power it once wielded; as a consequence, 'nationalist' agitation in the 1990s is likely to develop a localist aspect that emphasizes community over country, cultural and social ties over territory, the nation *tout court* over the specific qualities and advantages of the traditional nation-state and its physical borders.

This aspect of modern nationalism suggests we may soon need to decouple 'nation' and 'state', or perhaps return to an older definition of the nation, that is, the tightly defined community into which one is born. The nation-state hybrid was a peculiar feature of a world system in which national governments could be held responsible for the full range of economic and political aspects of nationhood, within specific territorial borders. The nation-state thereby became the repository of cultural ideals and the scribe of official history. It patrolled borders, and defined what those borders would include and exclude. The state remains in place, even if it must increasingly share power with other polities – supranational and subnational. But it can no longer effectively patrol those borders; certainly not on its own.

In Adam Watson's words: 'the modern successors of the European princes find themselves constrained by the pressures of a tightening system and by the institutions and practices of a more integrated society to act increasingly in ways that deprive them of independence *de facto*, externally and internally . . . while leaving intact the symbolic legitimacy of the state and varying degrees of real autonomy.'[14]

One cannot fail to recognize a concern among voters, particularly in the West, that the decline of nation-state autonomy is already affecting them deeply and not always in benign ways. Job losses in traditional industries and increased foreign investment in real estate, corporate ownership and the manufacturing base have incited considerable popular dissatisfaction. At the same time, a decade of deregulation, tax cuts, and market liberalization in most western nations has increased the gap between rich and poor. In the US, the richest one per cent of households owned thirty-seven per cent of private net worth in 1989, up from thirty-one per cent in 1983. Of the country's total private net worth in 1989, the top one per cent owned $5.7 billion while the bottom ninety per cent owned $4.8 billion.[15] A similar widening of the rich–poor gap was recorded in Britain and elsewhere in the West.[16] The emergence of two solitudes in parts of the industrialized world has threatened the consensus about the role of national governments in representing a broad range of interests within domestic society. Nowhere are those solitudes more obvious than in large cities such as Los Angeles, London, or New York, where rich suburban satellites exist cheek by jowl with poor neighbourhoods.

In the aftermath of the Los Angeles riots in the spring of 1992, the divisions between communities – based on race, income, perhaps culture – were painfully evident. As the *New York Times* reported from Simi Valley, scene of the trial which led to the acquittal of the white policemen charged with the use of unreasonable force against black motorist Rodney King, '. . . dozens of men and women spoke of the peace and pleasure of living among people with attitudes and aspirations that match their own; of sharing a community with others who own houses, work for a living, and obey the social contract.'[17]

The declining autonomy of national governments has not yet dissolved the ties of allegiance between the citizen and the nation-state. The 'nation' is still intact, as separatist movements in the former Soviet Union, the former Yugoslavia and elsewhere amply attest. Nationalists today continue to derive strength from perceived commonalities – historical, cultural, linguistic, ethnic. These belief-systems maintain their strength even when the believers are bereft of secure physical borders. Individuals who have never met, who indeed may never meet, are nonetheless convinced that they share a belief-system distinct from that of any other group. Such is the strength of this form of social organization that the nation will survive the weakening of the link between 'nation' and 'state' which inevitably will result from the challenges of the international economy and the increasing integration of national economies into a single, interconnected whole. Indeed, nationalism in this sense will do more than survive; frustration at the declining power of the nation-state is apt to fuel greater attachment to the community, as a buttress against the anchorlessness that the global economy engenders. The question becomes: what community, if not the nation-state?

The likely answer is: many. The erosion of the power of the nation-state has meant that there are several new claims on the allegiance of citizens when it comes to deciding how those commonalities are to be expressed. This creates the conditions for a multiplicity of allegiances: locally, in municipalities, even neighbourhoods; regionally, as with the growing numbers of west Europeans willing to define themselves as 'European' as well as 'French' or 'English'; provincially, when 'states within states' are granted a measure of autonomy in specific public-policy areas.

This multiplicity of allegiances is already manifest in Europe. 'The emergence of a diffuse sense of European identity has not led to a transfer of loyalties from the national to the European level, as some early theorists and proponents of European integration foresaw. What we have observed across western Europe over the last two decades is a shift toward multiple loyalties, with the single focus on the nation supplanted by European and regional affiliations above and below.'[18]

The shifts in communities and their allegiances affect not just small countries of eastern and western Europe. The United States, perhaps more than any other country, sought to find a way of accommodating communities so diverse in their histories, aims and cultures within a transnational ideology, one that promised much and sought to subvert the older allegiances. But now new patterns of allegiance are likely to replace the pre-eminence of affiliation to the nation that has typified the past two centuries. In other words, the famed melting pot, from which Americans emerged with a set of shared values, interests and concerns, is no longer bubbling. Multiple communities are replacing the single community. Pluralism is giving way to fragmentation. Indications that such alternative allegiances are not only possible but indeed probable can already be seen. For example, concerns about the state of the environment have encouraged citizens to fashion a global awareness that transcends national affiliation. While the band of 'internationalist' Greens is admittedly small, their influence is growing. Clearly, the ties to a specific nation-state are weakening, at least for some. At the other end of the spectrum, far narrower allegiances can be found, even at the level of the local neighbourhood.

In multicultural societies such as the US there has long been a tradition of hyphenated citizens – Italian-Americans, Polish-Americans, and so on. But the strength of US nationalism lay in its ability to turn its immigrants into citizens in seemingly effortless fashion. In recent years, that facility has faltered. The weakening ties between citizens and government have provoked growing frustration and encouraged people to look locally for comfort. In most large cities, 'looking locally' involves a retreat into one or another of urban America's ethnic enclaves. Particularly for the poor in the inner cities, neighbourhoods tend to be dominated by specific ethnic groups, and local services are apt to be provided in a language other than English.[19] The new localism has many origins, not least in the policy of the Reagan government to shift responsibility for social programmes onto state and local governments. As locally provided services become one of the primary foci of daily life, ethnic, racial and linguistic divisions tend to be reinforced. Poverty has also helped 'tribalize' American urban life, as the race riots in Los Angeles showed.

Localism is growing in Europe as well, again particularly in large cities. Riots on the housing estates in the suburbs of Paris in 1991 highlighted the degree to which immigrants have remained outside the mainstream of French culture. The multiracial societies of Europe and America are not new: the ratio of immigrants to natives in the US and France, for example, is roughly the same today as in the 1960s. But the processes of acculturation are no longer as effective, and one major reason is the decline in the role of the nation-state in determining and channelling national culture and values. That work is far more likely to occur at local level, a trend that strengthens the ethnic ties a newcomer brings with him to the new country.

While localism can act to reinforce ethnic divisions, it is apt to have a profound effect on native citizens as well. Local attachments are likely to grow wherever the nation-state abdicates its role as the prime mediator between the citizen and his nation. As a consequence, the 'nation' will find other means of expression, led perhaps by a reliance on smaller units of political affiliation – as small as the local community in which the citizen lives.

The prospect of such splintering has serious implications. How are relations among communities to be managed? With allegiances shared among international, national and local levels, the difficulties are enormous. Can one forge an international commitment to human rights, for example, that would effectively challenge any efforts to deny rights to minorities within communities? There have been recent calls for the creation of legal protection for minorities, under international law, perhaps sponsored by the United Nations Commission on Human Rights.[20] But in the absence of effective global policemen, what happens when wayward communities refuse to bend?

Security issues, though fraught, may prove easier to resolve than questions of accountability in the global economic system. The global economy also needs rules and regulations, and mechanisms to ensure that they are followed. Such a global system was maintained by the US in the years following the Second World War. It is no less necessary in an era where the focus of political allegiance is fragmented and multiple.

The changes we have talked about – rapid advances in the technology of communication, of industrialism, of military power and of capitalism – have been proceeding apace since the beginning of the modern age. Indeed, they are, in essence, what constitutes 'modernity'. Society has failed to keep pace with them on many occasions. The post-war acceleration of transnational linkages is just the latest in a long line of dislocating structural change that communities have found difficult to accommodate.

We do not know how to handle these changes. We have learnt a great deal about how to handle technical change; the theories we have about our own societies are weaker. We do not know much about economics – even about growth. We know little about the dynamics of societies, about what makes them stay together or come apart; and we know very little indeed about how to arrange political systems.

What we do know is geared to fundamentally nineteenth-century ways of thinking: and these are fast becoming irrelevant. Most of them are dependent on the nation-state, on a system of political organization that accords very poorly with the present reality, and even less with the probable future.

The predominant form of community that has developed in reaction to the forces of modernity has been the nation-state. It has evolved as the single most important form of social organization, as the main actor in international relations, as the fundamental economic unit and as the most familiar political landmark in discussions of how the world should operate.

But the forces of modernity do not inherently respect nationality. There is nothing national about capitalism, industrialism, warfare or technology, the principal motors of change. Each has developed within national frameworks, but that is no longer necessary nor even desired. We are reaching a point where the motors of change have outgrown nationalism, even if the rest of us have not. There is no reason to think that this process is over. The enormous changes which shook the world in 1989 are still reverberating. They do not represent the end of history: just one set of milestones.

This creates a set of conditions for diplomacy and inter-state relations that is decisively different from the pre-Cold War pattern, but yet reflects the forms that it generated. These are not national, but we have not found anything to put in their place; we may have transcended the old instabilities of mass violence, but our system is not in any sense stable. There are grave problems in building a post-national international society; but that does not undermine the need to do so, in view of the complex problems of organizing the linkages among modern societies. In the following sections we deal with the ways in which different actors cope with the uncomfortable reality of this new global society, and the emerging rules about how authority and power are dispersed and concentrated.

We first look at the extent to which regionalism and tribalism are already vying with the traditional nation-state as potent new political forces in a global age. We trace the emergence of trading blocs, and the effect these have on the international system and on the individual citizen. We next assess the characteristics of the modern transnational corporation and its relations with state and citizens; it, more than any other body, has helped to create the global dimension to the 1990s. The disenfranchisement of the citizen is the focus of Chapter Three.

The conventional reference points of citizenship in society, particularly guarantees of democratic accountability, are fast disappearing, or at least being rearranged. Part instrument, part subject of the process, the state is the subject of Chapter Four. We examine the ways in which states cope with the changing landscape of international relations, but also with their citizens.

All of these chapters are devoted to the ways in which different actors knit together a world society, and the pressures that this causes. But it implies that there is no possibility of opting out. In Chapter Five, we examine ways of challenging world society and the capitalist system: is the process we have described, which is so unstable, and so poorly equipped to handle change, liable to give way under the onslaught of a sustained, radical critique? Liberalism, capitalism and democracy, no longer effectively yoked together by the nation-state, have powerful enemies.

1

Tribalism, Regionalism and Globalism

'If I had my way, I'd pay a third of all my taxes to an international fund dedicated to solving world problems . . . a third to my community, where my children are educated and my family lives. And then a last third to my country, which each year does less and less for me in terms of security or well-being and instead subsidises special interests.'   KENICHI OHMAE[1]

The forces of globalization have gone a long way toward creating a single economic, political, military space. Trade, investment and information flows increasingly freely between nations. The sight of Pakistani and US soldiers fighting together in Africa no longer surprises us. Virtually every day, somewhere in the world, an international body is meeting to consider a problem that crosses borders, be it the environment, organized crime or settlement risk. At the same time, the decline of the US, the collapse of the Soviet Union and the growth of the international economy have incited or strengthened a host of tribalist tendencies worldwide. Fragmentation within existing nation-states – along ethnic, linguistic and religious lines – is occurring in eastern Europe, in Africa and in the states of the former Soviet Union.

Even in the traditional nation-states, tribalism is growing. Scots in the United Kingdom, Catalans and the Basques in Spain, and Lombards in Italy are increasingly vigorous in their demands for an even greater measure of self-administration. They seek a level of comfort in their communities to withstand the complexity and atomization that modern capitalism has wrought on their lives and to free themselves from domination by 'alien' elites.

We see in the chapters that follow where such tendencies might lead. Here, we outline the extent to which tribalism already vies with national affiliations for the hearts and minds of citizens, and the extent to which the concomitant growth in regional blocs and local organizations is undercutting the legitimacy of the nation-state as the basic form of political association.

Fragmentation and integration have helped undercut traditional forms of affiliation. They are breaking down the bases of traditional societies throughout the world as they have since print capitalism, the rising costs of war and shifts in agricultural production began the process that created the modern state. But in our age they are also weakening political elites, compromising their power to reallocate resources and to promote stability. The authority of governments is being undermined and there is nothing to replace it. The relationship of the individual to the economy in which he operates is increasingly unmediated by the forces of national government.

But atomization has not altogether destroyed the allegiances citizens feel. It has not convinced individuals that they have no right to seek redress if they are economically disadvantaged. It has not transformed their sense of community, their need to belong. It has displaced it, shifting allegiances to different levels, different centres. The individual will increasingly seek forms of association that are not dependent on the traditional nation-state. Yet he will do so in recognizable ways; for the power of nationalism – based on perceived commonalities of ethnic background, religion, language – is undiluted. There is no doubt that the terms of these tribalist demands are far from new. Reference to decades, even centuries, of common cultural development strengthen the claims of nationalists throughout the world. But the multiplicity of tribalist agitation, along with indications that demands for autonomy within nation-states are now likely to be met in many instances, are the results of a paradigm shift. The character of the nation-state itself is mutating, as the workings of the global economy undermine the sovereignty of national governments. Citizens of nation-states are reimagining their communities, seeking alternative forms of allegiance and affiliation. The age of cultural internationalism is far in the future, if it comes at all; nationalist feeling, virulent and vibrant, is finding narrower channels.

We have seen how the international economy has changed since the Second World War. One of the most significant effects has been to undermine the principle that economies must be of a certain 'size' to compete. The success of city-states such as Hong Kong and Singapore have shown that changes in technology and the evolving features of the international financial system have allowed even small economies to operate efficiently, provided they are integrated into the global system. That makes independence for small states appear far more realistic than might have been the case in the early years of the century. The impossibility of holding states together by force, and the lack of external assistance from the superpowers to do so, has increased the incidence of these *kleinstaaterei*.

At the same time, the changes have helped transform the character of the individual's relationship to the nation-state. The difficulty of determining economic policy on a national basis and the growing role of state-to-state co-operation together conspire to reduce the legitimacy of the nation-state in its nineteenth-century form. In the words of Daniel Bell, the nation-state is too big for the little things and too small for the big things.[2] This yields more than its fair share of contradictions in an age of nationalist revival. Responses to the contradictions inherent in the uncomfortable co-existence of tribalism and globalism have been understandably contradictory: the emergence of local politics that attract citizens wary of the weakened nation-state's ability to reflect their concerns; and the pressure to form regional associations that serve to protect citizens from the exigencies of the global economy but that, in the absence of democratic structures, reduce their control over decision-making.

Attachment to the local community, even as the reach of the global system is extended, poses dangers. The nation-state, in its heyday, was able to bridge that contradiction to some extent by determining a 'national interest', by judging the necessary balance between the public and the private spheres, by responding to demands for wealth-sharing and even treatment before the law. If the glue that kept multi-ethnic nation-states together is weakened, the ties that bind co-religionists, ethnic groups, or members of distinct cultural groups can only grow in strength. In Sarajevo, the capital of Bosnia, Muslims, Croats and Serbs lived together, often side by side in the same apartment block. The dissolution of the Yugoslav state created a vacuum filled quickly by tribalism, and a battle waged among imagined communities with all the fury that references to common culture and history can inspire.

In the former Yugoslavia, the ethnic and religious mixtures simply do not lend themselves to the type of territorial and political settlement dictated by the nineteenth-century nation-state. But if this is the most graphic example, others abound. The Caucasus, former Soviet central Asia, the rest of the Balkans, Russia itself, are all typified by a very high degree of ethnic and religious intermixture, sometimes the result of conscious effort, sometimes of historical evolution. The point is that increasingly every state is multi-ethnic, containing both historical minorities and new immigrants, in Europe and beyond. The assumptions of nineteenth-century nationalists do not apply even to France or Britain, those classic exemplars. It is, however, in the former Soviet bloc that this is most likely to lead to large-scale violence.

The Yugoslav case, sadly, may prove to be a prototype of tribalist agitation in the countries of the former Soviet bloc. The collapse of the Soviet state system, dedicated in part to containing ethnic differences by denying their existence, has allowed old hatreds to resurface. At the same time, forty years of communist rule, characterized by limits on political freedom and lesser or greater reliance on state planning (depending on the country) have produced a politics unused to democratic debate and decision-making. The electorate in the former Yugoslavia is distrustful of political leaders and far from adept at distinguishing truth from rhetoric. The result is chaos: ethnic and linguistic groups are manipulable by charismatic leaders willing to rewrite history in the service of nationalism; very real grievances (wholesale terror and murder during the war) are either dismissed out of hand or recast in the form of epic, genocidal war crimes, depending on which side you listen to; 'history' is invoked in mutually exclusive ways to bolster claims on all sides. By devaluing truth in the service of stability, the Soviet model stifled pluralism and legitimate debate. That legacy complicates the claims and counter-claims in the former Yugoslavia and in other countries of the old Soviet bloc.

As well, the collapse of the Soviet economic system has created acute problems that are only compounded by civil war. Shortages are chronic, distribution networks dogged by bottlenecks and incomes outstripped by price increases. The integration of command economies into the world capitalist economy has proved far more difficult than the purveyors of 'shock therapy' envisaged in 1989. Part of the problem stems from the rudimentary progress so far made on creating the framework for a market economy – particularly, the protection of private property and the rule of commercial law. Economic privation has made many people desperate, and increased the appeal of demagogues promising quick fixes. The answer, many leaders preach, lies in wresting control of historic homelands, of banishing the enemy, the 'other', of reclaiming control over our private lives. That control is best exerted within those communities that grant the greatest level of comfort and security: not the old Yugoslav state, with its associations of political interference from the centre; not even the successor states, with their pre-break-up borders; but new 'old' communities defined by a mixture of myth and reality.

Another element of the new tribalism can be seen in the rush by new states to seek membership of international clubs. Slovenia moved very quickly to assert its place in the European Community; so have the Baltic states. None of them seeks sovereignty *tout court*. All of them recognize limits to their autonomy and try to reconcile this with national independence. Estonia accepted the strictures of the Council of Europe over a proposed new citizenship law in 1993, despite opposition from nationalist factions. Co-operation is recurring because for purposes of security, prosperity and well-being, no small state can be an island. The fragmentation of existing nation-states has made it all the more important for governments to seek regional economic and political ties with neighbours and trading partners. The explosion in regionalism, as much as tribalism, is connected to the growing dominance of the global economy and the limits it imposes on states and domestic economies, and on political control exerted at national level. Barring the emergence of a truly international politics, such regional ties allow states to co-ordinate policy as a buffer against the dictates of international capitalism even as they are required to follow the general rules.

In attempts to resolve the contradictions of tribalism and globalism, the principal solution in sum has been to seek forms of organization beyond national sovereignty, either above it or below it. Within and among nation-states, a host of formal and informal associations has developed in the course of the past forty years. These are driven by a sense of common purpose, a desire to forge associations that go beyond or fall short of the territorial specificity of the nation-state. Free-trading arrangements, regional parliaments, sector-based special-interest groups, regional economic co-operation pacts – the form and function of these ties are myriad. They are not, however, inherently democratic, and ways to render them accountable have been too little explored.

Some such arrangements have a long pedigree. The British Commonwealth emerged from the ashes of the Empire and continues to have some measure of influence, albeit on a narrow set of issues. A free-franc zone was established, similarly, in the former French colonies of Africa, bolstered by a more broadly defined Francophonie linking French-speaking nations as economically varied as Quebec, Senegal, the Central African Republic, and Belgium. But the momentum toward the regionalization of economic management was established only with the creation of a world economy in the decades after the Second World War.

The impulses behind regionalism (whether within or among existing nation-states) derive from the relationship of groups to the functioning of the global economy and, increasingly, the relationship between the state and the transnational corporation. Alongside a global agreement on all forms of trade, under the auspices of the General Agreement on Tariffs and Trade, regionalism is emerging as an alternative, as multi-state organizations seek direct contact with the TNCs – and with other regional bodies – as the interdependent world economy demands.

The two main trading blocs are the European Union and the North America Free Trade Agreement (NAFTA). The EU is by far the most advanced, as we have described.[3] The non-EU countries of western Europe – grouped as the European Free Trade Association – have negotiated a separate agreement with the Community known as the European Economic Area. The EFTA nations (Switzerland, Austria, Finland, Sweden, Norway, Iceland and Liechtenstein) will accept the bulk of EU legislation in exchange for access to the Common Market.

The EU has also negotiated pacts with a handful of eastern European countries. Under the 'associate' membership formula with Hungary, the successor states of the former Czechoslovakia, and Poland, the EU has promised to remove most quotas at once; tariffs will be phased out over two to five years. The east European nations will in turn phase out their quotas and tariffs over four to ten years. In each case, sixty per cent local content is necessary for goods manufactured in the East to be imported duty-free into the EU. Further, albeit severely limited, concessions on food, textile, steel and coal have also been agreed. In return, Hungary, Poland, the Czech Republic and Slovakia will accept EU anti-competition laws, although they retain the right to subsidize backward regions. EU companies win guarantees on capital repatriation. The agreements extend to most services as well, although EU companies will be restricted in the

East European defence and financial sectors. Notably, the associate membership offers no freedom of movement for labour.[4]

The EEA and the associate membership agreements may end up being way-stations to full membership of the EU. Austria, Finland, and Sweden have already made applications, Switzerland has signalled its intention to do so, and Norway will not be far behind. Poland, the Czech Republic, Slovakia and Hungary have all declared their goal to be joining the EU as soon as possible.

The North American Free Trade Agreement (NAFTA) began life as the US-Canada Free Trade Agreement, signed in 1988, under which the world's largest bilateral trading relationship, worth $170 billion a year, would be governed by set rules and a mechanism for solving disputes.[5] Mexico negotiated with the US and Canada to join, while several Central and South American nations have expressed an interest in exploring closer economic ties with the US. The government of Chile has stated that it is ready to negotiate an FTA with the US as soon as it is allowed; it has already signed a separate economic co-operation agreement with Mexico, the first such bilateral pact in Latin America. Venezuela claims an interest in negotiating freer trade as a strategic supplier of oil to North America.

An independent study[6] suggests that Mexican-US trade will be boosted by $24 billion under NAFTA; Mexico would gain 609,000 net new jobs, while the US would gain 130,000. Canada stands to lose 5,000 jobs, but should achieve twenty per cent higher exports and forty per cent higher imports from Mexico. The study says the agreement could 'lock in and reinforce recent economic reforms in Mexico'.

Interest in the NAFTA model has now outstripped commitment to other regional trading groups that have a longer, if spotty, history. But most Latin American nations continue to hedge their bets. Costa Rica, El Salvador, Guatemala, Honduras and Nicaragua have agreed to revive their Central American co-operation pact of the 1960s, which collapsed in 1969 following the outbreak of war between El Salvador and Honduras. The new deal is meant to be in place by 1994. The Andean Pact also has recently been revived, and Venezuela, Colombia, and Bolivia agreed in early 1992 to phase out remaining trade barriers between them. Ecuador and Peru are to join later. The five are working on a common external tariff, a goal made possible because of progress in reducing domestic tariffs sharply in recent years. Meanwhile, Brazil and Argentina launched the Mercosur pact in 1988, joined by Uruguay and Paraguay in 1991. By 1994, there is meant to be a free market in goods, services, and even labour. The success of the agreement is still in doubt, not least because of Brazil's economic management problems and the social tensions created by Argentina's market reforms.

English-speaking nations in the Caribbean are kick-starting the near-moribund Caricom pact, established in 1973. But they, like the nations of Central and South America, are likely to seek membership in the emerging 'Enterprise for the Americas', a Reagan-Bush initiative. Their biggest fear is that the Caribbean Basin Initiative, which gave them duty-free access to the US market for an admittedly small number of products, will be superseded by NAFTA, leaving them out in the cold.

The FTA binge in the Americas has several proximate causes. The first stems from the degree of policy convergence in the region. From the high-water mark of state interventionism and 'industrialism behind barriers' of the 1960s and early 1970s, Central and South America are now privatizing and reforming with a vengeance, making effective economic co-operation much more likely to survive a host of political pressures from within. At the same time, fear of a failure at the GATT and the loss of real or potential support from the now-defunct Soviet Union together served to pressurize Third World nations in the Americas to seek a partnership with the regional power – the US. There is some hope that the partnership could reduce the level of US military interference in the region, a staple of Central American history for the last hundred years.[7]

The Americas are not alone in forming the embryo of a trading bloc based on the leadership of a regional economic power. In Asia, efforts are underway to expand the Association of South-east Asian Nations, which is comprised of the Philippines, Indonesia, Thailand, Singapore, Malaysia and Brunei, and boasts a combined population of 320 million. They agreed early in 1992 to reduce tariffs over the following fifteen years and to consider closer ties on security and defence issues as well. Some members are courting support for an expansion of the regional association to include newly industrializing nations such as South Korea and Taiwan, while Malaysia has even called for a East Asian Economic Grouping that would take in the region's leading power, Japan, but exclude Pacific Rim countries of the English-speaking world such as the USA, Australia and Canada.[8]

Even Africa has seen a revival of efforts to create effective regional trading arrangements, although sub-Saharan nations so far reject a role for South Africa and so are toying only with pacts among poor equals without the benefit of a regional economic power acting as anchor. There are two main associations, the biggest of them the eighteen-nation Preferential Trade Area of eastern and southern Africa (Angola, Lesotho, Malawi, Mozambique, Namibia, Zambia, Swaziland, Tanzania, Zimbabwe, Burundi, Comoros, Djibouti, Ethiopia, Kenya, Mauritius, Rwanda, Somalia, and Uganda). It wants to merge with the Southern African Development Co-ordination Conference (grouping the first nine of the PTA's membership list plus Botswana), set up in 1980 explicitly to lessen regional dependence on South Africa.

Elsewhere in the world, the Maghreb nations of North Africa are widening regional ties, while the Gulf states continue to co-ordinate policy within the Gulf Co-operation Council. Australia and New Zealand operate the Anzus agreement, while countries abutting the Baltic Sea are attempting to forge a modern version of the Hanseatic League. Turkey is wooing the Muslim states of the former Soviet Union with which it shares an ethnic-religious mix. The members of these emerging regional trading groups – at least those furthest along the road toward integration – recognize explicitly the need for co-ordinated reform of their domestic economies and as such are willing to accept the consequent loss of national sovereignty. The common thread of most of these regional arrangements is the convergence of policy agendas. As fewer and fewer countries find it possible to remain outside the global economic system, the incidence of supranational co-operation is set to increase.

But there are other kinds of regionalism that are already posing equally potent threats to the traditional functioning of nation-states. Subnational groupings – including regional parliaments and economic co-operation councils – have proliferated, particularly in Europe. Recognizing that several key economic issues are increasingly taken at supranational level, regions are keen to win greater authority from centralized government to provide local services.

Countries with strong federalist traditions – post-war Germany is an obvious example – already have potent state or provincial governments. But even traditionally centralist states such as France and Spain have expanded the role of regional parliaments and councils, awarding not only powers of expenditure but also of taxation to local regions. These tiers of government no longer concentrate solely on road-building and infrastructural development and maintenance, but may have economic planning departments and councils that group members of the educational community and local businesses.

In countries such as France, Spain, Britain, Germany, and even India and several developing countries in Latin America, regional governments are increasingly important. France provides a striking example.[9] The twenty-two regional governments (excluding, that is, overseas *départements* such as Martinique and Guadeloupe) have huge and growing influence over the relationship between the citizen and the seat of political power. Following a radical and extensive devolution of authority in the early 1980s, regional governments have seen their area of competence enlarged considerably. Infrastructural development (particularly of roads and industrial zones) has long been handled primarily by local government. Housing, the delivery of social services such as daycare, even retraining for the unemployed are now all seen as part of the proper task of the regions. Hand in hand has gone a restructuring of the political system under which local officials are elected. France has also granted taxation authority to the local governments, aligning political power with the fund-raising capability that truly accountable government needs. It also shares a portion of consumption tax revenues raised by the centre.

In France, the central government continues to redistribute general tax revenues to needy departments; but the spending of these funds is now labelled as co-operation rather than as brute redistributive transfer. Signs on highways in France often announce that roadworks are sponsored first by the locality and then by regional governments. Only then is the state's contribution noted. Partly as a result, local politicians have become media stars in France. Witness the rise to fame of Toulouse's activist mayor Dominique Baudis, credited with making La Ville Rose into one of France's 'technopoles', or high-tech centres. (The presence of the giant Aérospatiale facility on the town's outskirts, and the highly developed college and university system, no doubt helped. But Baudis has built his political base primarily through an ability to convince the local population that the success is largely his.)

France is only one – if the most extensive – example of the trend towards devolution of power in Europe. In Spain, seventeen regional governments exercise control over a broad range of services. Of the successful Spanish regions, Catalonia is as rich as Britain on a per capita basis, and its leaders expect per capita incomes to grow to 125 per cent of the EU average within five years.[10] Under Spanish decentralization, Catalonia makes payments to the centre in order to help finance the needs of less wealthy regions. In return, it exercises autonomy in a range of areas, including education, broadcasting, and regional economic policy. The regions of Spain include several with strong independent historical traditions – Andalucia, Galicia, the Basque country, and Catalonia – which never succumbed to Franco's attempts to impose a single, national culture. Demands for greater devolution have been voiced with growing vehemence in recent years.[11]

In Germany, the state governments are promoting decentralized structures for meeting local needs even within an already uniquely decentralized federal system imposed by the Allies after the Second World War. In Mexico, the northern states abutting the US border have a significant degree of autonomy in fashioning local political and economic policy. Even in Britain, where local-government financing is still dictated in large measure by the centre, attempts have been made to create local accountability through a revamped system of local taxation. Although the community charge, or poll tax, was withdrawn in the face of persistent criticisms from local populations over its cost, a modified financing system is now in place, and is likely over time to strengthen ties between local governments and the residents they represent. While the Conservative victory in 1992 ensured that a form of direct local taxation is unlikely to be implemented in the short run, the fact that both opposition parties campaigned for greater devolution to the regions suggests that a rebalancing of authority among the centre, the regions, and local government will remain on the political agenda.

In the US, states such as Arkansas have developed educational training programmes aimed at promoting local employment, while Massachusetts brought in a modified form of state-sponsored medical insurance. The US moves came in reaction to a diminution of the financing role of the federal government under President Ronald Reagan, but are set to continue under the Democrats.

Consider, too, the activities of multi-municipal associations in states such as California, and in countries such as Britain and France. Mayors of US cities in close proximity are co-ordinating policies ranging from transportation to waste disposal, all the while strengthening their political ties. They deal directly with companies operating in their jurisdictions, and compete to attract new investment. City officials have worked with suburban councils in the Paris region to produce a ten-year plan to develop the Île-de-France as a European financial and business centre. Both the Conservative and Labour parties in Britain went into the last national election promising a new regional structure for London, to provide the capital with a co-ordinating body answering to the perceived common needs of Londoners.

At the same time, various forms of inter-regional co-operation – sectoral, cultural, educational – have developed in Europe and elsewhere. Some of these already operate across formally national boundaries. Technical exchanges are part of the growing links of regions bordering the Rhine, for example, while extensive transport projects, coupled with technical and sectoral co-operation agreements, are bringing together regions on both sides of the Franco–Spanish border. Even municipal governments, often in association with neighbouring councils, are expanding their activities beyond the traditional sphere of waste disposal, sewage, street lighting, and so on by developing incentive programmes to attract new investment and by establishing councils that bring local employers and local educational institutes together to develop training and job-creation schemes. They are increasingly working with other, not necessarily contiguous, local governments with similar economic profiles – hence, for instance, the links between the governments of Calgary and Houston, both oil towns.

It is not surprising that the trend towards regionalism has been most evident in Europe.[12] As the European Union pressed ahead with its Single Market, and confirmed the importance of the European Commission in overseeing economic integration, direct lines of communication between the regions and the supranational centre in Brussels opened up, even when national governments were wary of being bypassed. In a recent example, environmental groups in the Twyford Valley appealed for EU intervention to halt the British government's extension of the M3 motorway through a rural site in southern England, although the Commission subsequently withdrew its opposition. Similarly, local activists enlisted EU support to establish a bird sanctuary on land in south-west France earmarked by the national government in Paris for a highway. In parts of the world where strong supranational structures have yet to emerge, the regionalist trend is more subdued.

As yet, these trends have not unhitched the citizen from the nation-state. In most countries, reference to the central government remains the obvious, primary reflex. At the very least, the state is relied upon to represent citizens at international level, on issues ranging from the global environment to international trading rules to financial services deregulation. But the emerging consensus on the global economy, to which no country is immune, has already reduced the nation-state's autonomy. The growth in regional trading blocs has already demanded some tentative pooling of sovereignty among member-states. Local and regional governments have already been awarded powers that encroach on the traditional role of the sovereign state.

The explosion in the number of local and regional organizations and networks has, however, generated the makings of a further contradiction between tribalism and globalism. Is it realistic to construct all these associations within one global structure? Or do the regional blocs that have emerged undercut global co-operation?

In the realm of international security the question has only raised its head in the past three years. Competition between Nato and the WEU, the EU's defence arm, was largely resolved in favour of the former. The alliance is a more global body and, crucially, includes the US, without which military action remains all but impossible. However, the Bosnian situation brought the UN and Nato into conflict over both strategy and tactics, weakening both organizations. The Somalian peace-keeping operation was stymied by the different strategies of competing national units. In general, problems between regional security and global security organizations seem likely to proliferate, with the OAS, UN, EU, CSCE, and CIS being only some of the acronyms in apparent conflict.

The conflict between regional and global organization is already much more apparent in economic co-operation. The GATT represents one of the last functioning elements of the US-backed international system established after the Second World War. Some of the institutions and agreements associated with that system have disappeared altogether, or have at least ceased to be meaningful. Bretton Woods and the Gold Standard disappeared in the 1970s. The Organization for Economic Co-operation & Development has lost a measure of credibility as the 'club of rich nations'. From its height of effectiveness in the mid-1980s, the Group of Seven leading industrialized nations is increasingly unable to establish common ground on relative currency-exchange rates and on the size of trade surpluses and deficits. The International Monetary Fund and the World Bank have been more successful, largely because their mandates have been so narrowly focused. They have become referees in the process by which 'national' economies in the developing world are subsumed by the global system.

Co-operation at regional level among several countries that share borders and histories is proving a more satisfying vehicle for the creation of common ground rules on economic issues. In this sense, the GATT is oddly retrograde: it posits a central role for the nation-state in the negotiation of international rules on trade. It requires signatories to accept a set of unified rules and guidelines governing trade between and among explicitly 'national' economies. With the emergence of a transnational economy, and one based increasingly not on industrial products but on a range of 'invisibles' such as financial services, computer software, or television programming, the rules established under early rounds of the GATT proved too narrow to be of long-term effectiveness. The Uruguay Round, launched at Punta del Este in Uruguay in 1986, promised to bring trade in services, protection of copyright and intellectual property, and trade in agricultural goods within the ambit of the GATT for the first time. That decision explicitly recognized the changing structure of the international economy, and the demand – voiced particularly but not exclusively by managers of transnational corporations – for common rules governing cross-border economic relations.

The difficulty faced by negotiators in finalizing the Round attested to the lingering strength of the nation-state in the world order. Governments were unwilling to give up advantage in the negotiations, challenged by domestic special interests ranging from farmers to biotechnology firms to seek concessions. A deal was ultimately reached, but it fell far short of the goals sketched when the Round was launched. Agricultural subsidies will not be phased out completely; full protection for intellectual property in the Third World will not be secured; the complicated matrix of local protectionisms will not be negotiated out of existence.

One reason for the difficulties at the GATT was the concomitant growth in other forms of economic co-operation that suit governments better. The reality of the world economy, however, is not simply expressed either in regional, national, local or international terms. The combination of financial deregulation, foreign direct investment and industrial change has created what Richard O'Brien calls 'the end of geography', a dramatic reordering of economic activity that pays little heed to borders. He has also suggested that for finance, at least, 'the region is the least coherent focus'. Once financial expansion has crossed national borders, 'there is no clear geographical limit to its scope ... interaction outside one nation or market can just as easily be with a market or players across the globe as in the region.'[13] Attempts by the European Union, for instance, to create a single financial marketplace have been complicated by the strong links all players have with extra-European markets, and by the sharp distinctions within Europe between markets.

There have been persistent worries about the effect of trade blocs on global commerce. The EU and North America have always claimed that their efforts at liberalization have been trade-creating rather than trade-diverting, but some critics – in particular of the EU – say that the Union has evolved into 'Fortress Europe'. Indeed, a recent study concludes: 'By 1990 EU members were trading sixty-eight per cent more with one another than proximity, income, and their countries' openness to imports would predict.'[14] There is no doubt that France would like to extend this. Before the Copenhagen Summit in 1993, President François Mitterrand explicitly referred to the need for 'Community preference'.

The relations between the blocs and their main trading partners are far from the open trading ideal. The US and Japan have reached agreements that strike European officials as being close to managed, as opposed to free, trade. Europe is keen on using anti-dumping policy and voluntary restraint agreements, such as that covering EU–Japanese trade in cars. Trade blocs seem to be emerging as a way of limiting, not just managing, a global economy.

Creating rules to handle foreign direct investment within blocs is even more difficult, as the EU has found. It has increasingly clashed with the US, Japan, and the NICs over the terms of production within its borders, notably those defining rules of origin. The Commission has tried to maintain vigilance about the level of subsidies offered to attract fresh investment, but both the EU and the US have had occasion to be concerned about the fierce competition among states, regions, even municipalities bent on enticing investors.

In short, the global economy does not dovetail very neatly with efforts to create either local or regional blocs. This should not come as any great surprise, given that the global economy has been created not by nations and states but by transnational corporations, entities which exist outside the politics of territoriality. Their marketplaces bear little relation to the efforts of politicians and officials to create new organizational structures, new ways to regulate and control and even less relation to the citizen, whose interests in the global economy are, in a formal sense, unrepresented.

2

State, Nation and Corporation

'Globalization is not an equalizing but, on the contrary, a very uneven process. Some business corporations, economic networks, social groupings and
cultures are highly advantaged by it while others are
seriously penalized or even condemned to extinction.'

ENZO MINGIONE[1]

The town of Greece in New York state wanted to buy an excavator.
These days, you have to watch your back – and, besides, patriotism
is a value that never goes out of style – so they tried to 'buy American'.
They rejected a used excavator from the Japanese company Komatsu,
in favour of one from good old John Deere, an emblem of American
agricultural life; the price advantage of the Komatsu machine was
disregarded. But they discovered on investigation that both were the
product of American-Japanese joint ventures. In fact the Komatsu
model was made in the US, whereas the John Deere one was made
in Japan. 'We would like to purchase American-made equipment and
keep Americans on the job,' said the perplexed town supervisor, 'but
it becomes a very complicated issue.'

The global economy is a very complicated place. The 'national
interest' becomes almost impossible to define as a web of connections
tie different elements of the nation to parts of the globe that are
geographically and culturally distant. Old policy tools, and their
rationale, lose their efficacy. New ones have failed to appear. The
result is not the neo-liberal dream of a world governed by commerce
and free of strife, nor the disappearance of sovereignty or nationalism.

Instead, it is a world of rapid change and conflict where the nation-state is not the main player, merely one of several.

The global economy has expanded through trade, through the creation of vast and deep capital markets, and through direct investment by companies. It is corporate activity, more than anything else, which has created a global space out of a world of nations and sovereignties. Fully one-third of 'private productive assets are under the common governance' of TNCs, according to UNCTAD.[2] Susan Strange says that 'by 1985 international production – production by transnationals outside their home base – actually exceeded the volume of world trade.'[3] Trade within firms, rather than between them, takes a growing proportion of world commerce.

The largest transnationals are titanic: in terms of size, the contest between countries and corporations is fairly unequal. In 1980 the sales of each of the top ten multinationals was over $28bn, more than the GDP of eighty-seven countries. Since then, the proliferation of small states, and the fracturing of larger ones, while corporations have expanded exponentially, has probably made the competition even more unequal. Exxon's sales in 1980 were larger than the GDP of ninety-six countries, well ahead of Austria, Denmark and Norway.[4] The order has changed over the decade, with Exxon losing out a little to finish between Indonesia and South Africa, and Austria gaining some ground[5]; but a report by the Conference Board of New York shows that if General Motors were a country, it would have the world's twentieth largest economy. Ford comes in just behind Denmark, and IBM behind Thailand. The point that the Conference Board makes is that there are more TNCs in the top hundred and fewer countries; 47 to 53 in the 1990 list, with only 39 to 61 in 1980.

The expansion and spread of transnational corporations has an importance that goes beyond industry or economics; it is part of a reshaping of the world's social and political structures. 'Multinationals are only the visible expression of a deeper change', says Susan Strange, 'as – in medieval Italy – the *condottieri* and their mercenaries were the visible expression of political change from a feudal state based on clan loyalty to a city-state based on wealth.'[6] She describes this internationalization of production as the 'second crucial change' in the structure of production, 'the first being the transition to a capitalist market-oriented production structure in Europe in the sixteenth century' which laid the foundations for the evolution of nation-states.[7]

TNCs operate very well in this environment; not surprisingly, perhaps, as they helped create it. But its evolution has not been peaceful. There has been no shortage of conflict, either between corporations locked in competitive struggle, or between TNCs and the governments with which they have been forced to live. In the early post-war years, frequent tensions arose between host states, into which the TNC invested, and the company and its home state. The politics of access was based on nationalism, but also on a broader opposition to US influence and the assertion of a different way of running the world economy to that put forward in Washington. It spawned the idea that sovereignty was at bay in the modern world; that by allowing in foreign companies, states were compromising their independence. This view – that global capitalism was undermining the differences between states and reducing their sovereignty – was also influential on those who predicted that a more open world economy would, ultimately, be a more peaceful world.

The struggle was a function, in part, of the times. Most TNCs in the post-war decades were in reality American 'multinationals'. They were operating in the area of raw materials and resources, oil, food products, or minerals; and the host was typically a relatively peripheral state, less committed to the market economy than the US, often less committed to its political values. This generated a trial of strength between host states and the US, often linked to the broader struggle for a greater share in the benefits of investment but also to the anti-colonial struggle. The ultimate assertion of host-country strength was nationalization, expropriation and confiscation of enterprises and assets. One study identifies 559 acts of takeover between 1960 and 1979.[8]

These were not limited to the developing world: France and Canada both experienced backlashes against foreign investment, in both cases linked to a rejection of American hegemony, and in France's case fear of *'le défi Américain'*.[9] It led Samuel Huntington to predict in 1972 that TNCs would increasingly have a hard time gaining access to Third World countries in particular.[10] Nations had a key card to play, he said: they had the only thing worth having, control of territory, and if they denied it, the TNC had a weaker hand.

In fact, the attempt to exclude the TNC was relatively short-lived and very unsuccessful. As one author has pointed out, 'Many of the governments that did nationalize TNC subsidiaries, particularly in the minerals sector, quickly found that ownership did not necessarily give them the control they expected over local operations. This was particularly true where governments had to continue to rely on the TNC for access to downstream activities and to final markets. In some notable instances, such as the nationalization of copper mines by Zambia and Zaire, governments found that they had no alternative but to reverse previous decisions and invite the TNC back to re-establish local production.'[11]

The pendulum swung back. In the 1980s, there was a growing wave of privatization programmes in the developed and developing worlds which reopened even very sensitive areas to foreign participation. The change in attitude was associated, above all, with the shortfalls in investment, growth and trade balances which followed the onset of the debt crisis in the Third World. Perhaps the TNCs had not paid enough taxes, had not invested enough, had not exported enough, but now nobody was paying any taxes, investing or exporting. As it turned out, the TNC also had cards to play that were worth far more than the state's control of territory: it had money, technology and the skills to put them together. To paraphrase Joan Robinson, the Cambridge economist, if there is one thing worse than being exploited by a trans-national, it is not being exploited by a transnational. But as states discovered, managing direct investment was not always a question of losing sovereignty: there were benefits as well. The turn towards the global economy had a lot to do with a realization that it was not necessarily a zero-sum game, with the nation-state losing out and the corporation winning.

If the decline in Third World economies and the debt crisis of the 1980s brought the politics of access to a lower key, it was followed by a more profound change, a step closer to a single global 'space' for the transnational. For our purposes, we can regard 1989 as the opening of a new phase for the world economy. No longer was there a significant divide between the East and the West, as a hamper on the development of truly global production and consumption; at the same time, the end of the Soviet bloc was the end of a certain kind of North–South rupture. The coming down of the Berlin Wall emphasized that from now on there was to be no support, financial or political, for an anti-capitalist agenda from Moscow; but as a cor-ollary, there was to be vicious competition for aid, trade and invest-ment. The growth of new sources of investment – in particular the European Union and Japan, but increasingly former developing coun-tries, such as Korea – meant that the global economy was no longer only, or even pre-eminently, about American capitalism, or about the exploitation of scarce resources, or about the centre against the periphery.

As well as the quantitative change in the role of transnational corporations, there has been a qualitative change. The expansion of TNCs has meant that, increasingly, all firms have a global aspect to their business. This is partly because the cost base of so many sectors is established by markets that operate beyond national borders. But it is also because TNCs have shown how global strategies can be profitable. Multi-country sourcing can be less expensive than local procurement; production can be spread among several facilities and final assembly done somewhere else again. 'Think global, act local' is a slogan for almost every company. Size has become less an indicator of importance; indeed the late 1980s and early 1990s saw a shift away from large corporations to smaller ones, as exemplified by mighty IBM's decision to decentralize and pare down. Corporations also increasingly merged their efforts with partners in joint ventures or marketing deals, sharing the costs of pre-competitive research, adapting their styles to a new age of so-called 'co-operative' capitalism. That they can do so owes much to the technological revolution. Communicating among far-flung subsidiaries is effortless; just-in-time manufacturing is possible because of powerful computer tracking of ordering and shipping. Multi-country banking has become very sophisticated, allowing TNCs to move funds, track investments, and maximize financial returns.

These new trends in the global economy have defused the politics of access: but they have also created a new kind of relationship between states and transnational corporations, which has had a profound impact on governments, more profound than simply threatening autonomy.

The interaction between the state and the global market hampers the ability of nation-states – even quite large ones – to determine their economic future. It weakens the role of exchange rates in a domestic context, complicates adjustment of trade balances, and undermines national attempts to control either trade flows or industrial policy. All of these are made subject to the effects of other countries' policies; and to those of the transnational companies. As well as undermining economic policy, TNCs put an additional set of demands on the state. Their functional need is for an environment which is secure, predictable and efficient. TNCs need physical security for their own plant and employees. They also need security of labour supply and access to the market. They need predictability in the macroeconomic and policy environments. They need secure rules of patent protection and other regulatory frameworks. Traditionally, these resources are all provided by governments.

Both the need to adapt the role of the state and commercial requirements mean that corporations are drawn increasingly into other, overtly political and social tasks. Being a good citizen is part of corporate practice for many TNCs. The basis dimension is obeying the laws and keeping within the rules. But this is increasingly broadened to observing local cultural practices, more costly but perhaps profitable for the country concerned. In Mexico, for instance, one assembly plant found that by providing a once-a-week barbecue they were more likely to keep staff than by offering extra pay. Beyond this, the good citizen TNC can contribute to local charities, or provide funding for other *pro bono* activities. Companies may, more broadly, find a new role as a provider of services and goods subsidiary to those of the main product. Ford in Britain, for instance, sponsors educational projects. These benefits in general are a larger and larger part of the corporation's activities.

The result is a significant change in the balance of power between the TNC and governments. Corporate information systems make them more flexible, and often more active in the international system than governments. They create new linkages at state-to-state level, often of a highly antagonistic nature. 'Change in the production structure changes the very nature of the state. Its capabilities are changed; so are its responsibilities.'[12] The new balance between the state and the global economy thus does not remove sovereignty, or deny it; but it devalues it and erodes its importance.

Parallel to the fear (of those who opposed the spread of transnational capital) that sovereignty would be erased by the spread of a global economy was a concern that by creating large, integrated markets that drew in all consumers, all producers, national differences would be erased or eroded. The expansion of global markets has also had an impact on nationalism, but again, it is not as clear-cut as either the opponents or proponents of transnational capitalism had believed. The concept of a 'community of fate' which is so central to sustaining the nation is undermined by the dislocations introduced by global markets.

The concept of a 'national interest' becomes harder to sustain, as the people who ran Greece, New York, discovered. By dissolving national boundaries, economic globalization allows in new sources of information, new views of the world, but makes room for new conflicts too. Fundamentally, the spread of a global economy can help to undermine the idea of a national identity. Different degrees of interaction with the global economy produce different attitudes. Local commerce may be disrupted, as competition with the global market destabilizes local labour relations and local culture. The use of incentives for foreign investment may distort this further. These conflicts have a strong internal dynamic, given that some sectors of society are more influenced than others. They will frequently bring the less educated, less international sectors of society into conflict with elites. The more peripheral areas of society have less in common with the global market than those at the top of the pile, and are more open to revivals of nationalist sentiment. Equally, the association with economic success can be important for reviving assertions of national or local independence. The increase in Catalan nationalism in the 1980s was fed by a realization of the growing commercial importance of Barcelona, and its location in one of the EU's fastest growing regions. Indeed regionalism in Europe has been largely reinvented by the changing patterns of comparative advantage; as in the US, the 'foreign policies' of US states are governed principally by their growing awareness of their industrial and commercial linkages. TNCs have had trouble defining national interest too. US automakers say they don't like competing with the Japanese at home, and invoke the 'jobs for Americans' argument with great regularity. Yet they are in the process of forming alliances with Japanese firms, switching component production runs to Mexico and have long been investors in Europe.

Dissolving nationality, either by claiming 'statelessness' or promoting a view of a wider, cosmopolitan community can be a tool in managing the competitive environment. This can have political or social motivations: during the Vietnam War, for instance, Coca-Cola stripped away its troublesome associations with America, and instead said that it would 'like to teach the world to sing'. It has also become a key part of the drive in the 1980s for 'global brands', which transcend nationality, claiming identity with some more motivational or aspirational value.[13] But asserting nationality can also be a key asset to the corporation: many English purchasers of French consumer products get cachet from their identification with a class structure and a way of life. One American producer of defence equipment ran a series of glossy ads using the photography of Ansel Adams, great panoramas of American landscape, implying that its products were an equivalent national resource. Indeed, companies often assert a nationality not their own: 'London Fog' rainwear conjures up images of misty City streets and well-dressed English gentlemen heading towards their desks at the Bank. The raincoats, of course, are made by an American company.

In this way, as Anthony Smith says, 'the impact of the transnational corporations has been contradictory. They may girdle the world through their networks of commodities, investments and operations, but they also provoke national opposition (or partnership) wherever governments are strong enough to make bargains or impose terms.' Nationalism has always invented and reinvented itself according to circumstance, and the expansion of a global economy has only encouraged this. 'Paradoxically, therefore, these transnational economic forces may end up reinforcing the nations and nationalisms they were expected to supersede.'[14] In the same way as global capitalism does not erase sovereignty, it does not compete with the national ideal: it subverts it, fragments it, enlists it, and provokes it. Marketing campaigns may be national; as often, they are transnational and increasingly regional, targeted to two or three countries or to one segment of a national population. Such campaigns are mounted because company management recognizes differences in consumer preferences and characteristics. But the campaigns themselves act to reinforce, even create, differing preferences. In short, the TNC is one agent in the reimagining of communities that characterizes the modern age.

In the same way as the transnational corporation has modified, not absorbed or removed, both sovereignty and nationalism, it has had to work within a framework established by the existing international system. While the expansion of a global economy has stimulated particularisms and undermined the power of individual states to mediate in conflicts, it has not created a parallel global political structure. There is little place for TNCs as an entity in international law and statelessness can be an asset. 'Legally, multinational corporations have many different national identities and are therefore subject to many different jurisdictions. Because no one entity or country is responsible for overall jurisdiction, and because jurisdiction is often unclear, it is sometimes difficult for states to exert legal control over the resident multinational corporations.' [15]

In general, corporations have a preference for loose, liberal structures at a global level. There is an obvious lack of consensus over how this is to be achieved. In the nineteenth and twentieth centuries, each state created for itself a legal, political and social structure to accommodate economic development, and capitalism. The norms establishing each of these were fundamentally national, based on the evolution of tradition, theory and practice over the two centuries of capitalism but also of nationalism in the different countries. There is no global liberal consensus on how capitalism should operate. Indeed, 'The two countries whose national policies evidence the greatest opposition to multinational corporations, France and Japan, are countries for which liberalism is not part of the national philosophical tradition.'[16]

The home state and its culture help to structure the TNC's attitudes towards its commercial relationships and regulatory frameworks. There is, for instance, a broad distinction between the financial culture of US-based companies, whose shareholders look fundamentally to short-term, quarterly growth in profits, and German companies, who are reliant on shareholders with a longer-term perspective, usually financial institutions. The latter are often partly owned by banks; the former, by pension funds or individual investors who trade their portfolios actively. The acquisition by Swiss-based Nestlé of British confectioner Rowntree aroused strong opposition, partly because the Swiss company was itself virtually immune from takeover. In Japanese TNCs, the shareholder structure is even more markedly along national lines.

Nor has any global pattern emerged to structure the ways in which business is done. Nationality has an effect, for example, on the relationships that develop between the TNC and the market, and the TNC and the client. In some countries, long-term relationships are established with price less important than quality, speed of delivery and adaptability. This leads to differences in the perception of competition, and of business. Japanese companies frequently invest abroad to serve other Japanese companies, leading to tighter clusters of commercial relationships than those which typify American transnationals. The TNC's attitude to labour relations will also be structured by its domestic experience. Some countries expect a lot, others less in terms of worker participation, consultation and information. Though the growth of global linkages has created some pressures for homogenization – forcing Japanese companies to reconsider staffing policies and German companies to open their books and adopt US accounting principles – we are a long way from a single model of corporate behaviour.

The evolution of institutions equipped to manage the conduct of transnationals and to impose a measure of accountability has been slow. Because foreign direct investment has played such a large role in reshaping the world economy, and since purely national efforts to manage the consequences have failed, there have been various attempts to reach broader solutions to the problem of policing the activities of TNCs through international organizations. The financial services sector, arguably the most global of them all, has been a central area for exploring policy co-operation, but the record has been very mixed. The decision to shut down the Bank of Credit and Commerce International was largely a success, in that it took place as the result of co-ordinated process; but the complaints of American and other bank regulators about the Bank of England's role, the subsequent political rows about responsibility, and the length of time before depositors could be compensated shows that the process is still at an experimental stage.

There has been little progress, either, in handling the new systemic risks that emerge from a global economy, and the costs springing from them. The risk of financial upset, for instance, was shown by the domino effect of the slide in the London property market on the Reichmann brothers' Canadian and US holdings. Unable to lease enough of their giant Canary Wharf development in London's docklands, the Reichmanns turned once too often to their bankers, and found that their credit had dried up. The shock in the Canadian banking system was palpable. The spectacular failure of Campeau Corp, the Canadian real estate developer, also set banks and securities firms reeling. The risk of environmental disaster from the liberalization of the shipping trade was graphically epitomized by the tanker MV *Braer*, which sank and broke up off the coast of Scotland. The cross-border consequences of environmental damage are the most tangible, identifiable evidence of the dangers. The pollution of the Rhine by chemical spill, accidents at chemical factories in Italy and India, oil spills in Scotland, Alaska and California all grab headlines. More complex, but more telling, are the attempts to establish responsibility, contain the damage and gain compensation.

Environmental mishaps and misdeeds have proliferated. In March 1992, for instance, a British-owned firm was accused of dumping toxic waste in South Africa and blamed for the poisoning of three workers. Greenpeace alleged that three million tons of toxic waste were shipped by Thor Chemicals from New Jersey to Natal, poisoning a river.[17]

Similar accusations have been levelled against companies doing business in Mexico. Though tough rules were agreed between OECD states, these were not extended in full to developing countries, with the argument being that much of the waste was going to be 'recycled'; in any case, South Africa was not a signatory to a 1989 agreement banning trade in toxic waste. This is just one – relatively minor – example of the difficulties of policing commerce in dangerous goods between countries, between continents and between worlds: the rich producers of waste and poor consumers of poison.

The result of rapid global economic change in a political vacuum has been a shifting, irregular pattern. The emergence of a global economy creates a new space for conflicts, one in which states are involved, but more often as mediators or as players than as the sovereign powers. Thus the arguments over access that characterized the 1960s and 1970s have been replaced by much broader debates, but also clashes, over the operation of a global economy. By linking distant regions and creating new divisions, geographical and social, the TNC has helped to create a new battleground. To some extent, as we have observed before, the evolution of a global economy creates new scope for particularisms, for the assertion of local identities even as it integrates and breaks down borders. At the other end of the scale, the creation of a global economy creates a new space for politics, working beyond the level of the nation-state, and a new basis for conflict.

There is a clash between global capitalism's mobility in the search for profit, its restless search for cheaper inputs and more lucrative markets, and the state's attempts to guarantee employment and investment. The decision by Hoover, for instance, to shift production from Burgundy to Scotland raised hackles in France not just because it involved jobs lost in France but because of where the jobs were going: to Britain – a country with looser rules on industrial relations, which had devalued its currency. Prime Minister Pierre Bérégovoy blamed 'savage liberalism' and condemned the practice of 'robbing Peter to pay Paul'.

The geography created by the expansion of transnational corporations has as it main co-ordinates just five countries: the US, France, Japan, Britain and Germany. These countries are headquarters to seventeen thousand TNCs, compared to fewer than three thousand in all developing countries, including the NICs. The EU, Japan and North America account for eighty-one per cent of FDI (compared to a forty-seven per cent share of world trade). At the other end of the scale it is clearly possible to identify a periphery, a spread of countries virtually untouched by the global economy. The bulk of the Third World has been virtually excluded from the bonanza of foreign direct investment. Third World countries, which have received little of anything in the last decade, have received a vastly declining share of foreign investment. Their resources are less important; their markets are comparatively small and underdeveloped; and their skills are nonexistent. Some exceptions are to be found among the NICs, where home-grown transnationals are emerging and where developed world TNCs are increasingly active. But the poorest nations have been all but excluded from the jamboree of cross-cutting international ties which capitalism has woven around the world in the last ten years. The Third World's incoming FDI is only twenty per cent of the total, down from thirty-three per cent in the 1970s. The United Nations estimates that the share of average annual foreign direct investment inflows in gross domestic capital formation in developed market economies was about 3.4 per cent in 1985–7, up from 2.9 per cent in 1980–2. By comparison, the figures for the developing countries were 6.1 per cent, up barely from 6.0 per cent.

But it is not in the nature of a system that is based on instantaneous, long-range communications to underpin a static relation between two regions. The geography, political and social, which a global economy encourages is one that is built around clusters of prosperity and zones of poverty often with direct and immediate linkages between the two. The 'periphery' displays some remarkable success stories: not just the Asian economies that are increasingly part of the developed world, but also the development of Mexico, for instance, as a site for overseas investment. Nor is the 'core' a homogeneous area. There is what might be called a 'periphery' within the developed countries, regions and states whose involvement in the global economy is small, whose economic prospects are poor. The political structures to handle the conflicts that emerge between these areas are simply not in existence.

It is easy, but misleading, to identify corporate and national interest. The argument that TNCs are politically subversive is one of the oldest accusations levelled against them – often accurately. In the early stages of overseas expansion, American and European business aggression was matched by military force at every stage. 'I helped make Mexico safe for American oil interests in 1914,' Major General Smedley D. Butler of the United States Marine Corps wrote in 1931.[18] 'I helped make Haiti and Cuba a decent place for the National City Bank boys to collect revenue from. I helped purify Nicaragua for the international banking house of Brown Brothers . . . I brought light to the Dominican Republic for American sugar interests in 1916. I helped make Honduras "right" for American fruit companies in 1903. Looking back on it, I might have given Al Capone a few hints.'

The idea of the rapacious transnational as the agent of political manipulation will be slow to die; justifiably so, given the continuing abuse of international and national law by some companies. But the real point of the expansion of the global economy is not that there is a close association between the goals of the state and private capital: it is that the political and social dislocations that follow in the wake of economic change are increasingly beyond the ability of any state to manage.

The breaking down of established borders and the erosion of traditional social patterns is, as has often been observed, part and parcel of the expansion of capitalism. Anthony Giddens, the sociologist, describes how it is the very nature of the modern world to create new risks, since it brings communities into closer contact. These new, risk-generating linkages are matched by the development of trust, layers of assumptions about how those other communities will act. A simple way of formulating what we have argued throughout this book is that the creation of risks has outpaced the development of trust. There has been, in the economic sphere in particular, a revolution fed by technological change. This explosion of global linkages, in a political vacuum, without any consensus about how the global economy or political system should be operated, generates a series of conflicts, contradictions and dangers, but no clear resolution of them in the form of organizations, rules or ways of behaving.

Corporations have been on the leading edge of these changes, and they have started to look beyond the world that is dominated by nation-states. 'The mark of the modern world is the imagination of its profiteers,' wrote Immanuel Wallerstein, and it is certainly true that the reshaping of the political context for business has made a difference to the way corporations conceive their roles. The evolution of a nation-state involved a change in the way that people saw themselves, others, and the rest of the world, by defining an exclusive community, which served the creation of new political and economic forms. Like a nation state, the TNC is, in Benedict Anderson's phrase, an imagined community: it is its very distribution across space and time that seems to define the TNC. But it is, of course, very different from the nation-state. It has no need for territorial borders; it has no citizens, just employees who are increasingly temporary; it has no requirement for sovereignty.

Like the nation-state, the TNC has become a variegated form with multiple loyalties and duties. Transnational corporations are becoming increasingly self-conscious, asking questions that are explicitly about management as a means of social organization. 'To whom is management accountable? And for what? On what does management base its power? These are not business questions or economic questions. They are *political* questions,' writes Peter Drucker.[19] 'Managers have not yet faced up to the fact that they represent power – and power has to be accountable, has to be legitimate.' His work underlines that the global economy is enmeshed in national and international structures, which have yet to adapt to what he calls its 'New Realities'; and that the TNC is in a position to change society and politics as much as business.

The head of a large transnational is a modern Prince, a strategist who must negotiate his way through a hostile world; he is also, in a sense, a revolutionary. 'We're helping Eastern Europe trade Marx for dollars,' reads an advert on the back of the Fall 1990 edition of *Foreign Affairs*, placed by a US bank, emphasizing its role in the transformation of a society. Most companies have seen an enlargement of what can be loosely called their political functions, with units devoted to 'public affairs' work, and 'embassies' in Brussels or Washington. This has been paralleled by the emergence of a class of strategic counselling for the TNC from consultancies and public relations firms. The firm's political activity may not help to shift product, but it will assist in entering new markets, in keeping a workforce, in developing links with local and regional government, and in the long run these strategic factors may be more important than a cent off the price of a product. The aims of the TNC are not purely profit-related; they include much longer-term considerations, including corporate survival. Companies can use networks of local, national and international regulation for defensive purposes as well. When BAT, the British tobacco and financial services group, bought Eagle Star insurance, it was forced to fight through state courts in the US to gain permission. When it was then, in turn, faced with a takeover bid, it used the same tactic, rerunning the battle.

States have made little progress in creating political checks on the global economy. For their part, labour unions are poorly placed in

this struggle; in the absence of any significant cross-border organization, they tend to be sucked into the fight for survival. As Susan
Strange wrote, 'in some ways it is arguable that the reshuffling of the
pack in the production structure has affected class relations more
directly than it has affected international relations.'[20] In the case of
white-goods manufacturer Hoover, seven hundred jobs were lost in
France and only four hundred created in Scotland when the company
transplanted its manufacturing operations and consolidated production. A union spokesman agreed that the Scottish workforce had
accepted certain conditions even to get this many jobs, such as a
one-year wage freeze. 'That's not exactly unusual in this economic
climate, and we were fighting to stop the plant's closure,' he said.
'Multinationals have the upper hand, there is really very little you can
do to stop them playing one country off against another.'[21]

Even IG Metall, the biggest union in the western world, has not
been immune from this. It fought BMW's plan to build a new car
factory in South Carolina without union representation, and accused
the company of deciding to build in the United States on political
rather than economic grounds. BMW Chairman Eberhard von
Kuenheim said the company would fight attempts to unionize the
plant. 'We don't need an outside, third party between management
and our employees,' Kuenheim said. In Germany it would be unthink-
able for BMW to open a new factory without union representation,
and German law requires that employees be represented on an oversight council with power to influence company policy.[22]

If unions cannot resist, what about consumers? There is a growing
network of transnational political campaigns which successfully
engage transnational companies. Perhaps the first example of this was
the targeting of US companies for their actions during the Vietnam
War in manufacturing chemicals for napalm, for instance. In many
respects, this was an extension of national politics by other means: it
was directed primarily against US companies, and was thus focused
on affecting the policies of the home-state from a distance. US transnationals have long become used to pressure exerted on them because
of their nationality. They have become increasingly skilled in managing their nationality as a corporate tool, and in defusing the conflicts
that result from being identified with a state.

The anti-apartheid movement targeted many companies over their
involvement in South Africa at the height of white rule and forced
several to pull out. In the case of Barclays Bank, British anti-apartheid

activists went to the lengths of defacing cashpoint machines. Where two such machines stood side by side in the high street, one would be marked 'whites' and the other 'blacks'. The effect was to demonstrate the practical effects of apartheid and the interconnections between a British high street and a South African township. This was matched with more sophisticated political campaigns forcing disinvestment by local government, universities and mutual funds. The result was a significant increase in the pressure on South Africa to shift policy.

But it is the limitations, rather than the scope, of those political methods that are so striking. These contingent forms of accountability – dependent on sustained political action within informal networks and on brute consumer power – are hardly the basis for a political system capable of managing, and at times reining in, the global economic system. One way to state the challenge is to reflect on the prime reason for having democratic mechanisms at all: the needs and aspirations of people. In the mix of globalism, regionalism and localism, where is authority to be located? Who has power? To whom are the TNC, the state, indeed the market, accountable? Any resolution of the problem of order will depend upon the degree to which the judgements and desires of citizens are rendered relevant.

3

The Disenfranchised Citizen

MENENIUS: ... you slander
The helms o'th'state, who care for you like fathers,
When you curse them as enemies.
FIRST CITIZEN: Care for us? True indeed! They ne'er
cared for us yet. Suffer us to famish, and their store-
houses crammed with grain; make edicts for usury,
to support usurers; repeal daily any wholesome act
established against the rich, and provide more piercing
statutes daily to chain up and restrain the poor. If the
wars eat us not up, they will; and there's all the love
they bear us.
WILLIAM SHAKESPEARE, *Coriolanus*, Act I, Scene I[1]

Citizenship is the foundation of the modern, liberal-democratic state. It provides a framework within which individuals are part of a political community, and as such is strongly linked to conceptions of the nation-state and sovereignty. Given that both these concepts are in crisis, it should not come as any great surprise that we believe citizenship, too, to be a beleaguered idea. The potential for an individual to play a political and social role has become increasingly constrained by a global economy, by the limits placed on states, and by social change.

This potential, at least in the West, has come to be associated with representative democracy, with the rights and responsibilities of the individual within the collective, with the recognition of popular sovereignty. The collective to which these rights and responsibilities were attached, historically, has been the nation-state. In Max Weber's classic topography of legitimate authority, the traditional, western nation-state falls under the category of the 'rational' – that is, 'resting on a belief in the "legality" of patterns of normative rules and the right of those elevated to authority under such rules to issue commands'.[2] But the nation-state can no longer be held accountable on the very issues which so directly and persistently affect the daily lives of those it purports to represent, mirror, sponsor, and protect. Once the citizen discerns this trend, the exercise of authority by the state is undermined, and authority necessarily shifts.

Provided they have the means, individuals can have a tiny, particularized effect on how the international economy operates. By pooling their consumptive power in some way – through consumer organizations, through co-operative structures such as food and bank co-ops, through the observance of boycotts – they can perhaps increase their influence. But that power, expressed in an economy based on mass consumption, makes them victims too – of the dominant culture, of consumption patterns that may not be their own. While their desires and tastes may be peculiar and personal, even the most independent-minded consumer will be influenced by the marketing strategies of business, by the taste-setters of the media, by the availability of goods in the store at an attractive price. The power that citizens have as consumers is not the kind of power they have been taught to expect in the era of the nation-state. It is misleading to argue, as some do, that consumerism is the ultimate form of democracy. For the power to consume is predicated on possession; without possessions, there is no power to express democratic free will, if that expression is to have as its vehicle the act of consuming. You cannot consume what you do not have; all the rest is politics.

As producers, individuals have seen their influence decline precipitously. Deindustrialization and the rise of a knowledge-based economy in the West have made the relationship between employee and employer a difficult one to analyse, but it is now without question far less likely to cultivate consciousness, let alone agitation, based on class. The nineteenth-century model of industrial development generated clearly discernible class tensions; while there is indisputably a power relationship based on control of the means of production even in the modern consumerist economy, the individual today is less able to grasp where he fits in. He may be a salaried employee with no shares in the company. But his pension fund probably owns stock, and its managers direct the portfolio on behalf of the fund's beneficiaries. Does that make the employee an owner?

Employees may believe they share interests with others, but these interests – except in a declining number of industries – are hard to place within the dialectic of class. Atomization of interest, coupled with a political system that preaches citizenship over other affiliations, has reduced the effectiveness of organized labour. Even when – and the incidence is shrinking in most developed countries – employees belong to industrial or perhaps clerical unions, they have little ability to dictate the terms under which their labour is sold. The ever-present risk that corporations will merely pick up and leave if they cannot get the concessions they demand from their workforce has cowed nationally bound unions, at least in the private sector (government workers still seek, and often win, concessions from their public-sector paymasters). Workers, on the whole, cannot or do not move easily to another country: tight immigration laws and nationalist narrow-mindedness have seen to that.

As a consequence, unions are nearly everywhere strictly national in scope, and have little recourse but to the nation-state when they seek political support in battles against employers. This provides them with little leverage. Most attempts to forge transnational labour federations have run aground. Given that there is no general mobility of labour transnationally, and in light of the persistence of national affiliation among most groups of citizens, there is little scope for co-operation among trade unions of different nations. There is a structural impediment as well. When, for example, transborder co-operation is attempted between the First and Third Worlds, organizers inevitably confront a structural divergence between the industrial economies of dynamic developing countries and the knowledge-based economies of the modern, western countries.

Indeed, unions no longer even subscribe to the ideology – much less to the practical aspects – of international labour solidarity. True, some European union leaders have paid lip service to the concept of transborder co-operation as a counterbalance to business-oriented reforms under the European Community's Single European Act, and there is firm support for a workers' charter that could harmonize labour relations throughout the Union. Elsewhere, without the benefit of even an embryonic supranationalism, transborder links among unions are unlikely. As Susan Strange writes, 'The obstinate fact remain[s] that change in the production structure plus the same immigration laws supported even by left-wing parties and voters had destroyed forever the idea that there was a common class interest for workers in every country. On this issue, it would take more than the singing of "the Internationale" to unite the human race.'[3]

In a useful, if sometimes impenetrable contribution to the debate about the relations between citizens and capitalist bodies, social theorist Jürgen Habermas has posited a topography of crisis in the capitalist system and its political structures based, in part, on the Weberian concept of legitimate authority. He writes, 'The political system requires an input of mass loyalty that is as diffuse as possible. The output consists in sovereignly executed administrative decisions. Output crises have the form of a *rationality crisis* in which the administrative system does not succeed in reconciling and fulfilling the imperatives received from the economic system. Input crises have the form of a *legitimation crisis*; the legitimizing system does not succeed in maintaining the requisite level of mass loyalty while the steering imperatives taken over from the economic system are carried through.'[4]

The nation-state faces just such a double crisis, both of rationality, whereby the state cannot adequately perform its traditional functions, and of legitimation, whereby the state is unable as a consequence to rely on mass loyalties.

David Held has sketched the problem of authority in an interconnected world: 'just as more and more people today are claiming the principle of democratic legitimacy for themselves – and asserting that they should control their destinies and that government must operate on their behalf if it is to be legitimate government – the very scope and relevance of this principle is ... being contested by the processes of global restructuring.'[5]

To understand the importance of this crisis, it is necessary to remember how the relationship between the citizen and the nation-state developed in the course of the nineteenth century. As we have seen, the nation-state became the focus of political allegiances, and the key policy player in the world system. By fulfilling this role, and gradually accruing additional powers to itself, nation-states became the building blocs of the world economic system.

At the outset, the nation-state was seldom a true reflection of the interests and desires of all its citizens. It legislated primarily for the strong, and catered to the dominant. To redress this imbalance, clusters of citizenship rights were gradually introduced. Civil rights, those necessary to individual freedom such as the rights of free speech, association, faith, etc., were gradually coupled with political rights in the nineteenth century. As we have seen, mass democracy and mass education together forced a further radicalization of the nation-state, obliging it to cater in limited ways to the less fortunate, and to soften some of the harsher aspects of the industrial-capitalist system. Social welfare programmes, government regulations on business, enlightened labour laws, and state interventionism developed in countries as different in ideology as Britain, France, the US, India, Brazil and Canada. Thus a clutch of socio-economic rights were added to civil and political rights. That such policies could be introduced at national level intensified the links between citizens and governments, making it a credo of nation-states that governments are meant to act in the 'national interest', not in the interests of one class or one region. This was a powerful ideological tool. It was developed yet further in the twentieth century, as women, ethnic minorities and other groups were brought into the political 'nation'. The explosion of activity that came with the post-war Keynesian state underlined the nature of a new social contract. This was supposed to weld the state to its citizens through patterns of socialization, education, health care, welfare and social security.

The ethos of citizenship and the rights that gave it content were created through national institutions. National parliaments debated them, national executives agreed them, national courts interpreted them. But more than this, they were the result of arguments and conflicts that reflected the strength of national groups: oil workers in Mexico, steel workers in Germany, farmers in France, the unions, churches, clubs and organizations of daily life. Civil society, the cluster of associations that exists apart from the state but that forms a key part of the nation, was overwhelmingly a national affair.

It has been this cluster of organizations, as well as the rights and the ethos of citizenship, that has been placed in jeopardy by the changes we described in the second part of this book. It has, however, been primarily in the political sphere that the crisis became evident in the 1980s and 1990s. Representative democracy on the western model no longer looks as healthy as it should at a time when it is the model for the newly democratizing nations of eastern Europe, the former Soviet Union, Africa and Asia.

Thrown now into confusion by the growing power of the global economy, and unable on its own to fashion economic policies purely in the light of 'national interest', the nation-state is in danger of losing an essential element of its authority. For it is now inescapably true that the citizen is no longer able – as much as he may like to try – to hold his elected officials accountable on the full range of economic issues that had formally been within the purview of national governments. Accountability means calling politicians to order. When decisions are made by officials, often at international rather than national level, or by transnational corporations, or by politicians in other countries, the myth of accountability is difficult to sustain. This is particularly the case when the decisions that count are made in the corporate sphere, resulting in environmental disaster, lost jobs, or financial risk.

The concept of a 'national interest' becomes all but impossible to sustain when it is evident that the concept of 'national' community is increasingly empty. The growing salience of local, regional and ethnic interest groups is one factor. Another is the presence of immigrant communities with little in common with their host country who are still entitled to citizenship. However, the widest discrepancies in the concept of national interest are revealed by differences of opinion over involvement in the global economy, which brings such great benefits to some and such huge costs to others that a single expression of 'interest' is meaningless. For many, its expression might be available jobs, goods in the stores, reliable communications, adequate health care, good roads, efficient public transportation, a social safety net. For others, it might mean affordable credit, *laisser-faire* regulations, low taxes, flexible work rules. But just how much can a national government deliver on these or any other demands? Every policy directed at the definition and distribution of public goods within a national economy – and it is the state's primary function so to define and distribute – will be judged by and through the market. Governments, alone, cannot buck the system, at least not for long. That does not mean they cannot do some of those things citizens clamour for. But more than just citizens will sit in judgement.[6]

Choice in national elections in most developed countries has become smaller, as party manifestos echo the limited agendas. Left-of-centre and socialist parties in Europe and elsewhere have painfully dismantled the more interventionist elements of their party platforms, either while in government (as in the case of Spain and France) or while in opposition (notably, Britain). Such is the strength and influence of the international economic order that those citizens seeking truly radical change have seen the virtual disappearance of any alternative within their own nation-states.

That is not to say there are no voices in the wilderness. But for the most part, radical – specifically socialist – parties, at least in the West, have accepted the central conditions of the consumerist-capitalist system, and those that have not have been marginalized. There is, of course, a proximate reason for this shift in the stated political policy of democratic socialists. Those espousing radical solutions had trouble getting elected in the 1980s. This may be partly because many of those sidelined by the fast-growth decade, particularly the working poor in the leading capitalist countries, often did not bother to exercise their franchise. In western nation-states where voting is not mandatory, the percentage exercising their right to vote has dropped precipitously in recent years. In the US less than half the adult population votes in congressional elections. Abstention cannot be assumed to mean approbation.[7]

The extent of transnational capitalism's autonomous character, its divorce from state power *per se* and its colonization of the individual through consumerization, have all but blocked the pathways to effective opposition. Class consciousness, as traditionally understood, has been obscured by consumerism, which Jameson calls 'a compensation for an economic impotence which is also an utter lack of any political power'. At the same time, other historical agents of political organization – for example, the Church or working-people's clubs – no longer figure in the daily lives of the masses in most developed countries.[8]

Governments, just as much as their citizens, feel the pressure. Action by independent nation-states is so circumscribed as to hinder the development and prosecution of national economic policy. Competitive forces have encouraged states to seek regional partners in an effort to improve their fortunes internationally. By operating within broader regional groupings, even at the risk of diluting sovereignty, it is hoped that states will be able to withstand the pressures of the global system, and to derive maximum benefit for their own citizens. Yet such emerging trade and policy links embody another set of problems that go to the heart of citizens' ability to be part of the political structures under which they live.

International action – through the mechanisms of intergovernmentalism – itself lacks a certain legitimacy, given that there is no direct democratically accountable structure accompanying the decision-making process. As Evan Luard writes, 'A government may have acquired power through free parliamentary elections, and won a majority of the votes ... but may nonetheless fail to represent the views of that majority within the international organizations concerned. Few, if any, make any attempt to consult the views of their electorate.'[9] In the absence of an international politics – in sum, a world government – the citizen is left relying on the nation-state, and its negotiations at intergovernmental level. These negotiations have proved difficult and inefficient in the extreme, at least since the world system built by the US after the war began to unravel in the 1970s. With the emergence of a consensus on international capitalism, multilateral discussions may now bear richer fruit. But accountability in fora as diverse as the GATT, the Group of Seven and the International Monetary Fund remains based exclusively on the assumed sovereignty of the nation-state.

For at the level of supranational groupings, the citizen finds himself far more explicitly disenfranchised. In attempts to create supranational bodies without effective elected executives or legislatures, governments lose sight of the democratic imperative. Nation-states throughout the world have already taken early, tentative steps towards the pooling of sovereignty over issues affecting their joint economic relations, yet in no case have their citizens been given a commensurate political voice at the supranational level. In the most advanced of the examples of supranationalism, the European Union, political leaders claim that the rights of citizens are protected as long as the member states maintain explicit control over each specific policy at the supranational level. This is, for instance, Britain's view, and helps explain that country's hesitant approach on the issues of monetary and political union – and their attendant pooling of sovereignty – within the Union. Attempts to boost the power of the European Parliament have been hesitant and limited.

This is even more acutely important in the case of supranational groupings that have as yet no explicit democratic element. A striking example is Canada, which entered into a free trade agreement with the US in 1989. The Canadians had sought guaranteed access to the US market (which already took seventy per cent of Canadian exports) and a mechanism to settle trade disputes. A bilateral panel was established to arbitrate in cases where disagreement on transborder trade arose. This proved unequal to the thornier disputes such as trade in lumber and fish, and led to tit-for-tat retaliation. Canada carries no weight politically within the US system, even though its monetary, trade, even defence policies are inextricably linked to those of the US. Canadians are essentially disenfranchised on such issues, although their government insists (as indeed they do themselves) on upholding the fiction that Canada operates fully independent policies.

As such supranational groupings grow in importance, calls for democratic accountability will intensify. But even if such calls are heeded, the citizen is unlikely to be satisfied, at least not at first. He requires a political voice but also a pact between the governed and the governing. He needs reassurance that his government operates on his behalf, whether at supranational or national level. He needs to believe in the power structure that dictates the conditions under which he lives, just as he now believes in the nation-state. Most people feel little attachment to supranational bodies such as the EU; super-states cannot elicit the same kind of loyalty and blind allegiance as the nation.

It is at this juncture that citizens will seek a more immediate, satisfying refuge as a way of asserting their identity. The surest sign of this can be seen in countries that harbour significant national movements. If the nation-state is prepared to give up some of its power to supranational groups, then minorities within may usefully argue that they no longer require the intermediation of the centre. 'Scotland – independent in Europe', runs the slogan of the Scottish nationalists. Quebec's French-speaking majority, a distinct cultural group within Canada, will have even more ammunition in its quest for self-administration if its citizens come to believe – as they may already – that an independent Quebec can sign an economic co-operation agreement with the US just as handily as the federal government did. The Québécois, by accepting links to a US-led North American trading bloc, may be content simply to administer the narrow set of policies that the international economy leaves to the nation-state (although that would not please a vocal and unnerved anglophone minority). In eastern Europe, states such as Croatia, Slovenia and Serbia can draw similar conclusions, if they can settle territorial issues and complete the bulk of their transition from command to market economies. Minority groups in Russia and throughout the former Soviet bloc (in Hungary and Romania particularly) will not be immune to the tribalist urge, emboldened by the possibility that, if they knock on the door hard enough and long enough, the EU might let them in.

The rising tide of ethnic consciousness and the declining effectiveness of multi-ethnic states has been evident for at least two decades.

In most states, there is a sizeable minority uncomfortable with the idea of living within a culturally or ethnically defined political community. The efforts after the First World War to cater to demands for 'national self-determination of peoples' proved difficult in the extreme. That similar attempts at forging ethnically distinct nation-states have resurfaced is testimony to the power of nationalism, to the extent of the power vacuum in the aftermath of the Cold War, and to the level of frustration so clearly in evidence in the face of structural economic change.

But tribalism is not confined to states harbouring ethnic groups with a nationalist consciousness. If the nation-state can only be held accountable on a diminishing number of policies, even states with no significant national movements will find similar pressures building in favour of local government. If accountability of the nation-state to the citizen is impossible to achieve on international issues, and if supranational bodies take time to develop significant direct links with member-state citizens, local government will become far more attractive as a reflective, personal, immediate, and responsive political entity. The scale is human; the company is familiar; the issues are simpler. Truly effective local government increasingly requires devolution of political power from the centre to the regions, if the citizen is to have even limited accountability. For here, yet again, citizens in many countries face disenfranchisement. Local-government structures are not everywhere well developed, nor are they necessarily empowered to deliver the range of services that citizens may require. Many central governments are loath to devolve power downwards, and seek to control the delivery of public goods from the centre. Even many states that pay lip-service to decentralization have in fact retained – and in some cases augmented – centralized power. For example, Britain's local-government reforms have not yet led to a significant shift of political authority, since the national government continues to impose limits and conditions on spending.

The erosion of nineteenth-century ideas of national citizenship – universal, classless, and irrespective of ethnicity – is rapidly exposing deep fault lines in western society. In the absence of rights that all can claim, social division is becoming more entrenched, the reverse of what was intended by the pioneers of citizenship. Bismarck introduced the beginnings of the welfare state in Germany to reduce the appeal of revolutionary politics, by giving all classes access to social benefits. It was an attempt to superimpose a universal community, that of the nation, onto a divided society. Reversing the process once more exposes those divisions, destroying the sense of social solidarity and cohesion which has been so crucial to the modern nation-state. Elites in many countries will be just as happy to work with, within and under the emerging supranational bodies, and will accept the decisions of the state to pool authority on issues where independent manoeuvring has become difficult or impossible. Especially after a decade of liberalization, the 1980s, the gap between rich and poor in the developed countries has widened. But more than wealth is at issue: elites are evolving a radically different view of their relationship to the nation-state and government; the better off in the US have more in common ideologically with elites in Britain and Canada than they do with their poor co-citizens. As Robert Reich has written: 'To improve the economic position of the bottom four-fifths will require that the fortunate fifth share its wealth and invest in the wealth-creating capacities of other citizens. Yet as the top becomes ever more linked to the global economy, it has less of a stake in the performance and potential of its less fortunate compatriots.'[10]

Indeed, elites may be sanguine about disenfranchisement, particularly those employed directly by transnational companies. The TNC executive, as O. Sunkel has described, operates increasingly on a global basis.[11] He (usually 'he') shares the social and political values of the international business community. He may move effortlessly from country to country, as the demands of his company dictate. Speaking, perhaps, a second language, and conversant at the very least with the terms on foreign-language menus, he feels more comfortable in other countries than would an assembly line worker from Paris or Detroit. A member of the TNC kernel may already be somewhat *depaysé*, and depoliticized; he is possibly uninterested in the precise issues of elections in his 'home' country and probably unable to vote in his 'host' country during his tenure abroad. He is able better to understand the form and function of the transnational economy, and derive maximum personal benefit from it. Like his parent company, he may even escape paying tax if his career moves are engineered carefully.

Even those educated members of the elite who do not operate specifically within the transnational culture will have less trouble accepting a transition in the nation-state's character. They will be prepared to accept a reimagining of the nation and of the state, confident that they will derive benefits in any event. They are more likely to be convinced, too, of the need for greater international co-operation on issues such as aid to the developing world and global warming.

Where does that leave everyone else? Perplexed and probably poor, for a start. As Nathan Gardels writes: 'Only the archipelago of the connected classes that reside in every mega-city from Bombay to Sao Paulo will prosper from the new capitalist order. The rest of the ever swelling ranks of the lumpenplanet face a fate worse than colonialism: economic irrelevance.'[12] And it is not just the Third World poor who face economic as well as political disenfranchisement. The old paradigm of economic organization, the Fordist model that allowed even many undereducated workers in the West to earn good money on the assembly line, is being replaced. The social safety net that developed around the concept of work – unemployment insurance, income tax on earned income, workers' compensation – is no longer easy to maintain at a time when structural unemployment is on the rise, and when the very nature of 'work' is changing. The developed world still largely dispenses education on the nineteenth-century model, turning out workers for nineteenth-century jobs. Those in the rich nations lucky enough to get manufacturing jobs in the new economy cannot earn the kind of money their parents received for similar work. In South Wales, the loss of mining jobs has been compensated for in part by the increase in light-manufacturing and assembly work at Japanese-owned electronic plants. The wages are low, however, and the prospects far from bright.

Major industrialized economies are producing and consolidating a perpetual underclass – unemployed and unemployable. A laid off forty-five year-old auto worker in Detroit is unlikely to be retrained for a job in the software industry in Ann Arbor. An inner-city Latino from Los Angeles might once have escaped the *barrio* through an assembly-line job; today, his choices are hopelessly straitened. Minimum-wage 'McJobs' there may be; high-paying industrial jobs generating enough income to support an average-sized family are few and far between. The recent trend toward the hiring of part-time workers – allowing companies to forgo paying expensive benefits and to hire and fire employees more easily – makes it even harder for workers to meet the basic costs of living. These part-time jobs are a growth industry in and of themselves. The largest employer in the US is not General Motors, not even IBM, but Manpower, the temporary employment agency. The handful of experiments with Japanese-style management in North America and Europe (for example, Toyota in

Britain or Honda in Ohio) have been lauded by locals for bringing in much-needed jobs. But these don't come with the sort of salaries assembly-line workers received, on a comparative basis, in the 1960s. Even those who work in the better-paying jobs struggle to make ends meet. Tax revenues amount to nearly forty-four per cent of GDP in France; in Canada, the figure is thirty-nine per cent. Even in the US the tax burden, at thirty per cent of GDP, is large. Taking into account cost-of-living increases, average income in North America has stagnated since the mid-1970s.[13]

There are simply not enough industrial jobs; and the western economies have failed to develop labour-market mechanisms to fill the gap. Despite a great deal of talk, particularly in western Europe, no government has introduced a shorter working-week, the mandating of job-sharing, or a revised system for the financing of social services that does not depend directly on taxation of the workforce. Yet the need to restructure the system is acute: in France, forty-eight per cent of the unemployed have been without jobs for more than a year.[14] The figure is very nearly as high (forty-seven per cent) in the UK. In Belgium, almost seventy per cent of the unemployed have been out of work for more than a year. This is unsurprising, given the radical restructuring of economies through the 1980s. Shipbuilding in France is a dying industry; in Britain, yet more coal mines are slated to close. 'Blue-collar' workers are unimpressed by claims that global economic forces will lead to the most efficient allocation of resources in the general interest of all. It is easier to blame South Korean autoworkers, Japanese robots, and your own government.

If the loss of political legitimacy for developed, stable states is dangerous, for the new states of eastern and central Europe it may be crushing, especially for those, such as Poland, Hungary, and the former Soviet states, that are simultaneously trying to introduce radical economic reforms. Mobilizing political support becomes more difficult; so does finding an effective valve for the expression of grievances. The risks of empowering demagogues and validating violence and extremism are great. In sum, winning political power in a nation-state in the modern age means inheriting the system's legitimization crisis too. The task of channelling tribalism becomes acutely difficult, particularly where – as in the former Yugoslavia – the state itself is the author of the destruction.

The disadvantaged, whether in South America, eastern Europe, or southern England, are far more likely to embrace narrow-minded nationalism, particularly in its economic-protectionist form. For them, the imagined community of the nation is the only option on offer. For these frustrated, marginalized, even just bewildered citizens, the transition to a global economy is far from easy. The hallmarks of the modern world – economic interdependence, instantaneous communication, large-scale immigration – lead to fear and desperation for those barred from the schools, clubs, and neighbourhoods of the elite. Bereft of the comforts of a sovereign nation-state charged with ruling in the 'national' interest, and confused by the contradictory supranational and international developments they see around them, many have already become so disillusioned that they have rejected traditional party politics altogether. The appeal of Ross Perot's phone-in lines and Clinton's electronic town halls lies directly in the degree to which both men appeared to be engaged in a new form of politics, one that harked back to the nation-building era of the nineteenth century. The individual was asked to tap into the process, to give vent to his particular frustrations and his private concerns. This kind of politics will be hard to maintain. The compromises of national government sit uncomfortably with governing by poll. What people do care about is jobs, income, and security – their own. Free-trade blocs and bailing out Russia are unlikely to be popular among those whose own livelihood is threatened.

In the former Soviet Union itself, such disillusionment will be all the more dangerous given how much work remains to be done to create the conditions under which consumerist capitalism can develop. Likewise, as some countries in the Third World extend their commitment to mass democracy, a similar frustration is bound to arise there. In both the developing and developed worlds, the clear and present danger is that populist, exclusionary politics become common: that those who are not afraid to manipulate violence, to encourage the extra-party political activity of the street, could win credibility amongst the dispossessed and fearful. Alienation breeds easy hatred. The re-emergence of neo-Nazi parties and the rise of ultra-nationalists are some symptoms of this. The attraction of Jean-Marie Le Pen in France rests explicitly on manipulation of such fears of disenfranchisement, couched in the retrograde language of far-right nationalism and fuelled by anti-immigrant resentment. It is in the states of the former Soviet bloc – where the pressures of integration into the world economy are coupled with radical reforms and severe dislocation – that ultra nationalism is most widespread.

The danger of narrow-minded nationalism, xenophobia and social exclusion shows the need to fashion a new and revitalized form of citizenship that offers an alternative. This cannot be exclusively at the level of the nation-state, nor based on existing institutions alone, nor centred on the form of citizenship that emerged in the nineteenth century. It must instead take account of the new realities – of changes in technology, in allegiances, and in levels of decision making. Multiple allegiances are possible, even as the importance of the nation-state system as an organizing principle has yet to be institutionally challenged on anything like a global scale. Individuals are increasingly encouraged to view themselves as members of groups – not national citizens exclusively, not members of a social class, but as blacks, as Slovaks, as Muslims, as French-Canadians, as born-again Christians, as gays, as environmentalists, and so on. The communications revolution has made such fragmentation all the more salient and far-reaching. The electronic mail systems that link scientists and historians at far-flung universities are one obvious new network of interaction. So are the chatlines that allow an individual telephonic access to strangers with similar interests (usually sexual). In an era of cable and the satellite dish, 'narrowcasters' target small groups to whose interests mainstream broadcasters cannot profitably cater. Hence specialist cable channels in major US markets can produce a steady diet for special interests – cooking programmes, horror shows, sports, science, pornography, and large amounts of ethnic programming for minority communities – where the national networks cannot. Community channels throughout North America allow amateurs to produce programming for tiny audiences. Manhattan's famed direct access channel is probably the best known.

The mass wiring of the developed world has created new networks of communication, the basis for the generation of new kinds of community. In the sixteenth century, Gutenberg's movable type helped launch a revolution by shifting power downward; modern communications represent a paradigm shift every bit as radical.[15] The fax machine's role in the 1989 revolutions has already been noted. In the US, Clinton's use of electronic town halls – when individuals, not the press, put questions to the candidate – held out the hope that a new form of direct democracy might be in the making, one that bypassed special-interest lobbyists and entrenched political positions. The same advances might even revolutionize the way we learn – bringing education into the modern era at last. New communication links may grow to become even more important, if plans to build an electronic information highway in several countries are realized. Using fibre optic lines, such as those developed by the telephone companies in the US, consumers can trade information, order films, book plane reservations, and arrange for a video conferencing call. The 'highway', indeed, is already in place: all that is required is the building of 'on' and 'off' ramps connecting individual homes to the network – and that could be done quite easily through existing telephone or perhaps cable networks, once regulation allows and once state-of-the-art connections are in place.[16]

But technological change so far has outstripped political development. The West still clings to outmoded ideas born of the industrial revolution, and the political system has yet to create ways of harnessing the effects of technological change. The individual may have a personal computer and a fax machine: he does not yet have a clear notion of how to use them. He may in a small number of countries be able to 'interact' with television programmes. So far, however, these are limited to determining the outcome of his favourite soap opera or 'voting' on an issue discussed on a talk show. The democratic potential in the new communications technology will not be realized by leaving all the decisions to the market. Concentration of ownership whereby the same firms produce the 'software' and distribute it through their own networks is no recipe for openness. Access to the new networks will need to be granted equitably if individuals are to derive maximum benefit. Even then, the kinds of community that may emerge are difficult to predict. New allegiances (on a basis other than national) may yet be born of the communications revolution: but the contours of this new society are only faintly visible.

As R. B. J. Walker writes, 'Modern political identities are fractured and dispersed among a multiplicity of sites.'[17] These allegiances are a form of reimagining society – particular ties are sought in an extension of personal identity within the general context of the state-sponsored collective culture. Jameson sees these allegiances to the group as 'offering the gratifications of psychic identity (from nationalism to neoethnicity). Since they have become images, groups allow the amnesia of their own bloody pasts, of persecution and untouchability, and can now be consumed: this marks their relationship to the media, which are, as it were, their parliament and the space of their "representation" in the political fully as much as the semiotic sense.'

A multiplicity of allegiances may suit capitalism. In a hierarchy of commitment, the individual can be a consumer first (of whatever he fancies), a Welshman second, and Britain be damned. Yet this multiplicity owes its very existence to the defining principle of sovereignty and the nation-state. As Walker concludes, 'it is this proliferation, affirmed by accounts of the modern state as institution, container of all cultural meaning and site of sovereign jurisdiction over territory, property and abstract space, and consequently over history, possibility and abstract time, that still shapes our capacity to affirm both collective and particular identities. It does so despite all the dislocations, accelerations and contingencies of a world less and less able to recognize itself in the fractured mirror of Cartesian co-ordinates.'[18]

It is by no means impossible to build new types of community, new types of citizenship on the basis of multiple allegiances, modern technologies, and multiple levels of decision making. Put another way, rights can be enforced by other bodies than the nation-state. We are slowly becoming used to the role of international and supranational bodies in doing this, and to the idea that our responsibilities may be broader than those that inhere in our membership in a national community. And there are already organizations, notably in the field of environmentalism, that are pressing for the idea of global citizenship rights and transnational political action, melding a wide conception of human rights with issue-specific agitation.

'Think global, act local,' is the (now rather hackneyed) phrase that typifies this approach, and one that has been taken up by transnational corporations. But to make it mean anything we need a revolution in political and social organization, one that extends the possibility of citizenships and raises our horizons beyond those of the nation. Ironically, there is only one body that can help us achieve this: and that is the nation-state.

There are still tasks the nation-state can accomplish, as we have seen. It can negotiate multilateral agreements. It can, in tandem with other national governments, put pressure on recalcitrant, outlaw states. It can impose embargoes and limit certain categories of trade (in military equipment and electronics, for example) in the service of the national interest. It can engage in state interventionism – to a degree – and can sponsor national welfare programmes. President Bill Clinton's promise of national health care, and his high-stakes call for higher taxes and targeted spending on infrastructure, suggest that governments still have some room for manoeuvre.

There are ways to minimize the dangers of fragmentation and integration, and the state itself must exercise its limited options if it wants to remain a force in a new political order. The nation-state must consider how best to aid in its own enforced transformation.

4

The New Agenda for Government

'A body representing the citizenship of the whole nation is charged with so much that it can do nothing swiftly and well.'   RAMSAY MACDONALD[1]

In considering the transformation of the nation-state it is important to remember how it evolved. As the guarantor of security to a community, it has a monopoly on legitimate force. It possesses not only its military and police but a wide array of powers to intervene in the lives of its citizens. These are balanced by civil and political rights, in different ways in different countries, with some putting the onus on state security, others on individual liberty. In its role as sponsor of a national economy, the nation-state traditionally has used a range of policy tools to accomplish tasks determined by its own formulation and elaboration of the 'national' interest, subject to (periodic) influence from the citizens it represented. These included, at various times and in varying mixes, credit controls, exchange-rate manipulation, tax incentives, business regulation, even direct state intervention by way of public control of companies. Particularly since the 1930s, but as early as the late nineteenth century, the state in the developed world undertook to 'humanize' capitalism, even as, in Herman Van der Wee's words, 'the competitive free-market system continued to hold sway'.[2] The nation-state grew in stature as it took on these responsibilities. It generated a climate of expectation: citizens, companies, and unions alike were invited to depend on the nation-state as arbiter, enabler, as impartial court of last appeal in the domestic economy.

The state, today, can no longer realistically claim to possess an independent arsenal of policy tools. It has become marginalized by the autonomy of companies operating in the transnational economy. Lacking firm connections to the seat of economic decision-making – increasingly supranational and in some cases global – citizens feel powerless to control the effects on their own lives of developments in the international economy. This results in citizens clamouring for immediate, tangible and full accountability from politicians (even where citizens may realize such clamouring is pointless), and, ultimately, in a retreat to ever more local forms of political association, where, at least, the citizen can expect a ready response to his needs. The state, if it is to retain any function at all, must respond to this clamour.

It has rather more leeway than might be supposed. For one thing, the 'global economy', as we have pointed out, is still in the process of emerging, and has in any event retained links to the system under which it first developed, the world community of nation-states. Even the largest transnational corporations are bound to take into account the role of governments. As Hobsbawm writes, 'Quite apart from the continued importance of state direction, planning and management even in countries dedicated in theory to neo-liberalism, the sheer weight of what public revenues and expenditure represent in the economies of states but above all their growing role as agents of substantial redistributions of the social income by means of fiscal and welfare mechanisms, have probably made the national state a more central factor in the lives of the world's inhabitants than ever before.'[3]

Above and beyond this, the nation-state has a reasonable claim to being the only sponsor of equity over efficiency, even if its power to impose conditions on the global economy is severely restricted. It can champion the rights of its citizens, and the need for a 'humanized' capitalism to the very limits of what the global economy will endure. If expressed carefully but forthrightly, claims that equity is being ensured under the system – while likely to be exaggerated – will improve the nation-state's standing in the eyes of its citizens.

Finally, it is hard to predict what would take its place. As James Mayall has written, 'The ultimate measure of [nationalism's] success is the difficulty that people have everywhere in envisaging an alternative political form to that of the nation-state.'[4] The nation-state remains the most legitimate form of political association because it is historically robust and bolstered by the level of allegiance citizens pay it. Any other form of political association – be it world government or supranational regional group – would face huge practical, political difficulties, not least those of making itself accountable to its citizenry and ensuring that it was broadly supported in emotional and personal terms by those it represented. For, despite rumours to the contrary, what the citizenry thinks remains very important. Its demands will be a potent ingredient in any state's recipe for coping with the exigencies of the global economy.

Given these constraints, and given the manoeuvring room afforded it by the persistent, if often misplaced, support it enjoys, how can the state best engineer a new role? Put another way, how does the state ensure its survival, even as it manages tribalism and obeys the constraints imposed on it by the international economy?

We believe that what is needed is a far more activist, interventionist approach to managing the world than has been demonstrated in the years since the end of the Cold War. That approach must put the citizen at the very centre of a new politics. Soothed by its apparent victories, concerned to minimize the costs of foreign policy and secure in the certainty that liberalism, capitalism and democracy had triumphed, the West took a back seat. Lately, most states in the developed world have experienced a backlash that has made them even less open to new ideas or initiatives. As in the period after the First World War, there has been a reactionary, conservative search for old nostrums and a return to 'normalcy'. This isn't working and if it continues the results are going to be very dangerous. The rethinking that has to be done might be compared with that analysis of the role of the state that permeated the nineteenth century, or that which followed both world wars. Revolutions, depressions and the ends of wars are good times to start reconsidering what went wrong and why.

In global security terms, the Somali troubles and the Yugoslav war have already initiated consideration of what needs to be done to assure greater stability. Order is increasingly being sought in untraditional ways, some of them breaching the long-standing principle of non-interference in states' internal affairs. The United Nations is being given a greater role as an autonomous body in managing security, and is developing new relationships with Cold War entities such as Nato. It is clear that force will have to play a more important role in policing global stability, and that this will involve *de facto* coalitions of allies built around national, regional and international bodies.

More than that is needed. The possibility of changing international arrangements to reflect new realities is one that has been all but excluded for forty years. This now needs to be rethought. Preventive diplomacy, honest broking and peace-keeping can all play a role; but before the next Yugoslavia comes along there is a need to develop ways of dismantling states peacefully and erecting new ones, while protecting minorities and respecting local sensibilities. It is also necessary to look more closely at the causes of instability, to see what can and cannot be prevented. Population fluctuations, environmental degradation and availability of resources need to be examined as causes of conflict.

There is also an urgent need to develop legal and moral principles for international security and to uphold what exists already. Rules are not made to be broken and states need to know that. The rules must be made, implemented and policed at regional and global levels. The cost of conflicts to neighbouring states needs to be more carefully considered, as does the whole issue of border sharing in times of war. If conflict is going to recur, it cannot be treated as an event only for the states directly involved: it is a common concern.

The global economy, too, needs appraising with a more activist eye. Free trade, freedom of investment and market access are all important principles and need strengthening. The efficiency of a world built on openness and trade is valuable and needs safeguarding through the GATT. Competition is important to promote, not just through rules but also through investment. But the system needs policing, to protect consumers as well as producers. The ever-increasing size in corporations is not necessarily the best guarantee of good behaviour. Nor are consumers' interests best protected by allowing the market to decide in other areas, including product safety, healthcare, transport, and security of investments. For all these reasons more powerful, effective agencies to manage the world economy are desirable.

Protecting the interests of individuals and communities also means establishing greater stability in the world economy, knocking off some of the hard edges, and establishing firmer forms of accountability for states and corporations over their behaviour. This includes finding ways of meeting the external costs to society incurred by the activities of private-sector players. The market is a discipline but more is needed – against unfair state practices for instance, or predatory pricing, or competitive subsidy packages that defy economic sense. That means putting new political structures in place, with more consultation of workers, citizens' groups and business as well as governments. Frameworks such as the European Charter are a start, and show that work can be done at regional as well as international or national level.

Market competition cannot be the only definition of what is fair, and ways to make the global economy more equitable need to be found. Competition between workforces with no social protection should not be the goal, and ways to prevent this from happening are crucially needed. This will mean establishing an effective way of taxing profit and income that is not so wholly fixed on the workplace, on manufacturing jobs – in short, on an old paradigm of economic organization. It will require ways of measuring 'value' in an era when much work is black market, or remunerated 'in kind' – in other words, untraceable because disconnected from the traditional models of the labour market. Equally, competition does not safeguard the environment. It may be time to add social and environmental chapters to the GATT, as both the EU and the US have suggested. More can be done at regional level, as the EU has sought to prove through its work on social policy and employment. In the nineteenth century, definitions of what level of protection was compatible with a liberal market economy changed dramatically with the rise in state activism: the process needs to be repeated in the global economy.

Much of this work is geared towards remedying flaws caused by the absence of any mechanisms for governance and democratic accountability in the global political and economic system. It seeks to establish structures analogous to those in nation-states, which have been so gravely weakened by a half-century of decline. But for it to work, it cannot be only a process of 'top-down' reformism with summits, new acronyms, and international secretariats: it needs to include people, by making the new structures democratic, tying them to new rights, and to the institutions that can allow civil society to expand beyond national borders.

A new concept of citizenship can be, indeed already is, built upon the rights established by two hundred years of social organization. The concept of human rights that are global, not national, is now well established if poorly respected. The United Nations and the Council of Europe have created mechanisms for passing judgements on states, and there is an intricate network of global, private-sector bodies established to pass on information and collate data. Amnesty International and Helsinki Watch are good organizational models for what can be achieved. But global civil rights can be extended, dispersed and turned into collective rights as well as individual rights. Minorities, ethnic fragments and other communities need protection; that should be an important test of the imagination for the next decade. Without more work on global civil rights, the promise of a more effective, fair global security structure will be empty.

Socio-economic rights, a second important nineteenth-century invention, also need a global and regional aspect. We do not live in communities bounded by national borders and our citizenship, too, should extend beyond them. This need not, indeed cannot, happen globally: economic progress has been far too patchy to impose the same standards on developing countries. But to pretend that western levels of social protection must simply yield to those of Thailand or Indonesia is equally unrealistic and dangerous. Defending these rights by region, by industry, or by other principles may be more tenable.

There is another cluster of rights that must be added in a globalizing world: those to education, information, and communication. Only by imposing all three can everybody in a society be given access to the basic tools of modern social organization. Being part of the global 'network' should not be a privilege but a right. Just as global security without broader civil rights is without meaning so a global economy without broader rights for workers, consumers and citizens is dangerously unstable.

All this shows how difficult it is to take the third category of citizen rights, political rights, and broaden their interpretation. Establishing new patterns of democracy, accountability and representation is a development in its infancy, beginning with parliamentary assemblies of international organizations and the European Parliament, the only directly elected supranational assembly. More needs to be done to tie together local and regional parliaments, representatives and officials. Political oversight for international bodies needs to be widened. Information on international organizations needs to be more widely available, and more effectively communicated. The strictures of nationalist politicians in Britain, France and other states notwithstanding, it is simply not plausible to pretend that politics can be kept within the water's edge. The test is to find ways to expand into wider areas, to find a new *agora* for a new age.

The agenda is not predetermined, not laid out already; nor have the key decisions already been made. To take place, and to be meaningful, political change requires acceptance by citizens, their active involvement. It was above all the absence of popular involvement, of sensitivity to what people wanted, that doomed the agenda of the New World Order, with its cool, reformist yet conservative instincts, emphasizing change from the top and 'leadership'.

What, then, must nation-state governments do? They must convince citizens that there are some decisions that are best taken at international or at least supra-national level, and that the state remains the best vehicle for protecting 'national interests' when sovereignty is pooled. It must, in the pursuit of those national interests, negotiate precise forms of political accountability within the supranational structure. At home, it must attempt to influence the decisions of business with as much finesse and subtlety as it possesses, even if the general guidelines imposed by the global economy are generally unalterable. It must then devolve a portion of its declining power downward. By one definition, this process is what 'subsidiarity', the Euro buzzword *par excellence* of the early 1990s, is all about. Power must be exercised at the lowest level consistent with efficiency and democratic accountability.

National governments must then convince citizens that a narrower set of domestic issues can be addressed directly by the state, and that government will continue to work in the best interests of citizens whenever these are threatened. There are many ways to do this, and some have been tried already.[5] Governments can finance special interest groups that are unlikely to be able to raise the funds needed to lobby representatives directly. These special interests need not be territorially based: communities demanding representation may have other interests in common than location – gender, for instance, or ethnicity, or language.[6] As well, governments can be vigilant in ensuring that regulators do not become captives of the industries they cover, and are open to solicitation by consumers and others affected by regulation and business activity. They can 'de-professionalize' hearings and inquiries, by limiting the role of lawyers and 'experts'. They can take decisions openly, without recourse to closed hearings and star chambers. They can ensure that communication channels work both ways, and that all information of use in decision making is widely and freely available.

They must combat distrust of the centralized state that is a part of the growing frustration among citizens. As Hobsbawn writes, referring to national movements within nation-states, 'most such movements appear to be reactions against the centralization – i.e. the remoteness – of state, economic or cultural power, against bureaucratization, or else they represent various other local or sectional discontents.'[7]

The state must be prepared to be hard on its citizens, too, in cases where special-interest demands are impossible to meet. This promises the perpetuation of social hierarchies, to be sure. Governments will continue to heed the loudest voices and to pay attention to their richest, most powerful citizens. But, at times, governments will have to be hard on their elites as well, particularly when the poor are roused enough by their condition to demand attention. All the signs indicate that the poor in the inner cities of North America and Europe and in the Third World are likely to be roused repeatedly in coming decades.

Part of the process of convincing citizens of the necessity of central-state action must sensibly be a public-relations exercise. The state must not only work to protect the dwindling number of services and activities it undertakes on behalf of its citizens, but must be seen to be doing so. It must explain carefully why certain tasks are better left to international organizations and to regional bodies, and be prepared to justify any decision to retain powers and areas of responsibility that might better be exercised and held by local governments – regional, state, provincial, or even municipal.

Various kinds of regionalism constitute the building blocks of a new political response to the demands of the international economy, and present the state with particular challenges. The most obvious form of regionalism is found in countries harbouring independence movements. It will be increasingly difficult for states to deny the calls for self-administration in their regions while they become demonstrably less accountable to the citizen in the political economy.

The activities of regions are largely limited to 'low politics': encouraging trade, tourism and investment for instance. 'High' politics, reflecting state-to-state relationships, trading rules, tax and treatment of investment capital have normally been handled by the unitary state. As many of these tasks are handed to various supranational and international organizations, the level of government responsible for low politics will become far more important. Government will have to decide how best to locate authority – including the power to tax. Local governments can be more innovative than the centre, and are usually more responsive to citizens' demands. Local governments can be better at consultation, and at responding quickly to changing environments. But local governments in most countries face severe constraints: they are inadequately financed, and often subject to excessive control by provincial, state and central governments. One solution is to provide greater powers of taxation; another is to transfer block grants to local governments.[8]

The trend toward greater reliance on local delivery of services may fit satisfyingly with a host of demands for greater autonomy voiced by groups within nation-states. Even in regions where a broad-based 'national' movement has yet to develop, or has faded over several years of rule from the centre, there will be demands for greater power at regional level. An example is Wales, which long ago was cowed by British rule. French regionalism is also instructive. With each passing year, the populations of towns such as Toulouse, Grenoble, and Reims are developing far closer ties of allegiance to local governments than to their deputies in the National Assembly in Paris. Granted, abstention rates at regional elections are still relatively high – perhaps thirty per cent. It will take longer than the ten years that have passed since the decentralized system was implemented in France to bring about a greater degree of political involvement. The speed with which political preoccupations shift to local level is at any rate bound to increase in the course of the next decade.

More generally, regions that have little notion of cultural separateness from the larger nation-state nonetheless will seek greater authority to offer basic services at local level. As political power is devolved downward, subdued regional differences could re-emerge, making even greater tribalist fragmentation likely. Candidates for this revival of long-buried cultural separateness include the traditional provinces of France, the pre-1870 German states, and – more obviously – the still culturally distinguishable states of Italy. This fragmentation will rely on efforts to revive notions of cultural distinctness by recourse to history (reinterpreted and refined). As A. D. Smith has cogently argued, the ideological and cultural content of 'nationalism' may be determined to a large degree by myth-making in the service of contemporary political goals; but while 'the nationalists were guilty of telescoping history, they were not altogether mistaken. They grasped that if a nation, however modern, is to survive in this modern world, it must do so on two levels: the socio-political and the cultural-psychological.'[9]

Even more reflective of the local imperative in the new political order is the example of transborder regionalism, wherein regions that happen to lie on two sides of an international border nonetheless seek to co-operate on issues of local competence. Significantly, these alliances often do not pass through the state explicitly, but take the form of cultural and educational contacts, and sometimes include an element of economic co-operation. Physical contacts across international boundaries are, of course, still controlled by the state. But moves by regional leaders in south-west France to open dialogue with neighbouring regions in France have nonetheless been extended to include regional bodies across the Spanish border. Franco-German co-operation extends across the natural and political border of the Rhine. Many examples of transborder co-operation in Europe have a strong historical component. The Rhineland is an obvious example: it has for centuries retained a Franco-German duality, and changing borders and pitched battles have managed to erase neither. This is true, too, of parts of the border regions of France and Spain, of the Netherlands and Belgium, and of southern Switzerland and northern Italy.

In similar if not so time-honoured a fashion, the Canadian provinces of British Columbia and Alberta have established ties with the states of the north-west US and with California. A magazine published in Vancouver, BC, and distributed as well in the Pacific states of the US (Washington, Oregon, California) recently ran a contest to choose a flag for Cascadia, a region that envelops states and provinces with more in common with each other (economic profile, ties to the Pacific Rim, mistrust of 'eastern' politicians) than with their national neighbours. Again, as we have seen, these forms of co-operation have developed along sectoral lines as well, grouping regions that share a dependence on a single resource or industry, for example.

A wise state might encourage such contacts, rather than concentrate on traditional forms of international co-operation. Such traditional links, whereby central governments negotiate terms of co-operation with other central governments on behalf of regions, are predicated on the nation-state's taking a central role. Examples include the Pacific Rim Region, which groups regions of several countries sharing a location on the Pacific Ocean. But there are cases where the state might profitably leave the terms of co-operation to the regions themselves. They must even be ready to see an erosion of their tax base: 'new' regions made up of erstwhile states and provinces of separate countries may make greater sense than old ones, and will need the power to tax and spend if they are to be accountable to emerging constituencies that transcend the old borders.

There is, of course, a third kind of regionalism of which numerous examples already exist in embryonic form. In its most advanced form, supranational regionalism consists of pooled sovereignty, whereby nation-states relinquish power to a central authority with independent powers. The European Union may become an example, provided the momentum established by the Maastricht Treaty is reaffirmed in coming years. Such a development would provide the nation-state with yet another constraint, in addition to the limits already or soon to be in place under the Single European Act on policy matters ranging from environmental protection, to taxation, to business regulations. For now, the member states of the EC have retained the concept of national sovereignty, insisting that the shared political structure is subject always to the wishes of the various governments that empower it.

It is far easier to allow such transborder associations to grow within the bosom of a larger, supranational grouping such as the EU. It is no surprise that the greatest number of transborder regional links have developed in Europe, where member states of the EU are creating a shared economic and political structure that sponsors both the nation-states and the regions themselves. The EU already enters into direct contact with regions within its member countries, and attempts by states to reduce this level of contact will be dealt with harshly by the European Union (witness the British government's difficulty in 1992 in controlling the flow of funds to former coal-mining communities in northern England).

Elsewhere, without even the embryonic form of a supranational state, regions inclined to co-operate with neighbouring but formally 'foreign' regions across international borders may find themselves in constant battle with the centre. Such is the case in Canada, where provincial governments have sought close ties with US states even when the federal government wished to funnel such efforts of co-operation through its own ministries and departments.

There are a number of points of sharp contour on this regionalist map. One is the question of democratic accountability and the so-called 'democratic deficit'. Devolution of authority to the regional level and tolerance of transborder associations are not enough: the state must help fashion a concomitant democratic structure at the local level and work to guarantee the civil, political and socio-economic rights we have described. Regional elections are one way; the awarding of powers of taxation to regional governments another. A third might be to introduce new forms of proportional representation aimed at reflecting special interests in the policy-making process. Seats can be set aside for certain groups – Aboriginals, members of minorities, women. Parties can draw up lists of candidates selected on the basis of their ties to specific communities, variously defined. We have seen the effects of disenfranchisement of the citizen globally; just as challenging will be the need to narrow the democratic deficit at local level. The state has an interest in seeing this happen, if only to bolster its own democratically determined, if much diminished role at the centre. This will require flexibility and imagination. States prepared to see transborder affiliations develop, for example, will have gone some way toward justifying their existence, even if such affiliations appear to reduce the authority and sovereignty of the nation-state.

Ultimately, the state will be required in some measure to capitulate in the face of demands by regions for the right to strike their own bargains. The wise state will have a hand in fomenting regionalism, if only to retain a justification for its own role at the centre. It will mount its own lobbying efforts, and be sensitive to the lobbying undertaken by its regions. It will choose when to act – primarily as a guarantor of equity and fairness domestically and as a conduit between citizens and international organizations – and when to withdraw in favour of local action. It will help fashion the political apparatus that must accompany tribalism.

The great task of the nation-state, then, is to pick and choose among the available options (pooled sovereignty, decentralization, membership in international organizations) showing as it does so why particular decisions have been made. That it must do so in its own best interests – insofar as through its actions it seeks to perpetuate the state – is obvious; it must, however, never lose sight of the demands placed on governments by citizens. The state can help fashion these demands by making certain choices appear inevitable. But it can only do this by convincing a majority of voters that the government has the interests of the citizen at heart.

The nation-state might profitably learn from the experiences of transnational corporations in fashioning its new role. TNCs, too, have had to decide at what level business should be done – local, say, in the case of purchasing; divisional when the operation concerns a series of interconnected manufacturing plants; or at head office in the case of capital-market activities. And like the state, the TNC has an identifiable set of constituencies – shareholders, governments, regulators, workers, the local community. The corporation must convince each of these constituencies of the wisdom of any single decision or risk criticism and possible withdrawal of support.

But unlike the TNC, the state has severely limited resources at its command and is anyway constrained in precise terms by the need to meet the expectations of its citizens. Still, if governments can convince their own electorates, and provided the state operates only within the rules imposed by the international economy, there is a fair amount of flexibility possible.

That flexibility suggests that not every state need make identical choices on particular issues. Aside from the handful of issues on which international co-ordination will become unavoidable – transparent and consistently applied rules on international trade, the conduct of world currency markets, perhaps environmental policy – there will be room for picking and choosing. Abroad, states will be able to select which international organizations they will join, for example, and have the ability to withdraw if they desire. The constraint will be the necessity of playing by the international rules, and the penalty of non-compliance will be ostracism from the global system. They will be able to pool sovereignty with others, establishing regional trading areas or regional co-operation programmes covering whole sectors of the economy, and balanced by strict forms of political power-sharing. At home, states will be able to control access to their territories (although illegal immigration may be difficult to control), run welfare programmes, establish and maintain national education and training standards, create or retain health-care programmes. They may even invest in infrastructure, subsidize businesses, dictate work rules. But their ability to do these things will be severely limited on several fronts: by the judgement of the international economy, as expressed in the private sector's willingness to operate in a given jurisdiction and in the response of international currency markets and international lenders; by the evolving policies within supranational groupings to which states have pledged allegiance (the European Union, the North American Free Trade Agreement); by their success in raising adequate taxes and justifying spending, or, in other words, by their success in promoting economic growth.

However, all these choices presuppose the support of the citizen. There will be great pressure on national governments to devolve power closer to the point where government services are consumed. Lacking its former role as the guarantor of a national economy, the state will have to convince its citizens that any power it retains necessarily must be exercised by a central authority. If the justification is weak, there will tremendous pressure to decentralize.

In decentralizing, governments will open themselves to political pressures on a local level. Politicians with a regional power base will be able to play on their opposition to the central government, proving in concrete and immediately identifiable terms – a new road, an industrial park, training programmes for the region's unemployed – that they have the interests of the local population to the fore, and that the central government is far too distant to be of any practical and profitable use in the community. Demagoguery at the regional level will be relatively easy to sustain precisely because local politicians have at their disposal a power of dispensation that bears immediate fruit. The state will have to keep close watch on the activities of the politicians to whom it devolves power at subnational level.

Making the right decisions about which international organizations to join, when to pool sovereignty, when to devolve power to the local community will be judged inevitably against the successes of other states. In a global environment where communication across international borders is commonplace, citizens in one state will have ample opportunity to see how well those in a neighbouring jurisdiction are faring, and will hold their politicians accountable whenever others are doing better. In Harold R. Isaacs' particularly apposite phrase, 'today's tribal caves are wired for sight and sound.'[10] Still, as we outline in the final chapter, states that pursue truly revolutionary policies may find it possible to build up a strong core of political support for a modified radicalism. There is room, particularly, for states and even local communities to veer toward extremism. The fear of the 'other', as embodied by the immigrant (a fear bolstered by a sense of helplessness and frustration), will give demagogues a ready audience. Those leaders who play on visions of creating an ethnically pure, politically empowered nation in the bosom of existing nation-states could meet with success, at least initially. That demagogues will be able, upon occasion, to manage tribalism on their own terms is one worrying aspect of the political order that is emerging.

In this environment, nation-state governments must focus on

protecting the set of citizens' rights we have described: civil, socio-economic, political. It is this role – one, broadly, of arbitrating – that gives the nation-state its legitimacy in the task of managing the tribal-ism of coming decades. Political reform will be one requirement: the interests of citizens, as far as possible, must be reflected in decision-making processes, through new forms of representation, improved access to information. The need for change at international level is no less crucial, in the dealings of nation-states with TNCs, other governments, regional blocs. In the course of the nineteenth and early twentieth centuries, governments developed a set of tools to tame, or at least contain, the economic system. They did so on a national basis, even if there were generally a convergence in at least the developed countries toward similar responses to economic challenge. Such efforts must now be made in many different arenas simultaneously: inter-national, regional, local. In short, a key item on the new agenda of government is the search for effective ways of regulating the global economy, and of managing the security order, on behalf of the citizen it represents.

The ideas that we have described are aimed at achieving a new balance among capitalism, liberalism and democracy, one that is better equipped to handle both the resurgence of nationalism and tribalism, and a more global system. Some readers will find them too conserva-tive; others too idealistic. There are clearly plenty of alternatives, some of them not based on finding essentially liberal solutions to problems. It is to these that we now turn; to the solutions that propose more radical answers to the same questions.

5

———

Rivals

' "I love the poor," Kennedy seemed to be saying with
his every motion, his every little petty, stock question
... As I left the auditorium, I said to myself: we don't
need a War on Poverty. What we need is a war on
the rich.'   ELDRIDGE CLEAVER[1]

'The most dangerous creation of any society is a man
who has nothing to lose.'   JAMES BALDWIN[2]

'The people for whom the form of government is
intended must be willing to accept it; or at least not
so unwilling as to oppose an insurmountable obstacle
to its establishment.'   JOHN STUART MILL[3]

Capitalism's most effective enemy is a single ideo-system that sets
itself up in opposition to it. It is worth remembering that the capitalist
system has had such monolithic rivals in the past. What Marxists
termed 'actually existing Socialism' (i.e., that prevailing in the states
of the Warsaw Pact) was the strongest or at least the most cogent of
these, positing a grand narrative that claimed to prove the inevitability
of capitalism's failure. Fascism, initially pro-capitalist, itself turned on
the free-market system, engaging corporatism in the service of political goals. Neither has been able, thus far, to impede the capitalist
system's steady march toward world domination, although each has
forced capitalism to mutate at key points in its history. The pressures
associated with socialist agitation in the early twentieth century, for

example, were a prime factor in the humanization of capitalism – the introduction of social welfare, anti-monopoly legislation, regulations on business practice, corporate tax, and so on.

In the current climate, a wholesale retreat into state socialism, typified by centralized allocation of resources without reference to the market mechanism, appears highly unlikely. Certainly single states, on their own, are effectively barred from operating command economies if they wish to function fully as part of the international economy.

But capitalism has yet to tame its enemies altogether, particularly at the end of a decade of liberalization and reform that has extended the market system's grip throughout much of the world. In its present form, capitalism has two central weaknesses that leave room for political challenges. It does not naturally encourage redistribution of wealth outside its own terms of reference. Wealth is indeed routinely transferred from one set of individuals to another, for example as a function of the success or failure of firms operating under the market system or of major changes in real estate values that can make or break private fortunes. But that redistribution does not occur with explicit reference to external, political desires – to narrow the general gap between rich and poor, for example, or to alleviate the poverty that appears to have a racial basis in many countries. This is only a weakness when those who routinely suffer under capitalism can be politicized to act against it. The system's second weakness is that it has not been called upon, nor does it desire, to meet the 'external' costs of its activities. Degradation of the environment and the dislocation of workers whose jobs are lost as a result of restructuring cost society dear, yet private companies are not, on the whole, asked to pay for these 'externalities'.

These two weaknesses suggest an opening for a radical alternative to consumerist capitalism, an opening for what one might call capitalism's 'rival'. Pitting itself against the capitalist system, the rival state can argue for greater wealth distribution, for greater equity, provided it can convince its citizens of the desirability or indeed viability of such policy goals. In so arguing, it can point to the obvious gap between rich and poor, and the fear that if wealth is not shared in a more equitable fashion, chaos will result. The rival state can thus marshal both positive and negative reasons for opposition to the international capitalist system: positive on the grounds of a moral need to ensure greater equity within the economic system; negative on the grounds of containing the system's propensity for instability and violence.

One such form of critique, radical environmentalism, has already gained limited ground in western countries. The Green movement is explicitly anti-market and communitarian, in that it generally argues in favour of low- or no-growth policies, massive income redistribution, communal decision-making, and the assignment of the costs of externalities to the corporation. It champions international agreements to reduce carbon emissions and other forms of pollution, and significant aid transfers to help the Third World develop 'sustainable' growth strategies. The movement has also attempted to highlight what its supporters see as a systemic weakness of capitalism, namely the possibility that there are absolute limits to economic growth – permanently depleted resources, a ceiling to how much individuals can consume – that militate against the system's long-term success.

But the Green movement, by operating as a political party in most democracies, has so far only been able to shape policy as part of the general political process. It is, in effect, but one special interest among many, whatever its claim to global responsibility. Arguments over global warming at the Rio Earth Summit in 1992 proved that the balance between economic growth and environmental protection is still unfairly weighted in favour of the former. The Green movement must also contend with a general belief in many quarters of the industrialized world that there is, in fact, no limit to the system's ability to remake itself: while free-marketeers might admit the possibility of reaching saturation point in the sale of particular consumer goods, they insist that – on past form – capitalism will engender new products to replace the old. Rather than cars, consumers can buy computers. Indeed, rather than physical products at all, beyond their basic needs, consumers can purchase images, knowledge, and ideas.

Another critique of capitalism approaches from the opposite end of the political spectrum. Fascism made common cause with capitalism during its history, but ultimately proved most successful when it imposed corporatism on the basic functioning of the market. In the service of national consensus, usually forged in terms of racial purity, the fascist state taps fear of the unknown and nostalgia for simpler times. In its purest form, fascism is uninterested in free markets if they bring too much fragmentation, too much openness. There are signs that while state socialism has lost its appeal in most parts of the world, fear and frustration could yet fuel the growth of neo-fascism.

Without a doubt, functioning fascism, complete with its traditional corporatist tinge, represents a challenge to the international consumerist-capitalist system now in the ascendant worldwide. Feeding it are a set of conditions last seen in the 1920s and 1930s, as open-minded nationalism took on a triumphalist, xenophobic tinge in the face of systemic economic change and a strong challenge from communism and socialism. Fascism may not have proved as fierce an enemy of capitalism as communism – after all, private fortunes, particularly in munitions, were protected and added to in Hitler's Germany and in Mussolini's Italy. Nonetheless, its anti-market bias, coupled with its isolationist political characteristics, made it an enemy of liberal capitalism. Mounting violence throughout the world political system could give a neo-fascist rival state adequate room to challenge the economic order. But it would require extensive chaos to convince most citizens of the need to impose fascism in the 1990s; sporadic recourse to totalitarianism can be by no means ruled out; but the longevity of any neo-fascist rival state would depend on significant and continuing violence and instability in the world political order.

Another form of radical politics, what one might called neo-progressivism, may also win converts. This would see a return to 1960s theories of the mixed economy, where the state plays a central role in redistributing incomes, building houses, providing extensive welfare, improving education and training, and so on. Mainstream journals and newspapers are again filled with Keynesian prescriptions and talk of a new New Deal after a decade dominated, even in the social-democratic nations of Europe, by monetarist and neo-liberal thought. But again, such an option is difficult to exercise at nation-state level. If proponents of neo-progressivism intend to have their economies remain within the global system, they will find their room for manoeuvre desperately tight, and their policies incessantly judged by the court of international competition.

While state socialism on a global scale currently seems beyond reach, the socialist critique has retained at least some of its power. Is there room, then, for a rival socialist challenge on a basis somewhat short of global? Certainly there are signs in eastern Europe that anti-market feeling can run high. There is a considerable constituency in Slovakia, Lithuania, and Russia, for example, calling for gradualism rather than radical reform. The gradualists want to keep a measure of state control to protect jobs, and argue in favour of continued and extensive price controls and income assistance. Critics of the transformation to market economics in eastern Europe are by no means limited to the core of former communist officials and activists. Signs of popular discontent with the costs of restructuring are evident in many countries.

Perhaps, then, the rival state can be 'socialist' – not so much the Soviet model of the command economy, but a communitarian, anarchist variety that has existed so far only in the imagination of theorists. But as with all these radical alternatives, the rival socialist state can only challenge the dominant system if enough states or regions or blocs are willing to co-operate to achieve the desired goals. At present, the basis for a consensus on such radicalism is far from achieved. Is there any likelihood that a consensus will emerge?

That depends on the degree to which citizens are radicalized. The source of frustration with the global economic system in the developed world centres on a large and expanding 'underclass' dominated by ethnic minorities, the undereducated, and/or the un- or underemployed. These citizens are to all intents and purposes unrepresented by politicians, and in most western countries – even where nominally left-of-centre governments are in power – are either unlikely to vote or are fodder for extremist, often right-wing, agitation. Flashpoints such as the riots in South-Central Los Angeles in May 1992 prove the virulence of frustrated feeling in the inner city; but they are not in themselves enough to galvanize a radical response to the global economic system.

The traditional organizing principle for the disadvantaged in the era of industrial capitalism has been class consciousness, broadly defined. If enough individuals view their place in society as a function of their relationship to the means of production (as owner or worker, in its simplest form), a critical mass of opposition to the dominant power group can be achieved.

But to what degree can class consciousness again form the basis of political agitation, in a system where economic relationships are far from obvious? In the modern variant of capitalism, the individual's relationship to the economic system is a highly atomized one. Individualism, not collectivism, typifies consumerist society, even for those who do not possess the wealth required to fulfil their desires: I consume, therefore I am.

As Marxist critic Fredric Jameson has written, 'Classes are few; they come into being by slow transformations in the mode of production;

even emergent they seem perpetually at distance from themselves and have to work hard to be sure they really exist as such.'[4] In industrial capitalism, class relationships were nonetheless easy to identify; the picture is far murkier in an economy where 'production' includes commodities such as images and ideas, where ownership is mediated via pension and mutual funds, where the individual is often far removed from the point at which production is undertaken. Jameson again: 'you don't want to have to think about Third World women every time you pull up to your word processor, or all the other lower-class people and their lower-class lives when you decide to use or consume your other luxury products: it would be like hearing voices inside your head; indeed, it 'violates' the intimate space of your privacy and your extended body. For a society that wants to forget about class, therefore, reification in this consumer-packaging sense is very functional indeed.'[5]

Added to this, the individual in western society is asked to share a primary commitment to the market, not as one possible mechanism among others but as the only, the true, the indivisible organizing principle of economic life. Work hard for yourself and you will prosper. Work hard for yourself, and, ultimately, the general good will be enhanced as a result of the unintended consequences of discrete, self-serving actions such as yours. Support for this view of the market is both wide and strong. Only by undermining commitment to the infallibility of the market can rival socialist states succeed. Socialists will have to convince citizens that the market is not the only or even the best basis on which to allocate resources and to empower consumption; that free choice does not exist in a market economy anyway; that the 'private' sector is in any event offered tax credits, guaranteed loans, and other government concessions without being held accountable for their use; and that the capitalist system is unable to ensure any degree of equity, whatever its claims to efficiency.

Even then, any rival to the international capitalist system will have difficulty remaining a part of the global economy unless it can convince others to join. What about those states that nonetheless choose outlaw status? Can rivals take a different route altogether, in effect forgoing integration with the global system?

Outlaw status is nearly inconceivable for the leading nations, where economic interests are so closely tied to the global system. In the Third World, there remain some anti-capitalist options despite the general trend toward the liberalization of domestic economies. Cuba,

China, and Vietnam retain state-socialist systems. Such rival states will only be able to survive provided they win support from their populations (or at least keep opposition in check) and provided they have the economic strength to withstand inevitable pressures from the international community. As the inviolability of sovereignty wanes, developed nations look increasingly likely to intervene in countries where international standards of human rights are ignored, or where perceived threats to regional stability are identified. Likewise, the number of outlaw states able to finance isolationism is severely restricted. The richest – usually oil-producing nations – will find it difficult to operate independently of the international community in the event that western nations believe their strategic interests are compromised. Access to oil is already well established as a strategic priority.

There is, however, scope for less specifically economic challenges to capitalism in the Third World that might preclude rich-nation interference in the domestic affairs of the poor. Some analysts[6] regard Islam as a new global enemy for the western alliance. Oil-rich nations such as Iran and Iraq (the latter admittedly in far less robust shape as a result of losing the Gulf War) may not, on their own, have the capacity to operate in relative isolation. But bolstered by a cultural and communitarian tradition that opposes liberal economic individualism, namely Islam, and joined by other nations of the Muslim world, could not the Islamic world as a whole represent a direct challenge to capitalism? Some even fear that an Islamic league, taking in nations of the Middle East, Turkey, and the newly independent, ex-Soviet Muslim republics of Central Asia, could challenge the dominance of the West. (It should be mentioned that the Turkish government has expressed an interest in having Turkey join the EU. Such a move might exacerbate tensions between the westernized elite and the fundamentalist camp.)

There are problems with this scenario, however. Islamic fundamentalism is very different in different places, and a basis for common cause is difficult to achieve. In Sudan, Islam represents a policy of spiritual and cultural renewal; in Iraq the basis for economic communitarianism. Turkey, even in league with the central Asian republics it is now wooing, represents, paradoxically, a secular Islam, with the emphasis laid on connections to the international economy via Europe and the US.

Islam is not the only fundamentalist religion that has gained ground in recent years. In the US, Christian fundamentalists have become a potent force in the elaboration of public policy, particularly in the social arena. At the same time, religious faith is openly reviving in the countries of the former eastern bloc, following the demise of Soviet state socialism. These trends could have an influence on the character of the capitalist system, particularly if religious fervour is combined with expressions of tribalism. As Anthony Smith has written: 'Religious nationalism, or the superimposition (or uneasy coexistence) of mass religion on nationalism, has made a remarkable comeback, primarily in the Islamic world, but also on the Indian sub-continent and in parts of Europe and the Soviet Union. This is hardly surprising. World religions have been long divided into specific ethnic liturgies and tradition, and have often come to serve not merely as badges, but as motors and repositories of popular myths, symbols and memories.'[7] But most of these religions have strong roots in the western tradition. More critically for capitalism, religion, if coupled with a staunchly independent and non-western culture, could empower some rival nations in a way western business may find difficult to overcome.

Karl Deutsch has argued that a common culture provides the vehicle for the extension of a single system (political and economic) throughout the world. But that common culture, or at least the beginnings of it, may truly be emerging only within the elites of developing countries. In India, the mass culture is not dominated by Hollywood films, western-style newspapers and magazines, or US television. India has the world's largest film industry, and simply does not 'buy' many of the cultural products exported so successfully by the US to Europe, Latin America and parts of Asia. The same is true of China. Despite concrete signs of economic reform in India, and the likelihood of further market reform in China, the hold of consumerist capitalism on those countries may not soon be strong enough to allow the success in the cultural sphere that US companies have posted in Europe and elsewhere. By retaining its own cultural language of signs (or idiom), and consumerizing it on its own, domestic terms, India (and perhaps other nations as well) may be able to withstand the pressures from the global economy, at least when it comes to the produce of the information and cultural industries. Indeed, a radically different idiom may represent protection from economic dominance in a more general sense. Western business may find itself unable to win markets for a range of consumer goods because it cannot 'speak' the idiom of homogeneous, communitarian cultures.

But can that degree of cultural independence be transformed into the basis of a rivalry great enough to withstand the pressures of the global economy? That depends largely on the form the rivalry takes. There may be room for an anti-western, anti-market ideology firmly rooted in cultural independence and shared communitarian values. Falling short of the united south's calls for a new economic order in the 1980s, this new challenge – culturally underpinned – may yet use some of the same tools prescribed by Third World radicals in the past. These include a form of blackmail on the three issues that worry the developed economies: debt, migration, and, increasingly, the environment.

Such approaches failed in the past in part because the developed world was able to divide and conquer and in part because of the heterogeneity of the developing world's economic experience. Mixing military interference and tied aid, the West in turn prodded and then punished Third World nations unwilling to accept the capitalist agenda; meanwhile, common cause was difficult to forge among nations with such diverging economic profiles and prospects. By emphasizing other forms of commonality – perhaps those culturally determined – some form of rivalry to capitalism might be achieved.

Radicals in developing countries have long argued for unilateral renunciation of debt, supported by a small group of western economists. If enough nations make common cause, demanding greater concessions from western banks, rejecting the austerity programmes established by lenders-of-last-resort such as the IMF and the World Bank, and insist that any repayments be tied to undertakings by creditor countries to open their markets fully to exports from the developing world, the West might be forced to act. A common front in the past has foundered on the varying levels of indebtedness and the range of economic profiles among the debtor countries. On the one occasion when several countries all at once reneged on some or all of their repayments, in the Latin American debt crisis of the early 1980s, banks were forced to make concessions. But the moratorium was not followed by common demands for further concessions, and the relationship between individual debtor nations and their creditors in the West returned to form – one of dependency, at the direction of the IMF.[8]

On migration, the challenge to the West is likely to be far greater, and governments of the leading economies will have difficulty refusing demands for a change in the relationship between developing and developed countries if the price of stasis is an huge increase in migration from poor to rich nations. Third World governments can extract concessions aimed at improving domestic economies to dampen the understandable desire on the part of the disadvantaged to seek better prospects abroad. The migration issue is all the more salient in light of global demographic trends. The poorer parts of the world continue to experience a population boom that will put greater strains on already stretched governments, and increase the pressures on the West to open its doors. China's population is growing by fifteen million a year, despite the 'success' of a government-imposed programme of birth-limitation.[9] Population growth is out of control in large parts of Africa. The implications for global resources and political stability are great, and the Third World will be able to bring significant pressures on the West to respond.

On the environment, the pressures developing countries can bring to bear are only now beginning to show. The Rio Earth Summit in the summer of 1992 highlighted differences over which countries should pay for the changes in development policy that would halt degradation of the biosphere. Many Third World nations demanded considerable funds to help them transform industrial processes and to protect endangered land and wildlife, and fought requests by industrialized countries to limit logging in rainforests. Indian officials have been blunt in maintaining their country's right to develop its raw resources and manufacturing base as it sees fit, without accepting emerging international rules on emissions. Negotiations on CFC emissions are a case in point. India has only recently begun to produce refrigerators in great numbers, and is using assembly-line technology that is now banned or being abandoned in western countries. On current projections it would cost fridge-makers in India too much to import the new CFC-free technology and still turn a profit. India argues that the West spent over a hundred years developing industrial and then post-industrial economies, without heeding the effect on the environment; why should poor, industrializing nations now bear the cost of externalities in their own economies?

Debt, migration, and the environment are all areas where levers can be applied by the Third World. The successful rival state or group of states may be able to extract concessions from the West in exchange for accepting western guidelines. There are precedents. The Montreal Protocol included the establishment of a fund to help Third World nations phase out the use of CFCs by the target date of 2000. But the use of levers such as these is unlikely to constitute a challenge to capitalism *per se*, unless accompanied by other demands (massive wealth-sharing, privileged market access, control of domestic economies) that are not at the present time on the agenda in most developing countries. There is scope for rivalry, certainly, but as yet no indication that the political will is strong enough.

We have emphasized the room for a challenge to capitalism at the level of the rival state, or a bloc of nation-states. But there may be limited scope for opposition on a smaller scale. Violence in the inner cities of some developed countries is bound to be a hallmark of the 1990s. If such uprisings can engender a common cause capable of uniting those disaffected citizens, the embryo of opposition to the system will have been created. Riots in Los Angeles did not come complete with an agreed agenda for wealth-sharing, better education, improvements to housing and local services. But if, as we suggest, citizens are prepared to dilute their primary allegiance to the nation-state in favour of increased commitment to their community, variously defined, is there not some prospect of opposition at community level to the capitalist system?

This is certainly the hope of some commentators on the left in the US, who have already begun to argue that local radicalism may be the only option for those formerly committed to 'grand narrative' theories of global revolution. Marxist historian Immanuel Wallerstein suggested recently that the left should concentrate on organizing groups within nation-states rather than hold out hope of achieving state power, and to develop 'alternative visions of possible futures ... [through] the open imagining of alternative institutional structures'.[10]

Such an approach is unlikely to work on a small scale. Neighbourhoods, cities, and districts can push for changes in their relationship to the capitalist system, but run the obvious risk of being abandoned by the purveyors of economic growth if they do so. If such small-scale radicalism is to work at all, it will have to start slowly, through the creation of local-produce co-operatives for example, or the setting up of communal daycare centres. It will need to emphasize education and training on a collective basis. As David Held has suggested, 'If individuals and peoples are to be free and equal in the determination of the conditions of their own existence there must be an array of social spheres – for instance, privately and co-operatively owned enterprises, independent communications media and health centres – which allow their members control of the resources at their disposal without direct interference from political agencies or other third parties.'[11]

Such a scenario also leaves room for forms of allegiance that are non-territorial – dependent, that is, on forms of community other than country or even region. 'Nations' determined by gender or by sexual orientation or by any number of social, linguistic and ethnic characteristics can create a political 'space' that competes with the nation-state. This communitarian-anarchist option, operating at a local level, is perhaps the most likely to flourish, at least in some form. It allows for the multiple allegiances that individuals feel; it emphasizes individual choice; it gives the citizen a sense of power over the particularities of his day-to-day existence. There are some interesting examples already: in the form of co-operatives in the Basque country where employees make all decisions, including those affecting wages and benefits; in Oregon, where political radicalism has helped place an array of legal protections on the books – anti-discrimination laws, affirmative action policies, and so on. While such community-based alternatives to consumerist capitalism might grow in importance, one would do well to remember that the history of the modern capitalist economy is littered with noble communitarian attempts. It will take time, and concerted effort, for these local initiatives to acquire the necessary strength to defy the world economic order; to influence decision-making at international level on issues ranging from the environment to north-south fiscal transfers, to the drugs trade; and in turn to promote the creation of a successor to the system, a potent rival. All the same, by targeting the community, such rudimentary reimaginings of our political and social relationships may eventually help determine the broader institutional, social and political structures with which liberal consumerist capitalism will one day be forced to compete.

The strongest impetus toward the reimagining of our communities will come from the realization that without political opposition, capitalism will not of its own accord create the conditions for a narrowing of the gap between rich and poor, a redistribution of wealth globally, nor even much more than a basic measure of security and stability. Without the articulation of a political balance to the international economy, the likely result will be a perpetuation of the system's inequities. The rival's goal, sensibly, will be to reject the concept of the market's infallibility, to defeat the proposition that 'there is no better way,' to say no to half-measures, to battle the complacent view that some social problems simply cannot be solved, and should therefore be ignored, to demand incessantly that corporations be required to meet the full costs of production – including environmental degradation – and that meaningful limits to the global economic system be established through political action. Without Wallerstein's 'alternative visions of possible futures', better-off citizens may elect to cordon off those communities that function poorly – drug-infested, black and Hispanic inner cities in the US for example – and retreat behind ever higher walls in the sunnier suburbs. It is instructive that there have been calls in the richer suburbs in greater Los Angeles to reduce the size of school districts, relieving better-off parents from the need to subsidize schools in poor areas.[12]

Retreat behind walls does not hold out the promise of long-term escape; barbed wire may yet be pulled down. But barring a radicalization of the disenfranchised, the elites in most countries will continue to be the primary beneficiaries of the economic system. Being rich is the best way of avoiding some of the dislocating features of new-age capitalism.

Such a scenario leaves capitalism in control but has some major, and troubling, implications for democracy. Democratic accountability found its most obvious expression through the nation-state. To replace that accountability with a form of consumerist democracy – voting with one's consumptive power – disenfranchises the poor. The answer to the inequities of the system lies in creating political checks on capitalism. As we have argued, the vehicle for the channelling of capitalism that has dominated the past two hundred years, namely the nation-state, is being transformed. A new political system, a mix of international, supranational and local components, is emerging. The exact mix will be determined by the choices we make in the coming decade: choices about democratic accountability, collective rights, the limits of sovereignty. As we choose, we would do well to remember that opposition to the capitalist system is still possible, and our political accommodations may yet be found wanting by those whose interests capitalism does not serve. The emerging socio-political system, this high-modern mix of tribalism, regionalism, and globalism, gives a lease to capitalism, not a freehold, no matter how elegant our new political hybrids, no matter how judicious our choices about how to live – in peace – together.

CONCLUSION

The High-Modern World

'L'Imagination au pouvoir!'
SITUATIONIST SLOGAN
OF THE 1968 *ÉVÉNEMENTS*

Nation-states have a difficult task. Radical socio-economic change is reducing the importance of territory and borders; and yet nation-states remain territorial entities in the extreme, linked to frontiers and sustained by defined relationships with their populations.

Sovereignty has been a key idea in the evolution of the modern world, although – like both the nation and the state – it takes its meaning from societies that have long since gone, and in particular from the problem of order in seventeenth-century Europe. Its evolution has altered the term, gradually, by adding the concepts of national self-determination, democracy, economic management and social justice. But the core meaning lies in the anarchy of the world of states, where a monopoly on legal violence was once the principal weapon in a sovereign's political armoury. In the twentieth century, sovereignty was fractured and the nation-state diminished.

The most important structuring relationship in most peoples' lives has been their relationship to the nation-state. The nation, the people who have hitherto had a privileged link to the state, has this no longer. Citizens are seeking new forms of organization, which involve asserting their identities in different ways. The effects are manifold. Local communities, seeking a greater share of resources, will sometimes see that their interests lie in underpinning nation-states, at other times in subverting them. International organizations will seek greater legitimacy, and one way is to be sure that the sponsoring countries have legitimacy of their own.

As we have seen, neither the nation nor the state is about to disappear as a result of this. For a start, there are no substitute structures that can perform all the functions traditionally associated with the nation-state. At the same time, people are not prepared to give up a state-centred nationalism altogether, even if they are prepared, increasingly, to divide their loyalties. Even so, patterns of allegiance are shifting, and multiple loyalties will be the inevitable result.

What we are seeing, then, are the outlines of a global system that has been in the making since the French Revolution; in the process, the principal defining element of it – the autonomous nation-state – is losing its privileged position. As Anthony Giddens has put it, this is in some ways more a heightened modernism than a post-modernity. The dynamics of change continue in many respects to be identical albeit on a much larger scale, and the effects – the redefinition of the social world that has been in train since the French Revolution – are similar.

What is clear is that this involves political and social change on a very grand scale: the map is changing, literally and metaphorically. The political principles behind this shift in social organization have been the source of much pondering in recent years: witness Francis Fukuyama's *The End of History* or Eric Hobsbawm's *Nations and Nationalism*. Fukuyama clearly believes that the era of struggle between capitalism and socialism is over. There can be no more disputing capitalism's dominance: it has won its war. Hobsbawm, meanwhile, attempts to show that the underlying dialectic still obtains. By his lights, there is room still for radical opposition to the capitalist system and its social effects.

It is doubtless true that the role of political ideologies in the twentieth century has been undermined. At the level of practical principles, clearly the ability of the communist societies of eastern Europe and the Soviet Union to react to global economic change was extremely weak. As a consequence, socialism is in trouble; so is social democracy, at least in its anti-capitalist incarnation. Yet so too is traditional conservatism. Autocratic, centralized and traditional rule has been in crisis for decades. Franco's Spain was no more capable of reacting to the changes in Europe than Honecker's East Germany. The middle way which has emerged, forged from elements of the right and left, is usually referred to as liberalism. But it is no more fundamentally capable of handling the transitional state of today's nation than is socialism.

All of these ideologies were geared towards steering the state, and they took for granted the existence of a fairly wide spectrum of choice about what was to be done and what tools were available to do it. As we have said, the territorially bound state can no longer be the sole vehicle of public policy. The task handed to the state for the next century will be to co-manage capitalism, promote social peace, temper the excesses of tribalism, and battle persistent forms of economic fragmentation. Its tools will be submission to international rules, manipulation of democracy and the democratic principle, and a supple willingness to shift power down towards the local level and up towards international organizations, which the state has a hand in running. Liberalism, in one form at least, finds this easier because it is in any case predisposed to shift power to other levels of society.

The end of ideology that has been mooted has clearly not taken place. In fact, the end of history debate is meaningless, because it merely elicits the question: how do you know? Instead, sharply contrasting reactions to the geopolitical tumult of the 1990s have destabilized political systems throughout the world. Hard-line nationalism, racism, regionalism, environmentalism, radical feminism, and many other broad and narrow perspectives on the world are all contending for loyalties. What is true is that the competition between communism and capitalism, at the level of geopolitics, has evaporated, and no one single set of conflicts has replaced it. The best way to run an economy is clearly still disputed. But these are disagreements about details not about the system itself. Communism not only criticized capitalism but posited an alternative. It sketched a grand narrative that told us where we had been and where we were going. There is no such grand narrative left; only the odd chapter or two.

We have argued that there is still room for opposition to capitalism. Such opposition will require a consistent critique of the nature of economic organization to be credible; it will need to be persuasively anti-market. Given these constraints, the prospects for a successful sustained challenge to capitalism appear dim. That is not to say that there will be no crises, no conflicts, no unrest as a result of dissatisfaction with the economic system: just that there will be no one focus for dissent, no one counter-attracting pole.

This fragmented political response to change is what might be expected. The individual sits at the very centre of a consumerist

society, and is confirmed in his singularity by the economic system
of which he forms a part. His political responses are apt to be personalized, individuated. He will seek out other like-minded individuals, the fodder of his imagined community. But there is no single
delineating factor – nationality, class, race, gender, sexual orientation
– that dominates. Instead, the individual will embrace a multiplicity
of allegiances.

But this fragmentation makes the task of making political systems
work harder, not easier. How will the relations between citizens of
vastly different backgrounds and interests be managed? We have
argued strongly that it is impossible to analyse the changes of 1989
simply in terms of a geopolitical shift in Europe. The causes of the
decline and fall of the Soviet Union are affecting all states, which,
though better able to handle them, still find them very problematic.
The effects of the end of the Soviet Union on other nations and
regions, in particular Europe and Asia, will not easily be contained.
Everywhere, the challenge for political systems is acute: in terms of
social order, justice, efficiency, and stability.

The trick will be to make democracy work, and to place the citizen
at the centre of politics. The citizen may find that local government
is the most appealing of his options, but he will have to be encouraged
to pay allegiance to other policy-making levels too: regional and international. In all these spheres, one of the central problems will be
deciding how authority can be located. This is partly a question of
deciding who, for instance, should decide the rules for competition
policy, or intervention in the affairs of states, or the right of voters.
It is a question of deciding how powerful supranational organizations
should be, how their work will be made accountable to the citizen,
how much power must sensibly be devolved to a level closer to the
individual. The difficulty arises because the edges of societies and
markets are eroding and are less easy to draw on a map. New boundaries are needed; new ways of dividing the tasks of government; new
ways of relating the diverse interests and concerns of citizens. This
might mean that social services will be financed and delivered locally;
that environmental protection will be mandated internationally; that
consumption, not income, will be taxed by the various levels of government. These boundaries are not just a question of an organizing principle but a principle of legitimacy. The weakening of nation-states
makes finding a single national purpose, a national interest, more
difficult. Multiple loyalties, and the right system to arbitrate among

them, must be addressed. Therein, at least, resides a role for the nation-state: it is well placed to arbitrate among these loyalties, securing international ties when necessary, devolving power downward whenever possible; championing equality and justice where the economic system sees only efficiency.

The process is apt to be violent. As we have tried to explain, this is not just because of the vast differences in resources and aspirations that remain – a process of arrested development that could in theory be restated, as the Third World focuses its claims for a fairer share of global wealth or as the poor in the developed world replace loyalty to their political systems with commitment to radical realignment. It is also because of the sharp contrast between the integrating and disintegrating tendencies of the world economy, and their impact on social structure. The violence of Iraq against Kuwait is one example; but so is that of angry men and women in Los Angeles or Seoul.

In sum, managing international order in an age of fragmented loyalties will not be easy, however many resources are brought to bear. The task is made even harder by the difficulty in forging a consensus on handling outlaw states, migrants, insurgents, irredentists and xenophobes.

It is not the violence of the modern world alone that justifies us in saying that the end of history is not about to happen. Looked at in another way, what is happening is perhaps the most exciting period since the birth of the modern world. The underpinning principles are being swept away: there is a bonfire of the certainties,[1] and nothing to put in their place. But we will retain features of the system we inherited. Nationalism has not evaporated. The need for international rules has not disappeared.

New ways of conceiving the relationship between communities, and between individuals and communities, are being tested out. The markets' realignments in the 1970s and 1980s, like the individualist reaction in philosophy, were the first sign of that. This should not surprise us, given that the post-war period – for contingent reasons – was characterized by a shift towards social democratic solutions. But that shift in turn has produced a counter-revolution.

The rejection of grand theory in the intellectual sphere over the past twenty years has been characterized by some as distinctively post-modern. The post-modern phenomenon reacts primarily to the death of the subject: the end of one way of conceiving the individual as a creative, active and involved participant in the affairs of the world. In politics, economics and sociology, the challenge is different but related. The problem is to analyse changes in the way in which communities are defined, and indeed the extent to which they can be defined at all. Rising to this challenge in its own backyard, sociology, which took a decisive knock from the individualist reaction of the 1980s, has emerged probably brighter and more vibrant than for decades. But economists have been less supple: the conventional framework of macroeconomics is still reacting to the shocks of the 1970s, which saw much of the apparatus of economic theory discarded. Political theory finds as many problems, in fact more. The certainties of boundaries are essential to political organization, or at least they have been, and political theorists are having trouble establishing a fresh analytical framework. For these experts, indeed for all of us, the challenge of the new age is tremendous. It is partly a challenge to the way we do things, the way we organize, work, communicate, associate, vote, and live. But it is no less a challenge for the imagination too.

The enormous increase in the scale, scope and number of communication technologies is a central cause of the changes we have discussed. Through its impact on the military, financial, industrial and cultural spheres, new-age communications has revolutionized not only what we perceive but how we perceive. Technology is not, as some writers who foresaw the future believed, always an instrument of oppression, totalitarianism and domination. It can be used to create new kinds of community. In politics, the creation of new networks of communication and new types of interaction have already been demonstrated by, for instance, the use of computer networks to spread information during the attempted *putsch* in the Soviet Union. But the new technology can also be used in more local ways, for instance in 'pirate' radio and even television stations, in electronic mail networks, in access television, and in fax campaigning.

Technology and globalization together allow us to create new links between the individual and the community; they can help forge a network of the personal, the local, the national and global, enabling individuals and communities to reclaim some of the dignity and power that they have lost through the advance of modernity and its consequent atomizing effects.

With information goes education. Currently, education is the privilege of a few, despite the vast advances of the last century. At the same time, our educational systems are outdated, stuck in a nineteenth-century timewarp. As long as this state of affairs is allowed to persist, the benefits of economic and political change will be the monopoly of a few. But the need to develop human potential to build stable, prosperous societies will lead to the expansion of education; skilled non-manual workers are increasingly necessary. Another dynamic which is likely to speed the spread of new skills throughout the world is the need to shift goods. The consumer, too, must be educated to receive new, knowledge-based products.

As we have shown, the development of technology and the technical skills that go with it cannot be disentangled from the broader aspects of social structure. Teaching new skills is only part of the answer. Creativity in the technical process is as essential as the ability to manipulate new technologies. Innovators, as Schumpeter pointed out, are as necessary as entrepreneurs. In this sense, at least, he has triumphed over Weber, who thought that the iron cage of bureaucratic rationality would trample the human spirit in the modern age.

Benedict Anderson's book on nationalism[2] was in key respects the foundation stone of this book. It explained the way in which technological change worked to create a new world, but with a difference. It showed how the printing press could become the instrument of social liberation, and how new states were forged out of the colonial world, when ignited by human imagination and spirit. The explosion in print made the work of imagining our society far easier: we could invent, perfect and disseminate tradition, and make it the basis of new communities. We could write history in our own image, and give form and substance to our longing to belong. Anderson reassures us that man, individual men and women, can still make history, though things do not always turn out the way they intend. Mass communication not only makes the process of reimagining quicker; it can allow a greater variety of communities to develop.

There is a need for new ways of perceiving the world, for a new paradigm of social change. The nation-state is primarily a way of imagining the world, and its institutions. Its emergence and development allowed us to reorder our communities in the absence of outmoded traditions. It gave us new traditions, tied to the permanence of borders and the eternity of our relationship to others like us. It made us whole when the collapse of the old hierarchies threatened to divide us. That it was such a powerful model is proved by the difficulty of imagining what comes after it. That does not mean that no one will do so. There are three mistakes that people make when trying to imagine the future. The first is to believe that it will not be constrained by what has gone before, that it will be entirely different. The second is to believe that it will be exactly the same, that nothing ever really changes. The third, and the worst, is not to think about it at all.

NOTES

In addition to the sources listed below, we have relied on several periodicals and journals published over the past four years, notably: *Harper's*, the *New Republic*, the *Financial Times*, the *Independent*, the *Independent on Sunday*, the *New York Times*, the *New York Review of Books*, *International Affairs*, *Foreign Affairs*, the *International Herald Tribune* and the *Economist*.

INTRODUCTION

1. Karl Deutsch, 'Nation and the World,' in Ithiel de Sola Pool (ed.), *Contemporary Political Science: Toward an Empirical Theory* (New York: McGraw Hill, 1967), p. 217; quoted in Peter Alter, *Nationalism* (London: Hodder and Stoughton Ltd., 1989), p. 123.
2. Paul Kennedy, *The Rise and Fall of the Great Powers: Economic Change and Military Conflict from 1500 to 2000* (New York: Random House, 1988), p. 2; E.J. Hobsbawm, *The Age of Empire, 1875–1914* (London: Weidenfeld and Nicolson, 1987), especially pp. 1–12.
3. The works of Ernst Haas, David Mitrany, Robert Keohane and Joseph S. Nye are but a few of those who have covered some of this ground, although they reach very different conclusions. In particular, Ernst Haas' *Beyond the Nation-State: Functionalism and International Organization* (Stanford: Stanford University Press, 1964) should be mentioned in this context, a book whose title and contents obviously relate to our project.
4. See C. Freeman and Carlotta Perez,

'Structural Crises of Adjustment: Business Cycles and Investment Behaviour,' in F. Dosi, C. Freemand, R. Nelson, G. Silverberg and L. Soete (eds.), *Technical Change and Economic Theory* (New York: Pinter, 1988).
5. We follow, to an extent, Anthony Smith, a leading English-language historian of and commentator on nationalism. Under Smith's 'Western' model (by far the most influential) 'the nation tended to emphasise the centrality of a national territory or homeland, a common system of laws and institutions, the legal equality of citizens in a political economy, and the importance of a mass, civic culture binding citizens together.' A.D. Smith, 'National Identity and the Idea of European Unity,' in *International Affairs*, Vol. 68, no. 1 (January 1992) p. 61. See also A.D. Smith, *The Ethnic Origins of Nations* (Oxford: Oxford University Press, 1986). Smith adduces a second form of nationalism, largely 'Eastern,' which for historical reasons was explicitly ethnic in nature, and empowered national movements in the Austro-

Hungarian and Ottoman empires of Eastern and Central Europe. While the work of Smith is helpful in reminding us of the perceived ethnic underpinnings of nationalist agitation, he pays less attention to economic issues. Other analysts of interest on definitions of nationalism include: Ernest Gellner, *Nations and Nationalism* (Oxford: Oxford University Press, 1983); John Breuilly, *Nationalism and the State* (London: Manchester University Press, 1982); Elie Kedourie (ed.) *Nationalism in Asia and Africa* (New York: Meridian, 1970); Hugh Seton-Watson, *Nations and States: An Enquiry into the Origins of Nations and*

the Politics of Nationalism (London: Methuen & Co. Ltd., 1977).
6. For a discussion of the way 'traditions' are created and disseminated, see E.J. Hobsbawm and Terence Ranger (eds.), *The Invention of Tradition* (Cambridge: Cambridge University Press, 1983).
7. Alter, *Nationalism*, especially pp. 28–34.
8. Quoted in E.J. Hobsbawm, *Nations and Nationalism Since 1780* (Cambridge: Cambridge University Press, 1990), pp. 44–5.
9. Benedict Anderson, *Imagined Communities*, revised ed. (London: Verso Books, 1991), especially pp. 5–6. See also Alter, *Nationalism*, p. 61.

PART ONE: The Nation-State From Westphalia to the Wall

CHAPTER ONE: When and Why Was the Nation-State?

1. Peter Alter, *Nationalism* (London: Hodder and Stoughton Ltd., 1989), p. 77.
2. In addition to works specifically cited, this chapter draws on many general sources: Perry Anderson, *Lineages of the Absolutist State* (London: Verso Books, 1979); Jerome Blum, *The End of the Old Order in Rural Europe* (Princeton, NJ: Princeton University Press, 1978); Paul Johnson, *The Birth of the Modern* (New York: HarperCollins Publishers, 1991); E.J. Hobsbawm, *Industry and Empire* (London: Penguin Books, 1968); Simon Schama, *Citizens* (New York: Viking Press, 1989); George Rude, *Revolutionary Europe 1783–1815* (New York: Harper & Row, 1964); Alan G.R. Smith, *The Emergence of a Nation State: The Commonwealth of England 1529–1660* (London: Longman, 1984); Albert Soboul, *Histoire de la Révolution française*, 2 vols. (Paris: Gallimard, 1962); Alfred Cobban, *History of Modern France*, Vol. 1 (London: Penguin Books, 1957); Fernand Braudel, *The Identity of France*, Vol. 1 (London: HarperCollins Publishers, 1986); Fernand Braudel, *The Mediterrean World in the Age of Philip II* (New York: Harper and Row, 1972); AJP

Taylor, *The Hapsburg Monarchy 1809–1918* (London: Penguin Books, 1948); Peter N. Stearns: *The Revolutionary Tide in Europe* (New York: W.W. Norton & Co., 1974; Ernest Gellner, *Nations and Nationalism* (Oxford: Oxford University Press, 1983); Hugh Seton-Watson, *Nations & States: An Enquiry into the Origins of Nations and the Politics of Nationalism* (London: Methuen & Co. Ltd., 1977).
3. Immanuel Wallerstein, *The Modern World System: Capitalist Agriculture and the Origins of the European World Economy in the Sixteenth Century* (New York: Academic Press, 1974), p. 18.
4. A useful guide to the debate can be found in Rodney Hilton (ed.), *The Transition from Feudalism to Capitalism* (London: Verso Books, 1978).
5. Paul Kennedy, *The Rise and Fall of the Great Powers: Economic Change and Military Conflict from 1500 to 2000* (New York: Random House, 1988), p. 90.
6. Charles Tilly, 'Reflections on the History of European State-making,' in Charles Tilly (ed.), *The Formation of National States in Western Europe* (Princeton, NJ: Princeton University Press, 1975), p. 42.

7. Fernand Braudel, 'European Expansion and Capitalism 1450–1650,' in *Chapters in Western Civilization*, Vol. 1, 3rd ed. (New York: Columbia University Press, 1961), p. 260.

8. A good, if traditional history of this period is Geoffrey Parker, *Europe in Crisis 1598–1648* (London: Fontana Press, 1979); see also Kennedy, *The Rise and Fall of the Great Powers*, pp. 39–93 and Mark W. Zacher, 'The Decaying Pillars of the Westphalian Temple: Implications for International Order and Governance,' in James N. Rosenau and Ernst-Otto Czempiel (eds.), *Governance Without Government: Order and Change in World Politics* (Cambridge: Cambridge University Press, 1992), pp. 58–101.

9. Cobban, *A History of Modern France*, p. 165.

10. A.D. Smith, 'National Identity and the Idea of European Unity,' in *International Affairs*, Vol. 68, no. 1 (January 1992) p. 62.

11. E.J. Hobsbawm, *The Age of Revolution 1789–1848* (New York: New American Library, 1962), pp. 74–75.

12. David Landes, *The Unbound Prometheus: Technological Change and Industrial Development in Western Europe from 1750 to the Present* (Cambridge: Cambridge University Press, 1969).

13. On the importance of economic analysts in the spread of liberal ideology, see Robert Heilbroner, *The Worldly Philosophers: The Life, Times and Ideas of the Great Economic Thinkers*, 4th ed. (New York: Simon and Shuster, 1972), pp. 40–72. The seminal work, of course, is Adam Smith, *An Inquiry into the Nature and Causes of the Wealth of Nations* (London: J.M. Dent & Sons, 1977).

14. E.J. Hobsbawm, *The Age of Empire 1875–1914* (London: Weidenfeld and Nicolson, 1987), p. 25.

15. Smith reminds us, however: 'If the nation seems in many ways modern, it is also deep-rooted. The nationalists were guilty of telescoping history, but they were not altogether mistaken. They grasped that if a nation, however modern, is to survive in this modern world, it must do so on two levels: the socio-political and the cultural-psychological.' Anthony D. Smith, *National Identity* (Harmondsworth: Penguin Books, 1991), pp. 69–70.

16. Alter, *Nationalism*, pp. 28–34.

17. Quoted in E.J. Hobsbawm, *Nations and Nationalism Since 1780* (Cambridge: Cambridge University Press, 1990), p. 44.

18. The transformation in the case of France has been diligently described by Eugen Weber in his *Peasants into Frenchmen: The Modernization of Rural France, 1870–1914* (Stanford: Stanford University Press, 1976).

19. John Stuart Mill, *Principles of Political Economy* (Toronto: University of Toronto Press, 1965).

20. As Anthony Smith puts it: 'Ethnic mythologies and symbolisms can restore the collective heritage and explain 'who we are' to ourselves and to others, by clearly demarcating what is authentically 'ours' from what is alien, much the same way that traditional religions distinguished the sacred from the profane.' A.D. Smith, *The Ethnic Origins of Nations* (Oxford: B. Blackwell, 1986), p. 202.

21. Kennedy, *The Rise and Fall*, p. 21.

22. Graham Ross, *The Great Powers and the Decline of the European States System, 1914–1945* (London: Longman, 1983), p. 2.

23. Hugh Brogan, *Penguin History of the United States* (Harmondsworth: Penguin Books, 1990), p. 401.

24. Adam Watson, *The Evolution of International Society* (London: Routledge, 1992), p. 247.

25. David Halberstam, *The Reckoning* (New York: Morrow, 1986).

26. E.J. Hobsbawm, *The Age of Empire*, pp. 101–107.

27. Samuel Eliot Morison, Henry Steele Commager and William E. Leuchtenburg, *A Concise History of the American Republic* (New York: Oxford University Press), pp. 382ff.

28. On the importance of these, see Gilles Deleuze, *Le Bergsonisme* (Paris: Presses universitaires de France, 1988); Robert

Bocock, *Freud and Modern Society: An Outline and Analysis of Freud's Sociology* (New York: Holmes and Meir, 1978);

Julian Schwinger, *Einstein's Legacy: The Unity of Space and Time* (New York: Scientific American Library, 1986).

CHAPTER TWO: A World of Nations, a Society of States

1. From 'Petition' (1930), in M.H. Abrahams (ed.), *The Norton Anthology of English Literature*, 3rd ed. (New York: W.W. Norton & Company, 1974), p. 2345.

2. In additional to sources specifically cited, we have drawn for this chapter on a number of general political and economic histories of the period 1914–1989. In particular, we have used Peter Calvacoressi, *World Politics Since 1945*, 6th ed. (London: Longman, 1991); William R. Keylor, *The Twentieth Century World: An International History* (New York: Oxford University Press, 1992); the three volumes from the *Pelican History of the World Economy in the Twentieth Century*: Derek H. Aldcroft, *From Versailles to Wall Street, 1919–1929* (Harmondsworth: Penguin Books, 1987), Charles P. Kindleberger, *The World in Depression, 1929–1939* (Harmondsworth: Penguin Books, 1987) and Herman Van der Wee, *Prosperity and Upheaval in the World Economy, 1945–1980* (Harmondsworth: Penguin Books, 1987); Joan Edelman Spero, *The Politics of International Economic Relations*, 4th edition (London: Routledge, 1992). We have drawn on many of the arguments used by Hedley Bull, *The Anarchical Society* (London: Macmillan, 1977) and Hedley Bull and Adam Watson, *The Expansion of Intenational Society* (Oxford: Oxford University Press, 1984); Robert O. Keohane, *After Hegemony: Co-operation and Discord in the World Political Economy* (Princeton: Princeton University Press, 1984); Robert O. Keohane and Joseph Nye, *Power and Interdependence* (Boston: Little Brown, 1977); James Mayall, *Nationalism and International Society* (Cambridge: Cambridge University Press, 1990); Adam Watson, *The Evolution of International Society* (London: Routledge,

1992); and many of the essays and extracts in Michael Smith, Richard Little and Michael Shackleton (eds.), *Perspectives on World Politics* (London: Croom Helm, 1981).

3. On the Great Power system, its breakdown and the failure to construct a replacement, see: Graham Ross, *The Great Powers and the Decline of the European States System, 1914–1945* (London: Longman, 1983); Paul Kennedy, *The Rise and Fall of the Great Powers: Economic Change and Military Conflict from 1500 to 2000* (New York: Random House, 1988), especially chapters 5 and 6; F.H. Hinsley, *Power and the Pursuit of Peace* (Cambridge: Cambridge University Press, 1963; Norman Stone, *Europe Transformed, 1979–1919* (London, 1983); A.J.P. Taylor, *The Struggle for Mastery in Europe, 1848–1918* (Oxford: Oxford University Press, 1954 and E.H. Carr, *The Twenty Years Crisis, 1919–1939: an Introduction to the Study of International Relations* (New York: Harper & Row, 1964).

4. Ross, *The Great Powers*, p. 111.

5. Regarding the impact of nationalism and the idea of national self-determination on the political and economic structures of the inter-war years, see also: E.J. Hobsbawm, *Nations and Nationalism Since 1780* (Cambridge: Cambridge University Press, 1990), p. 138; Aldcroft, *From Versailles to Wall Street*, especially chapters 2 and 3; and Hugh Seton-Watson, *Nations and States: An Enquiry into the Origins of Nations and the Politics of Nationalism* (London: Methuen & Co. Ltd., 1977).

6. Evan Luard, *The Globalization of Politics: the Changed Focus of Political Action in the Modern World* (Basingstoke: Macmillan, 1990), p. 166. On the foundation and weakness of the United Nations system, see also A. LeRoy Bennett, *International*

Organizations: Principles and Issues (Englewood Cliffs, N.J: Prentice Hall, 1991).

7. *Financial Times*, June 20, 1992, p. 3.

8. Adam Watson, *The Evolution of International Society* (London: Routledge, 1992), p. 289. For accounts of the emergence of the bipolar system, see: John Lewis Gaddis, *The United States and the Origins of the Cold War, 1941–1973* (New York: Oxford University Press, 1992); Adam Ulam, *Expansion and Co-Existence: the History of Soviet Foreign Policy, 1917–1973* (New York: Praeger, 1974); and Walter LaFeber, *America, Russia and the Cold War, 1945–1980* (New York: Wiley & Sons, 1980).

9. Phyllis Deane, *The State and The Economic System: an Introduction to the History of the Political Economy* (Oxford: Oxford University Press, 1989), p. 166. On the economic programmes of the post-war years and their influence on government, see: Andrew Graham with Anthony Seldon, *Government and Economies in the Post-War World: Economic Policies and Comparative Performance, 1945–1985* (London: Routledge, 1990); Robert Skidelsky (ed.), *The End of the Keynesian Era: Essays on the Disintegration of the Keynesian Political Economy* (London: Macmillan, 1977), especially chapter 3 by Skidelsky himself, chapter 6 by Samuel Brittan and chapter 13 by Geoffrey Barraclough; Herman Van der Wee, *Prosperity and Upheaval*; Phyllis Deane, *The State and The Economic System: an Introduction to the History of the Political Economy* (Oxford: Oxford University Press, 1989); and J.K. Galbraith, *A History of Economics: The Past as Present* (Harmondsworth: Penguin Books, 1987).

10. The shifts in society, government and political attitudes that came about the 1950s and 1960s are documented in literature of the period, including: two books by J.K. Galbraith, *The Affluent Society* (Harmondsworth: Penguin Books, 1962) and *The New Industrial State* (Boston: Houghton Mifflin, 1967); Andrew Shonfield, *Modern Capitalism: the Changing Balance of Public and Private Power* (Oxford: Oxford University Press, 1965); J.H. Goldthorpe, D. Lockwood, et al., *The Affluent Worker in the Class Structure* (Cambridge: Cambridge University Press, 1969).

11. On the political and economic nature of the post-war Soviet bloc in central and eastern Europe, see Ulam, *Expansion and Co-Existence*; two books by Alec Nove, *The Soviet Economic System* (London: George Allen & Unwin, 1977) and *An Economic History of the USSR* (Harmondsworth: Penguin Books, 1980); Jacques Rupnik, *The Other Europe*, revised ed. (London: Weidenfeld and Nicholson, 1989).

12. See Benedict Anderson, *Imagined Communities: Reflections on the Origins and Spread of Nationalism*, revised ed. (London: Verso Books, 1991) and E.J. Hobsbawm and Terence Ranger (eds.), *The Invention of Tradition* (Cambridge: Cambridge University Press, 1983). On anti-colonist nationalism and the retreat of the European empires, see also Elie Kedourie (ed.) *Nationalism in Asia and Africa* (New York: Meridian, 1970); and two books edited by Anthony D. Smith, *Nationalist Movements* (London: Macmillan, 1976) and *Nationalism in the Twentieth Century* (New York: New York University Press, 1979).

13. James Mayall, *Nationalism and International Society* (Cambridge: Cambridge University Press, 1990), p. 49.

14. Calvacoressi, *World Politics Since 1945*.

15. Watson, *The Evolution of International Society*, p. 290.

16. On the workings of the bipolar system, there is, of course, a vast literature. We have used two books by John Lewis Gaddis, *Strategies of Containment: a Critical Appraisal of Postwar American National Security Policy* (Oxford: Oxford University Press, 1982) and *The Long Peace: Inquiries into the History of the Cold War* (Oxford: Oxford University Press, 1987), as well as: Fred Halliday, *The Making of the Second Cold War*, 2nd. ed. (London: Verso Books, 1986); Mike Bowker and Phil Williams, *Superpower*

Detente: A Reappraisal (London: Sage Publications for the Royal Institute of International Affairs, 1988).

17. Calvacoressi, *World Politics Since 1945*, p. 139.

18. See Mayall, *Nationalism and International Society*.

19. Aldcroft, *From Versailles to Wall Street*, p. 55.

20. For accounts of the negotiations at Bretton Woods and afterwards, discussions of the early history of the world trading system after the Second World War and the demise of hopes for a more supranational system, see: Van der Wee, *Prosperity and Upheaval*, chapters IX, X and XI, and Spero, *The Politics of International Economic Relations*.

21. Van der Wee, *Prosperity and Upheaval*, p. 471.

22. Deane, *The State and the Economic System*, p. 191.

23. Galbraith, *A History of Economics*, p. 266. On the contradictions and complexities of combining democracy and demand management, see also Skidelsky (ed.), *The End of the Keynesian Era*, particularly the chapter by Samuel Brittan. The theoretical discussion of this can be found in David Held, 'Democracy, the Nation-State, and the Global System,' in *Political Theory Today* (Stanford: Stanford University Press, 1991).

24. For these figures and a general discussion of FDI and the role of transnational corporations, see United Nations, Transnational Corporations and Management Division (UNCTC), Department of Economic and Social Development, *World Investment Report 1992: Transnational Corporations as Engines of Growth* (New York: United Nations, 1992). p. 3.

25. DeAnne Julius, *Global Companies and Public Policy: the Growing Challenge of Foreign Direct Investment* (New York: Royal Institute of International Affairs, 1990), p. 36.

26. UNCTC, *World Investment Report*, p. 3.

27. Peter Drucker: *The New Realities in Government and Politics, in Economics and Business, in Society and World View*

(New York: Harper & Row, 1989), p. 109.

28. On the debt crisis, see Pedro-Pablo Kuczynski, *Latin American Debt* (Baltimore: Johns Hopkins University Press, 1988); Harold Lever and Christopher Huhne, *Debt and Danger: The World Financial Crisis* (Boston: Atlantic Monthly Press, 1986); and Anatole Kaletsky, *The Costs of Default* (New York: Twentieth Century Fund, 1985).

29. On the new economic liberalism of the 1980s and 1990s in developing countries, see the chapter by Thomas Biersteker in James N. Rosenau and Ernst-Otto Czempiel (eds.), *Governance Without Government: Order and Change in World Politics* (Cambridge: Cambridge University Press, 1992).

30. Van der Wee, *Prosperity and Upheaval*, p. 397.

31. Philip Hanson, 'The Soviet Union,' in Andrew Graham and Anthony Seldon (eds.), *Government and Economies in the Postwar World: Economic Policies and Comparative Performance* (London: Routledge, 1990), pp. 205–224.

32. Anders Aslund, *Gorbachev's Struggle for Economic Reform: The Soviet Reform Process*, 1985–88 (Ithaca, N.Y: Cornell University Press, 1989), p. 3. See also Martin McCauley (ed.), *The Soviet Union under Gorbachev* (New York: St. Martin's Press, 1987).

33. Drucker, *The New Realities*, pp. 117–18.

34. Mark W. Zacher, 'The Decaying Pillars of the Westphalian Temple: Implications for International Order and Governance,' in James N. Rosenau and Ernst-Otto Czempiel (eds.), *Governance Without Government*, pp. 58–101.

35. On the declining use of force – a highly controversial topic and the subject of considerable debate both during and after the Cold War – see Evan Luard, *War in International Society* (London: IB Taurus, 1986); John Mueller, *Retreat from Doomsday: The Obsolesence of Major War* (New York: Basic Books, 1989) and the review essay by Carl Kaysen reprinted in Sean M. Lynn-Jones (ed.),

The Cold War and After: Prospects for Peace (Cambridge, Mass.: The MIT Press, 1991); and Mueller's essay in the same volume.

36. Gaddis, *The Long Peace*.
37. David Held, 'Democracy, the Nation-State, and the Global System,' in *Political Theory Today*.

CHAPTER THREE: Breaking Down the Borders

1. E. Gibbon, *The Decline and Fall of the Roman Empire*, Vol. I (London: Dent, 1910), p. 7.
2. *Financial Post*, Feb. 2, 1990; reprinted in 'Tapping the Markets,' (offprint, Toronto: Financial Post Co, March 1990), p. 10.
3. Susan Strange, 'States, Firms and Diplomacy,' in *International Affairs*, Vol. 68, no. 1 (January 1992), p. 4.
4. United Nations, Transnational Corporations and Management Division (UNCTC), Department of Economic and Social Development, *World Investment Report 1992: Transnational Corporations as Engines of Growth* (New York: United Nations, 1992) p. 15.
5. Susan Strange, *States and Markets* (London: Pinter, 1988), p. 81.
6. Herman Van der Wee, *Prosperity and Upheaval: The World Economy 1945–1980*

(Harmondsworth: Penguin Books, 1987).
7. Joan Edelman Spero, *The Politics of International Economic Relations*, 4th edition (London: Routledge, 1992), p. 280.
8. Strange, 'States, Firms and Diplomacy,' p. 5.
9. *International Herald Tribune*, March 24, 1992.
10. Fredric Jameson, *Postmodernism, or The Cultural Logic of Late Capitalism* (New York: Verso Books, 1991), p. 3.
11. Jonas Widgren 'International migration and regional stability,' *International Affairs*, Vol. 66, no. 4 (October 1990), p. 762.
12. Harold R. Isaacs, *Idols of the Tribe: Group Identity and Political Change*, 2nd edition (Cambridge, Mass.: Harvard University Press, 1989), pp. 16–17.

PART TWO: New World Orders

INTRODUCTION: The End of the Cold War

1. James Mayall, *Nationalism and International Society* (Cambridge: Cambridge University Press, 1990), p. 64.
2. See Mary Kaldor, 'After the Cold War,' in *Europe From Below: An East-West Dialogue* (New York: Verso Books, 1991), pp. 29ff.
3. A formulation that became known as the Sinatra Doctrine.
4. Quoted in Adam Roberts, 'A New Age in International Relations,' in *International Affairs*, Vol. 67, no. 3 (July 1991), pp. 509–26.
5. George Bush, 'Towards a New World Order,' US State Department Dispatch 1:3, September 17, 1990, p. 91. The speech, delivered to a joint session of both Houses of Congress on September

11, is quoted in Roberts, 'A New Age in International Relations,' which contains as useful discussion of the idea of 'a new world order' and its relevance to present and past ideas about international relations.
6. As analyzed by William Pfaff, *The Los Angeles Times*, March 16, 1992.
7. See International Boundaries Research Unit, *Boundary Bulletin*, no. 3 (January 1992).
8. Lawrence Freedman, 'Order and Disorder in the New World,' *Foreign Affairs*, Vol. 71, no. 1 (1991–92), p. 25.
9. Hugh Seton-Watson, *Nations and States: An Enquiry into the Origins of Nations and the Politics of Nationalism* (London: Methuen & Co. Ltd., 1977), p. 322.

10. Francis Fukuyma, *The End of History and the Last Man* (New York: Free Press, 1992).
11. In private conversation with the author.
12. Alan Ryan, 'Professor Hegel Goes to Washington,' *The New York Review of Books*, March 26, 1992, p. 12.
13. Paul Kennedy, *The Rise and Fall of the Great Powers: Economic Change and Military Conflict from 1500 to 2000* (New York: Random House, 1988), pp. 639–40.
14. 'Eastern Europe: Tapping the Markets,' series in the *Financial Post*, February 26–March 2, 1990).

15. *International Herald Tribune*, May 5, 1992, p. 11.
16. 'Russians search for logic in market's magic,' *The Toronto Globe and Mail*, March 18, 1992.
17. See, for example, Václav Havel, 'Paradise Lost,' in *The New York Review of Books*, April 9, 1992, pp. 6–8.
18. In private conversation with the author.
19. See Strobe Talbott, 'Post Victory Blues,' in *Foreign Affairs*, Vol. 71, no. 1 (1991–92), p. 60.
20. The CSCE did however take a handful of largely ineffectual decisions despite member country Yugoslavia's protests.

CHAPTER ONE: The Return of the Nation: Tribalism Triumphant?

1. Quoted in Elie Kedourie (ed.) *Nationalism in Asia and Africa* (New York: Meridian, 1970), p. 59.
2. E.J. Hobsbawm, *Nations and Nationalism* (Cambridge: Cambridge University Press, 1990), p. 181.
3. Tom Nairns, 'Demonizing Nationalism,' in *London Review of Books*, February 25, 1993.
4. Hobsbawm, *Nations and Nationalism*, p. 63.
5. Oxford Research Group, *New Conflicts in Europe: Prevention and Resolution*, as discussed by Edward Mortimer in The Financial Times, July 29, 1992.
6. In private conversation with the author.
7. See Gerhard Simon, *Nationalism and Policy Toward the Nationalities in the Soviet Union: From Totalitarian Dictatorship to Post-Stalinist Society* (Boulder, Col: Westview Press, 1991).
8. Quoted in *The Financial Times*, July 10, 1992. Havel might have added that people are being encouraged in many cases to consider their past by politicians

with a clear agenda to protect and expand their own power base.
9. On ethnic relations, see Janusz Bugajski, *Nations in Turmoil: Conflict and Cooperation in Eastern Europe* (Boulder, Col: Westview Press, 1993).
10. See Roy Porter, *The National Question in Europe in Historical Context* (New York: Cambridge University Press, 1993) and Susan Watkins, *From Provinces into Nations: Demographic Integration in Western Europe, 1870–1960* (Princeton NJ: Princeton University Press, 1991).
11. Stanley Hoffmann, 'Delusions of World Order,' *New York Review of Books*, April 9, 1992, pp. 37–43.
12. See Hugh MacLennan, *Two Solitudes* (Toronto: Collins, 1945).
13. See Canada, *Consensus Report on the Constitution, Final Text* (Ottawa: Minister of Supply and Services, 1992).
14. Gregory F. Treverton, 'The New Europe,' in *Foreign Affairs*, Vol. 71, no. 1 (1991–92), p. 95.
15. See James Bovard, *The Free Trade Fraud* (New York: St. Martin's Press, 1991).

CHAPTER TWO: Going Global

1. Susan Strange, *States and Markets* (London: Pinter, 1988).
2. Phyllis Deane, *The State and the Economic System: an Introduction to the History of the Political Economy*

(Oxford: Oxford University Press, 1989).
3. M. Panic, *National Management of the International Economy* (Basingstoke: MacMillan, 1988), p. 56.

4. Joan Edelman Spero, *The Politics of International Economic Relations*, 4th edition (London: Routledge, 1992), p. 67.
5. Panic, *National Management*, p. 49.
6. Panic, *National Management*, p. 49.
7. Reginald Dale, 'Punchless pageantry,' in the *International Herald Tribune*, July 6, 1993; and the editorial in *The Financial Times*, September 25, 1993.
8. Organization for Economic Co-operation and Development, *Unemployment Outlook, 1992* (Paris: OECD, 1992).
9. European Community, *Unemployment Outlook, 1992* (Luxembourg: Office for Official Publications of the European Communities, 1992).
10. Reuters, 'EC Sounds Alarm Bells over Unemployment,' July 22, 1992.
11. Reported in *The Economist*, April 25, 1992, p. 76.
12. Reuters news wire, June 30, 1992.
13. DeAnne Julius, *Global Companies and Public Policy: the Growing Challenge of Foreign Direct Investment* (New York: Royal Institute of International Affairs, 1990).
14. *International Herald Tribune*, July 9, 1992, p. 1.
15. *International Herald Tribune*, July 9, 1992, p. 1.

CHAPTER THREE: The Limits to Hegemony

1. J. Ungar (ed.) *Estrangement: America and the World* (London: Oxford University Press, 1985).
2. Ungar (ed.), *Estrangement*.
3. E.H. Carr, *The Twenty Years Crisis, 1919–1939: an Introduction to the Study of International Relations* (New York: Harper & Row, 1964), p. 132.
4. Hume quoted in Carr, *The Twenty Years Crisis*, p. 132.
5. Paul Kennedy, *The Rise and Fall of the Great Powers: Economic Change and Military Conflict from 1500 to 2000* (New York: Random House, 1988), p. 689.
6. Kennedy, *The Rise and Fall*, p. 559, table 42.
7. For variants of the declinist thesis, discussions of the Kennedy book, arguments both for and against and Kennedy's own extension of his thesis, see: Walter Russell Mead, *Mortal Splendour* (Boston: Houghton Mifflin, 1987); David Calleo, *Beyond American Hegemony: the Future of the Western Alliance* (New York: Basic Books, 1987); Samuel P. Huntington, 'The US – Decline or Renewal?', in *Foreign Affairs*, Vol. 67, no. 2 (Winter 1988–89), pp. 76–96; Peter G. Peterson, 'The Morning After,' in *The Atlantic Monthly* (October 1987), Joseph S. Nye, *Bound to Lead: The Changing Nature of American Power* (New York: Basic Books, 1990).
8. On the relationship between US domestic economic policy and the international system, see Robert O. Keohane, *After Hegemony: Co-operation and Discord in the World Political Economy* (Princeton: Princeton University Press, 1984); David P. Calleo, *The Imperious Economy* (Cambridge, Mass: Harvard University Press, 1982); Stephen Marris, *Deficits and the Dollar: the World Economy at Risk*, revised ed. (Washington: Institute for International Economics, 1987; Strange, *States and Markets*; and Susan Strange, 'The Persistent Myth of Lost Hegemony,' in *International Organisation*, Vol. 41, no. 4, pp. 551–74.
9. DeAnne Julius, *Global Companies and Public Policy: the Growing Challenge of Foreign Direct Investment* (New York: Royal Institute of International Affairs, 1990), pp. 41ff.
10. Margaret Sharp, 'Tides of Change: The World Economy and Europe in the 1990s,' in *International Affairs*, Vol. 68, no. 1 (Janaury 1992), p. 21.
11. Sharp, 'Tides of Change,' p. 21.
12. For other discussions of the impact of liberalization, deregulation and globalization on the American political economy, see Robert Reich, David Obey and Paul Sarbanes (eds.), *The Changing American Economy* (New York: Basil Blackwell, 1986).

13. Julius, *Global Companies and Public Policy*, p. 81.
14. Kevin Philips, *The Politics of Rich and Poor: Wealth and the American Electorate in the Reagan Aftermath* (New York: Random House, 1990), p. 14.
15. Philips, *The Politics of Rich and Poor*, p. 52.
16. William G. Hyland, 'The Case for Pragmatism,' *Foreign Affairs*, Vol. 71, no. 1 (1991–92), p. 46.
17. David Gergen, 'America's Missed Opportunities,' *Foreign Affairs*, Vol. 71, no. 1 (1991–92).
18. Kennedy, *The Rise and Fall*, p. 665.
19. Kennedy, *The Rise and Fall*, pp. 684–5.
20. Gergen, 'Missed Opportunities,' pp. 15–16.
21. Robert Reich, *The Work of Nations: Competition in the 21st Century* (New York: A.A. Knopf, 1991), p. 301.
22. Lester Thurow, *Head to Head: the Coming Economic Battle Among Japan, Europe, and America* (New York: William Morrow and Co., 1992).
23. Smith, *National Identity*, p. 150.
24. In private conversation with the author.
25. Ungar (ed.), *Estrangement*, p. 14.

CHAPTER FOUR: Europe: *La Grande République*

1. *Agence France Presse*, November 20, 1992. Tackling the growth in illegal drug trafficking and transnational crime was one priority of the new policies on home and justice affairs introduced by the Maastricht treaty, and the focus for proliferating networks of regional co-operation throughout the 1980s.
2. Reuters, August 21, 1992.
3. The implications of removing borders, and the problems in achieving that goal, are set out in Sarah Collinson, *Europe on the Move* (London: RIIA/Pinter, 1993), amongst others. At the time of writing, the Schengen group had just chosen – for the fourth time – to postpone removing their borders, and had failed even to set a new deadline for doing so.
4. For analysis of the political problems for Western Europe that followed the end of the Cold War, see William Wallace, *The Transformation of Europe* (New York: Council on Foreign Relations Press, 1990) and the same author's work in *The Dynamics of European Integration* (London: Pinter/Royal Institute of International Affairs, 1990); and Gregory Treverton (ed.), *The Shape of the New Europe* (New York: Council on Foreign Relations, 1992).
5. The economic situation in Western Europe, including both the prospects after the single market and the problems of the early 1990s, is set out in Loukas

Tsoukalis, *The New European Community: The Politics and Economics of Integration* (Oxford: Oxford University Press, 1992) and in Wallace, *Dynamics of European Integration*. It is also summed up, in a rather grimmer and more policy-oriented way, in the White Paper on Economic Renewal agreed by the EU leaders in Brussels in 1993.
6. Adam Watson, *The Evolution of International Society* (London, Routledge, 1992), p. 8 and see chapter 18.
7. Ibid. For other views of the enlightenment concept of European unity and its precursors, which were important not just for European integration but also for broader conceptions of world order, see also Immanuel Kant, *Perpetual Peace*, trans. Lewis Beck (Boston: World Peace Foundation, 1950) and Fernand Braudel, 'Civilisation and Capitalism': Vol. 3, *The Perspective of the World* (London: Collins/Fontana Press, 1984).
8. Gordon Smith, *Politics in Western Europe* (Aldershot: Dartmouth, 1989) p. 284.
9. For the ideas of the founding fathers of post-war European integration and their successors, see Jean Monnet, *Mémoires* (Paris: Fayard, 1976); Lord Gladwyn, *The European Idea* (London: New English Library, 1966); Robert Marjolin, *Memoirs 1911–1986: Architect of*

European Unity (London: Weidenfeld and Nicholson, 1989); and Walter Hallstein, *Europe in the Making* (London: Allen and Unwin, 1972).

10. The place of thinking about security in the drive for European integration, and the relation between Europe and the two superpowers, is explored in Alfred Grosser, *The Western Alliance: Euro-American Relations since 1945* (London: Macmillan, 1978); and A Deporte, *Europe Between the Superpowers* (New Haven: Yale University Press, 1979).

11. The social and economic ideas that underpinned European integration were undergoing fundamental re-examination while this book was in the course of completion, with new plans from the European Commission to revitalise economic production casting a shadow over the networks of social protection accumulated over the previous four decades.

12. The British conception of Europe is of course multidimensional and the Conservative ideas that sprang out of the debates of the mid-1980s continued to express different versions for different audiences, reflecting the splits within the party as much as within the country. For a representational spread of British approaches and analyses of them, see Geoffrey Smith, Britain in the New Europe, '*Foreign Affairs*', Fall 1992; David Martin MEP, *Europe: An Ever Closer Union* (Nottingham: Spokesman, 1991); William Wallace, 'What Price Independence? Sovereignty and Interdependence in British Politics', in *International Affairs*, Vol. 62, no. 2, Summer 1986; the publications of the Bruges Group; and the writings and speeches of, amongst others, Margaret Thatcher, John Major, Douglas Hurd, Geoffry Howe, Nigel Lawson and Tristan Garel-Jones, the main British policymakers during the period in question.

13. The federalist idea and the alternative approaches are examined in Helen Wallace *et al.*, *Policymaking in the European Community* (New York: Wiley, 1983) and in much of the theoretical literature relating to the EU and its antecedents.

14. Haas' view of supranationalism is quoted in Smith, *Politics in Western Europe*; see Ernst Haas, *The Uniting of Europe: Political, Economic and Social Forces* (Stanford: Stanford University Press, 1958) and *Beyond the Nation State: Functionalism and International Organisation* (Stanford: Stanford University Press, 1964).

15. The crumbling of parties and political systems and the rise of regionalist and nationalist movements seemed at the time of writing likely to be the defining result of the European elections in June 1994.

16. For explorations of subsidiarity and its implications, see Andrew Adonis and Andrew Tyrie, *Subsidiarity: No Panacea* (London: European Policy Forum, 1992); Centre for Economic Policy Research, *Making Sense of Subsidiarity* (London: CEPR, 1993); Andrew Duff (ed.) *Subsidiarity within the European Community* (London: Federal Trust, 1993); Anthony Teasdale, *Subsidiarity in Post-Maastricht Europe*, in Political Quarterly, April 1993; Mark Wilke and Helen Wallace, *Subsidiarity: Approaches to power-sharing in the European Community* (London: Royal Institute of International Affairs, 1990).

17. William Pfaff, p. 4.

18. The implications of enlargement of the European Union, including the countries of the European Free Trade Areas and central and Eastern Europe, are set out in several publications from the Centre for Economic Policy Research including *Is Bigger Better* (London: CEPR, 1992), and from the Royal Institute of International Affairs including Anna Michalski and Helen Wallace, *The European Community: The Challenge of Enlargement* (London: RIIA, 1992).

19. The waning of faith in the old ideologies of unity was not replaced by any new conception of European integration,

however. The federalist groups have remained influential and the path to union through federalism remains the rallying call of Europe's Christian Democrats, as enshrined in the party programme agreed in Brussels in December 1993.

20. Anthony D. Smith has enlarged on this theme in 'National Identity and the Idea of European Identity' in *International Affairs*, Vol. 68, no. 1 (January 1992).

21. The use of an external threat to generate unity was evident in both the closing stages of the Gatt round in Europe, where France and its allies rallied against US trade practices, Hollywood and American farmers; and in the frequent references to the 'Islamic menace' of fundamentalism that accompanied statements on the Bosnian conflict from Tehran.

22. See 'Choice for Europe May Be Two Speeds – or Twelve', by Andrew Marshall in the *Independent on Sunday*, July 21, 1993).

23. The White Paper on growth, competitiveness and employment agreed by European heads of state and government in Brussels in December

1993 sets out many of the main lines of the new policies advocated by Jacques Delors, Commission President, and his colleagues.

24. The parallels between the European and American responses to the arguments about competitiveness were increasingly obvious after the election of Bill Clinton, whose analysis as a right-wing Democrat was very similar to that of Europe's social and Christian democrats – and at odds both with the conservatives who had preceded him and the European socialists.

25. The possibility of a clash between Europe and the US is examined in Henry Brandon (ed.) *In Search of a New World Order: The Future of US-European Relations* (Washington: Brookings, 1992); Jeffrey E. Garten *A Cold Peace: America, Japan, Germany and the Struggle for Supremacy*, (New York: Times books, 1992); Lester Thurow, *Head to Head: the Coming Economic Battle among Japan, Europe, and America* (New York: William Murrow and Co., 1992) and Paul Kennedy, *Preparing for the Twenty-First Century* (London: HarperCollins, 1993).

CHAPTER FIVE: The Politics of the Periphery

1. Elie Kedourie (ed.) *Nationalism in Asia and Africa* (New York: Meridian, 1970), p. 23.

2. John Ravenhill, 'The North-South Balance of Power,' in *International Affairs*, Vol. 66, no. 4 (October 1990), pp. 745–46.

3. Kedourie, *Nationalism in Asia and Africa*, p. 61.

4. Hugh Seton-Watson, *Nations and States: An Enquiry into the Origins of Nations and the Politics of Nationalism* (London: Methuen & Co. Ltd., 1977), p. 328.

5. Peter Calvocoressi, 'World Power 1920–1990,' *International Affairs*, Vol. 66, no. 4 (October 1990). p. 666.

6. See Susan George, *A Fate Worse Than Debt* (New York: Grove Press, 1988).

7. Ravenhill, 'The North-South Balance,' p. 732.

8. For a discussion of global demographics, see Paul Kennedy, *Preparing for the Twenty-first Century* (London: HarperCollins, 1993), particularly pp. 21–46.

9. Michael Chege, 'Remembering Africa,' *Foreign Affairs*, Vol. 71, no. 1 (1991–92), p. 150.

10. George Hicks, writing in the *International Herald Tribune*, May 19, 1992, p. 8.

11. See articles in 'Nafta and Beyond,' in *Policy Options*, Vol. 14, no. 1 (January–February 1993).

12. Lawrence Freedman, 'Order and Disorder in the New World,' *Foreign Affairs*, Vol. 71, no. 1 (1991–92), p. 27.

13. See Susan George, *Debt Boomerang: How Third World Debt Harms Us* (London: Pluto Press, 1992).

CHAPTER SIX: Order and Change

1. *The Independent*, May 1991.
2. John Mearsheimer, 'Why We Shall Soon Miss the Cold War, *Atlantic Monthly*, Vol. 266 (August 1990). See, also, a longer version of the article, 'Back to the Future: Instability in Europe After the Cold War,' reprinted in Sean M. Lynn-Jones (ed.), *The Cold War and After: Prospects for Peace* (Cambridge, Mass: The MIT Press, 1991), and other chapters in the same volume.
3. David Calleo, *Beyond American Hegemony*.
4. 'Still Chairman of the Board,' in *The Financial Times*, January 8, 1994, p. 8.
5. Peter Calvacoressi, *World Politics Since 1945*, 6th ed. (London: Longman, 1991);p. 138.
6. James Mayall, *Nationalism and International Society* (Cambridge: Cambridge University Press, 1990).
7. A. LeRoy Bennett, *International Organizations: Principles and Issues*

(Englewood Cliffs, N.J: Prentice Hall, 1991), p. 408
8. Malcolm N. Shaw, *International Law*, 2nd ed. (Cambridge: Grotius Publications, 1986), p. 616.
9. Bennett, *International Organizations*, p. 52.
10. Bennett, *International Organizations*, p. 52.
11. Quoted in E.H. Carr, *The Twenty Years Crisis, 1919–1939: an Introduction to the Study of International Relations* (New York: Harper & Row, 1964).
12. Bennett, *International Organizations*, p. 12.
13. Bennett, *International Organizations*, p. 255.
14. Robert O. Keohane and Joseph Nye, *Power and Interdependence* (Boston: Little Brown, 1977), pp. 23–37.
15. Adam Roberts, 'A New Age in International Relations,' in *International Affairs*, Vol. 67, no. 3 (July 1991).
16. Robert O. Keohane and Joseph Nye, *Power and Interdependence*, pp. 22–37.

PART THREE: Reimagining the Nation

INTRODUCTION: Breaking Up the Communities

1. Niccolo Machiavelli, *Discourses on the First Decade of Titus Livius* (London, 1883), p. 175.
2. Fernand Braudel, *The Mediterranean World in the Age of Philip II* (New York: Harper and Row, 1972).
3. Abraham F. Lowenthal, 'Vanishing Borders and New Frontiers,' *The Oxford International Review*, Vol. 2, no. 2 (Summer 1992), pp. 8–9.
4. Lowenthal, 'Vanishing Borders,' p. 8–9.
5. Lowenthal, 'Vanishing Borders,' p. 8.
6. Christopher Coker, 'The Special Relationship in the 1990s', *International Affairs*, Vol. 68, no. 2 (July 1992), pp. 407–22.
7. *The Independent on Sunday*, July 19, 1992.
8. Eldridge Cleaver, *Soul on Ice* (New York: Dell, 1968).
9. David Clark, then Labour agriculture

critic, quoted by the Press Association in 1992.
10. In private conversation with the author.
11. See, for example, Susan Strange, 'States, Firms and Diplomacy,' in *International Affairs*, Vol. 68, no. 1 (January 1992), p. 3.
12. Witness the soaring sales of products sold for the first time via newspaper advertising in Poland, as documented in the *International Herald Tribune*, May 9, 1992.
13. Reported by Reuters, July 23, 1992.
14. Adam Watson, *The Evolution of International Society* (London: Routledge, 1992), p. 307.
15. Federal Reserve Board, *Triennial Survey of Consumer Finances*, 1992.
16. Britain's wealthiest ten per cent earned four times more than the poorest ten per cent in 1989, up from three times a

decade earlier. In 1989, the poorest tenth were marginally worse off, after inflation, than they were in 1979, while the richest tenth saw their real incomes climb by more than seventy per cent over the same period. Figures from Central Statistical Office, as reported in *The Guardian*, June 6, 1992.

17. *The New York Times*, May 5, 1992.
18. William Wallace, *The Transformation of Europe* (New York: Council on Foreign Relations Press, 1990), p. 33.
19. For example, fifty per cent of the population in Dade County and thirty-eight per cent in Los Angeles County is Latino. See Lowenthal, 'Vanishing Borders,' p. 8.
20. See, for example, Michael Hager, director of the International Development Law Institute, writing in the *International Herald Tribune*, July 30, 1992.

CHAPTER ONE: Tribalism, Nationalism and Regionalism

1. Keniche Omae, *The Borderless World: Power and Strategy in the Interlinked Economy* (New York: Harper Business, 1990), p. 268.
2. Daniel Bell, *The Coming of Post-Industrial Society: A Venture in Social Forecasting* (New York: Basic Books, 1976).
3. See Richard S. Belous and Rebecca S. Hartley (eds.), *The Growth of Regional Trading Blocs in the Global Economy* (Washington DC: National Planning Association, 1990).
4. *Financial Times*, February 28, 1992, p. 3.
5. See Government of Canada, *Nafta: What's It All About?* (Ottawa: External Affairs and International Trade, 1993) and Steven Globerman and Michael Walker (eds.) *Assessing Nafta: a Trinational Analysis* (Vancouver: Fraser Institute, 1993).
6. Gary Hufbauer and Jeffrey Schott, 'North American Free Trade: Issues and Recommendations,' Institute for International Economics, as reported in *The Financial Times*, February 28, 1992.
7. See Walter LaFeber, *Inevitable Revolutions: The United States in Central America* (New York: Norton, 1983).

8. *The Guardian*, January 29, 1992.
9. See Vivien Schmidt, *Democratizing France: the Political and Administrative History of Decentralization* (Cambridge: Cambridge University Press, 1990).
10. *The Guardian*, May 22, 1992, p. 27.
11. See European Community, *The Regions in the 1990s: Fourth Periodic Report on the Social and Economic Situation of the Regions of the Community* (Luxembourg: Office for Official Publications of the European Communities, 1991); P.J. Donaghy, *Spain: a Guide to Political and Economic Institutions* (Cambridge: Cambridge University Press, 1987); Robert J. Bennett, *Local Economic Development: Public-Private Partnership Initiatives in Britain and Germany* (London: Belhaven Press, 1991).
12. For a pertinent discussion of local government, see Jeffrey M. Berry, *The Rebirth of Urban Democracy* (Washington, DC: Brookings Institution, 1993).
13. Richard O'Brien, *Global Financial Integration: the End of Geography* (London: Pinter, 1992).
14. National Bureau of Economic Research, *Digest*, August, 1993.

CHAPTER TWO: State, Nation and Corporation

1. Enzo Mingione, Twenty-First Century Trust conference, Klingenthal, 1993.
2. Joan Edelman Spero, *The Politics of International Economic Relations*, 4th edition (London: Routledge, 1992), p. 132.
3. Susan Strange, *States and Markets* (London: Pinter, 1988).

4. Conference Board of New York, *Report*, 1992.
5. Conference Board.
6. Susan Strange, *States and Markets* (London: Pinter, 1988), p. 63.
7. Strange, *States and Markets*, p. 62.
8. Stephen J. Kobrin, 'Expropriation as an

Attempt to Control Foreign Firms in
LDCs,' quoted in Stefan H. Robock and
Kenneth Simmonds (eds.), *International
Business and Multinational Enterprises*, 4th
edition (Homewood Ill.; Irwin, 1989),
p. 304.

9. Jean Jacques Sevran-Schreiber, *Le défi
américain* (Paris: Denoel, 1967); Pierre
Vallieres, *White Niggers of America*
(Toronto: McClelland and Stewart, 1971).

10. Samuel P. Huntington, 'Transnational
Organizations in World Politics,' in
World Politics, Vol. 25 (Princeton, N.J.:
Princeton University Press, 1973),
pp. 333–68; exerpted in Michael Smith,
Richard Little and Michael Shackleton
(eds.), *Perspectives on World Politics*
(London: Croom Helm, 1981),
pp. 198–213.

11. John Ravenhill, 'The North-South
Balance of Power,' in *International Affairs*,
Vol. 66, no. 4 (October 1990).

12. Susan Strange, *States and Markets*
(London: Pinter, 1988), p. 87.

13. On this subject, see Christopher Macrae,
World Class Brands (Wokingham:
Addison Wesley, 1991).

14. A.D. Smith, *National Identity*, p. 157.

15. quoted in Malcolm N. Shaw,
International Law, 2nd ed. (Cambridge:
Grotius Publications, 1986), p. 157.

16. Joan Edelman Spero, *The Politics of
International Economic Relations*, 4th
edition (London: Routledge, 1992),
p. 152.

17. *The Daily Telegraph*, March 30, 1992.

18. Stefan H. Robock and Kenneth
Simmonds (eds.), *International Business
and Multinational Enterprises*, 4th edition
(Homewood Ill.; Irwin, 1989), p. 313.

19. Peter Drucker: *The New Realities in
Government and Politics, in Economics and
Business, in Society and World View* (New
York: Harper & Row, 1989), p. 219.

20. Strange, *States and Markets*, p. 81.

21. The Independent, March 1992.

22. Quoted in a report from Associated
Press.

CHAPTER THREE: The Disenfranchised Citizen

1. William Shakespeare, *Coriolanus* (New
York: The New American Library, 1966),
p. 56.

2. Max Weber, *The Theory of Social and
Economic Organization* (New York: Free
Press, 1964).

3. Susan Strange, *States and Markets*
(London: Pinter, 1988), p. 81.

4. Jurgen Habermas, *Legitimation Crisis*
(Boston: Beacon Press, 1975), p. 46.

5. David Held, 'Democracy, the Nation-
State, and the Global System,' in *Political
Theory Today* (Stanford: Stanford
University Press, 1991), p. 226.

6. France, New Zealand, Sweden and most
recently Canada have discovered how
difficult it is to meet the demands of
citizens – jobs, social protection, health
and welfare services – and at the same
time keep foreign lenders happy. Canada,
with the G7's largest share of public debt
held by foreigners, was formally warned
by the IMF in mid-1993 to temper the
trend toward higher federal and
provincial indebtedness.

7. J.K. Galbraith, *The Culture of Contentment*
(London: Sinclair-Stevenson, 1992).

8. Fredric Jameson, *Postmodernism, or The
Cultural Logic of Late Capitalism* (New
York: Verso Books, 1991).

9. Evan Luard, *The Globalization of Politics:
the Changed Focus of Political Action in the
Modern World* (Basingstoke: Macmillan,
1990), p. 66.

10. Robert Reich, *The Work of Nations:
Competition in the 21st Century* (New York:
A.A. Knopf, 1991), p. 301.

11. Quoted in John M. Stopford and Susan
Strange, *Rival States, Rival Firms:
Competition for World Market Shares*
(Cambridge: Cambridge University Press,
1992), p. 21.

12. *International Herald Tribune*, April 14, 1993.

13. 15. *OECD Outlook, December, 1992*
(Paris: Organization for Economic Co-
operation and Development, 1992).

14. 16. *OECD Outlook, December, 1992*.

15. See, for example, Francis McInerney and
Sean White, *Beating Japan* (New York:
Dutton, 1993).

16. Robert Wright, 'Voice of America,' in *The New Republic*, Vol. 209, no. 11 (September 13, 1993), pp. 20ff.

17. R.B.J. Walker, 'State Sovereignty and the Articulation of Political Space/Time', in *Millenium*, Vol. 20, no. 3 (Winter 1991), p. 445.

18. Walker, 'State Sovereignty,' p. 445.

CHAPTER FOUR: The New Agenda for Government

1. Quoted in Carl Cohen (ed.), *Parliament and Democracy* (New York: Random House, 1962), pp. 533–54.

2. Herman Van der Wee, *Prosperity and Upheaval: The World Economy 1945–1980* (Harmondsworth: Penguin Books, 1987).

3. E.J. Hobsbawm, *Nations and Nationalism Since 1780* (Cambridge: Cambridge University Press, 1990), p. 175.

4. James Mayall, *Nationalism and International Society* (Cambridge: Cambridge University Press, 1990), p. 25.

5. For a discussion of representation, citizen access, and government-citizen relations, see F. Leslie Seidle (ed.), *Rethinking Government: Reform or Reinvention?* (Montreal: Institute for Research on Public Policy, 1993).

6. On various issues involving representation, consultation and the political rights of citizens, see F. Leslie Seidle (ed.), *Equity and Community: The Charter, Interest Advocacy and Representation* (Montreal: Institute for Research on Public Policy, 1993), especially pp. 61–90.

7. Hobsbawm, *Nations and Nationalism*, p. 178.

8. David Osborne and Ted Gaebler, *Reinventing Government: How the Entrepreneurial Spirit is Transforming the Public Sector* (Reading, Mass: Addison-Wesley Publishing Co., 1992).

9. A.D. Smith, *National Identity*, pp. 69–70.

10. Harold R. Isaacs, *Idols of the Tribe: Group Identity and Political Change*, 2nd edition (Cambridge, Mass.: Harvard University Press, 1989), p. 2.

CHAPTER FIVE: Rivals

1. Eldridge Cleaver, *Soul on Ice* (New York: Dell, 1968), p. 48.

2. Quoted in *The Guardian*, July 29, 1992, p. 21.

3. J.S. Mill, *Considerations on Representative Government* (Oxford: B. Blackwell, 1946), pp. 207–8.

4. Fredric Jameson, *Postmodernism, or The Cultural Logic of Late Capitalism* (New York: Verso Books, 1991), pp. 346–47

5. Jameson, *Postmodernism*, p. 315.

6. See for example, James Dale Davidson and William Rees-Mogg, *The Great Reckoning* (London: Sidgewick & Jackson, 1992).

7. A.D. Smith, 'The Nation: Invented, Imagined, Reconstructed?', in *Milennium*, Vol. 20, no. 3 (Winter 1991), p. 364.

8. For a review of the Latin American debt crisis, see the survey in *The Financial Times*, July 30, 1992.

9. Paul Kennedy, *Preparing for the Twenty-first Century* (London: HarperCollins, 1993).

10. Ralph Millband and Leo Panitch, *The Socialist Register* (San Franciso: The Merlin Press, 1992).

11. David Held, 'Democracy, the Nation-State, and the Global System,' in *Political Theory Today* (Stanford: Stanford University Press, 1991), p. 234.

12. *Time Magazine*, April 19, 1993.

CONCLUSION: The High-Modern World

1. A term first used, we believe, by George Robertson.

2. Benedict Anderson, *Imagined Communities*, revised and extended ed. (London: Verso Books, 1991).

INDEX

Adams, Ansel, 206
Aérospatiale, 194
Afghanistan, superpower interference, 75
Africa: borders, xvii, 29–30, 75; economic
and political reforms, 74; economic
problems, 151; ethnic groups, 78, 148;
federations, 29; French-speaking, 190;
nationalist leaders, 139; nationalist
movements, 30, 31; nineteenth-century,
14; political changes, 147–9; population
growth, 142, 143, 258; Preferential Trade
Area, 193; regional trading arrangements,
192–3; sub-Saharan, xiv, 142, 193; tribal
conflicts, xvii, 143; US policies, 31;
violence, 74; wars, 19
agriculture, 7–8, 175
aid, foreign, 100, 150
air transport, 47
Airbus, 95
Albania, Macedonia issue, 68
Algeria: Islamic fundamentalism, 149;
politics, 149
Alter, Peter, xvii, 3, 11
America First movement, 115
Amnesty International, 238
Andean Pact, 191
Anderson, Benedict, 212, 271
Angola, politics, 148
Anzus agreement, 193
Aquino, Corazón, 145
Argentina: economy, 146, 192; Mercosur
pact, 192
Armenians, 248
Asia: economies, 144, 151; foreign
investment, 211; nationalist leaders, 139;
nationalist movements, 28; political
systems, 144–5; regional co-operation, 152;
US policies, 31

Association of South-east Asian Nations,
192
asylum-seekers, 58, 87, 120
Atlantic Monthly, 155
Auden, W.H., 23
Australia: Anzus agreement, 193;
colony, 14; economic policy, 98; immigration
policy, 58
Austria: ethnic group, 79; EC status, 132,
190, 191; fascism, 131
Austro-Hungary: Concert of Europe, 10;
Empire, 80
authority, xviii, 194, 215, 244
automobile: industry, 206, 214; influence of,
22
Azeglio, Massimo d', 12
Azerbaijan, 68, 81, 248

Baca, Muzaffer, 55
Baker, James, 93
Baldwin, James, 249
Balkans: borders, 79; ethnic and religious
mixture, 188; minority populations, 79;
nineteenth-century, 10
Baltic states: EC status, 189; independence
struggles, 158; minority populations, xv,
79; Soviet acquisition, 31; trade bloc plans,
193; Western recognition, 75; *see also*
Estonia, Latvia, Lithuania
Bank of Credit and Commerce International
(BCCI), 209
Bank of England, 209
Bank for International Settlements, 96
Barclays Bank, 214
Barré, Siad, 159
Basques, 84, 131, 185, 260
BAT, 213
Baudis, Dominique, 193

287